P9-CMX-029

CONSUMING KIDS

Consuming Kids

The Hostile Takeover of Childhood

Susan Linn

THE NEW PRESS

NEW YORK
LONDON

Published in the United States by The New Press, New York, 2004
Distributed by W. W. Norton & Company, Inc., New York

LIBRARY OF CONGRESS CATALOGING-IN-PUBLICATION DATA
Linn, Susan E.
Consuming kids : the hostile takeover of childhood / Susan E. Linn.
p.   cm.
Includes bibliographical references and index.
ISBN 1-56584-783-0
1. Child consumers—United States.   2. Advertising and children—United States.
3. Marketing research—United States.   I. Title.

HF5415.32.L56   2004
658.8'34'0830973—dc22   2003066600

The New Press was established in 1990 as a not-for-profit alternative
to the large, commercial publishing houses currently dominating
the book publishing industry. The New Press operates in the public interest
rather than for private gain, and is committed to publishing,
in innovative ways, works of educational, cultural, and community value
that are often deemed insufficiently profitable.

The New Press
38 Greene Street, 4th floor
New York, NY 10013
www.thenewpress.com

In the United Kingdom:
6 Salem Road
London W2 4BU

Composition by dix!

Printed in the United States of America

2   4   6   8   10   9   7   5   3   1

FOR SASHA LINN CRAINE, WITH LOVE.

Contents

Foreword

Tweak this book just a little and it would be credible as a novel: a third millennium *1984*, perhaps. A science-fiction picture of our world in the near future—recognizable, yet subtly and horridly different from reality. But *Consuming Kids* is not a novel. This account of corporate America's use and abuse of children and their families is fact, not fiction, and that is why it is as terrifying as it is timely.

Everybody knows that corporations need to make money; to make more and more they need to expand their products and their markets, selling as many things as they can to as many people as possible. Even as they head for the mall on a wet Saturday afternoon, most people are aware that many of their purchases will not be things they need, should have, or even want for more than a moment, but will be things they are conned into buying by marketing ploys that are as irresistible as they are recognizable. We're told we'll look or feel or perform or smell better if we buy this, that, or the other. We don't exactly believe it, but we still buy. We buy two for the price of one or choose the special-offer giant size, even when we only need one or we're trying not to overeat, because they're presented as good values. We buy because this is cool and that's the latest and because being able to afford it—even at the credit card's limit—feels successful.

Until they've read this book, though, most people probably won't have realized that they buy for their children and grandchildren in response to the same kinds of pressure and for many of those same reasons. Susan Linn's "consuming kids" are the latest huge market for corporate America: not just teens, nor even preteens, but little children: preschoolers, toddlers, anyone old enough to recognize brand-name packaging in the supermarket and plead until the sugary stuff is in the shopping cart. It's not

all food and toys, either. Soft drinks, toiletries, makeup, sexy lingerie, violent videos and computer games (and personal computers and bedroom
TVs to play them) are being marketed to children from preschool age up,
with a completely cynical disregard for their well-being or that of the parents who have to withstand or accede to those cries of "All the other kids
have one. . . . ," knowing that the "wrong" schoolbag or outfit really can
reduce a child's social standing and popularity. No wonder recent surveys
find that more parents describe children as "expensive" than "enjoyable."

    People like to avoid unpleasant truths, but by piling instance on in-
stance, example on example, Linn forces us to see a world in which it is
considered legitimate to treat children and their tastes as market potential
and to manipulate them accordingly. How has it happened? Why do we let
it go on? A great many of the people who are financing, commissioning,
designing, producing, packaging, advertising, and marketing these "products" have children and grandchildren themselves, and every single one of
them was once a child, so how do they manage to believe that ethical concerns about the effects of commerce on kids are not their business?

    Perhaps because business today is about individual wealth, not about
social concern. Extreme individualism and notable materialism are the
hallmarks of modern life. We have become a society of workplace-centered
adults for whom money is not only a means of exchange but also the principal arbiter of value. That's a crucial difference; once money is intrinsi-
cally valuable, nobody can ever have enough; more is better, so the search
for profit, for a raise, for a quick buck, a bold investment, a second job, or
more and more overtime is never-ending. The notion of "working to live"
sounds definitely old fashioned. It is not just workaholic city types who
"live to work"; we all do.

    A society devoted to individualistic enterprise feeds on itself because it
offers no rewards for the caring activities that might modify or change it.
Commercial interests are not interested in the personality-shaping relationships children have with parents but in the taste-dictating relationships they have with peers. They know how difficult it is for parents to
refuse to buy the things children want. And in case parents get better at resisting, marketers are even teaching children to nag more effectively, as
Linn discovers. So now more than ever, and just when many of them are
most pressed for time, mothers and fathers need to spend more time and
energy trying to prevent children from following each other into the latest
fad and fashion; feeding less materialistic adult values and controls into the

peer group; and diluting the excitement of commerce and of the herd with large doses of individual attention. Unless, of course, all those captains of industry, advertising executives, and salespeople—many of them grandparents and parents themselves—could be persuaded (or compelled) to start treating children as children rather than as commercial opportunities.

Penelope Leach, PhD
November 2003

Acknowledgments

I could not have written *Consuming Kids* without Chris Kochansky and Barbara Sweeny. Chris's talent made it possible for me to begin. Barbara's made it possible to finish. I am indebted to them both.

Several people read and commented on versions of the manuscript: Arnold Fege (Public Advocacy for Kids), Allen Kanner (Stop the Commercial Exploitation of Children), Marge and Richard Amster, Sherry Steiner, Jim Metrock (Obligation, Inc.), Rheta Rubenstein (University of Michigan–Dearborn), Jan Hamer, Nancy Pearl (Washington Center for the Book), Todd Anderson (Judge Baker Children's Center), Velma La-Point (Howard University), Marie Woods, Rhoda Trietsch, and Judy Salzman. Others read and commented on individual chapters: Enola Aird (The Motherhood Project), David Jernigan (Center for Alcohol Marketing and Youth), Diane Levin (Wheelock College), Alex Molnar (Commercialism in Education Research Unit at Arizona State University), Jean Kilbourne, Phyllis Menken, Susan Wadsworth, and Jane Levine (Kids Can Make a Difference). Thanks also to Jane for the title.

Jane Brown (University of North Carolina), Ellen Bates-Brackett (Workman's Circle), Akil Amar (Yale University Law School), Noam Chomsky (MIT), Priscilla Hambrick-Dixon (Hunter College), Joe Kelly (Dads and Daughters), Anne Mahon, Elizabeth Whelan (American Council on Science and Health), Dan Anderson (University of Massachusetts), Marjorie Heins (The Free Expression Policy Project), Don Ernst (Association for Curriculum and Development), Gary Ruskin (Commercial Alert), Rachel Barr (Georgetown Early Intervention Project), and Sarah Finn (Manville School) were generous with their time and expertise on topics ranging from child development to the First Amendment.

Josh Golin, Michelle Beacock, Megan Meaghan, and Naomi Greenfield were the best of research assistants. Chuck Howell (American Library of Broadcasting) sent a slew of useful resources and confirmed my husband's suspicion that Arthur Godfrey drank Lipton Tea. Dr. Pamela Hunter (University of Connecticut) supplied relevant survey data. Alex Amster led me safely through cyber-combat. Lynda Paull went out of her way to be helpful.

Ellen Reeves has been a first author's dream editor—a great combination of clarity, kindness, and high expectations. Thanks to everyone else at The New Press, especially Jessica Colter, editorial assistant; Ben Kuperman, editorial intern; and Ed Davis, legal counsel. Sue Goldberger told me to write a book about kids and commercialism only a few weeks before my agent, Andrew Stuart, suggested it. Thanks to Andrew for shepherding me through the proposal process and finding the manuscript such a good home.

I have been fortunate in my mentors, William Beardslee, MD, Alvin Poussaint, MD, and Fred Rogers. Each has had a profound effect on my work and has been a stellar model of effective advocacy for children. Dr. Beardslee and Dr. Poussaint continue to be ongoing sources of support, guidance, and excellent advice. I am especially grateful to Dr. Poussaint, first for founding the Media Center at Judge Baker Children's Center, and second for inviting me to work with him. I couldn't have a better boss. Camille Cosby has generously supported the work that inspired me to write this book.

Celia Shapiro, Linda Zoe Podbros, Linda Barnes, and Stephen Sniderman provided encouragement when I most needed it, as did Karen Motylewski, who was always available to sort through various complexities—often at a moment's notice.

To my husband, Cliff Craine: I am thankful as always for your integrity and vision. Through endless drafts you have helped me—not just to keep my eye on the big picture, but to see things in it I didn't know were there.

CONSUMING KIDS

Introduction:
The Marketing Maelstrom

My DAUGHTER is a popular kid these days. Taco Bell wants her, and so does Burger King. Abercrombie and Fitch has a whole store devoted to her. Pert Plus has a shampoo she'll love. Ethan Allen is creating bedroom sets she can't live without. Alpo even wants to sell her dog food.

With a single-minded competitiveness reminiscent of the California gold rush, corporations are racing to stake their claim on the consumer group formerly known as children. What was once the purview of a few entertainment and toy companies has escalated into a gargantuan, multi-tentacled enterprise with a combined marketing budget estimated at over $15 billion annually[1]—about 2.5 times more than what was spent in 1992.[2] Children are the darlings of corporate America. They're targets for marketers of everything from hamburgers to minivans. And it's not good for them.

Even while I, like all American parents, am held responsible for the behavior of my child and for safeguarding her future, corporations bombard her with messages that undermine my efforts. One advertisement for a violent movie, a few sexual innuendos to get her to buy a certain brand of jeans, or a couple of commercials urging her to eat junk food are not going to harm my daughter. But kids today are growing up in a marketing maelstrom. That children influence more than $600 billion in spending a year[3] has not been lost on corporate America, which seeks to establish "cradle to grave" brand loyalty among the purchasers of its goods and services.[4] Every aspect of children's lives—their physical and mental health, their education, their creativity, and their values—is negatively affected by their involuntary status as consumers in the marketplace.

There's no doubt that advertising works. Its success stories are told and retold within the industry. At mid century the phrase "A Diamond Is Forever" succeeded so well in bolstering a faltering diamond market that by 1951, 80 percent of American marriages began with a diamond engagement ring. In the mid-1950s only 7 percent of American women dyed their hair; six years after Clairol introduced their "Does she or doesn't she?" campaign, one study reported that 70 percent of all women were coloring their hair. In 1970, just before McDonald's began telling moms that they "deserve a break today," annual sales were at $587 million; by 1974, after four years of that catchy little jingle, annual sales jumped to $1.9 billion.[5]

So what's the big deal? What's wrong (leaving aside for the moment the questions of where those diamonds come from, and whether hair dye and fast food enhance your well-being or physical health) with trying to get people to buy a diamond engagement ring, or dye their hair, or indulge in the occasional Big Mac with fries? Well, all of these legendary campaigns were aimed at adults, who presumably can bring a certain amount of information and judgment to their decisions about what's good for them. Because children are unable to employ such judgment, they are more vulnerable to marketing.

Preschool children, for instance, have trouble differentiating between commercials and regular programming on television.[6] Slightly older children can make the distinction, but they are concrete thinkers, tending to believe what they see in a fifteen-second commercial for cookies or a toy.[7] Until the age of about eight, children can't really understand the concept of persuasive intent—that every aspect of an ad is selected to make a product appealing and to convince people to buy it.[8] Older kids and teens might be more cynical about advertising, but their skepticism doesn't seem to affect their tendency to want or buy the products they see so glowingly portrayed all around them.[9]

I recently sat with a group of elementary school kids who all told me that commercials do not tell the truth, yet when asked, they all had strong opinions about which was the "best" brand of sneaker. Their opinions were based not on their own experience but on what they'd seen on TV and in magazine ads. Advertising appeals to emotions, not to intellect, and it affects children even more profoundly than it does adults.

Unfortunately, marketing is so ingrained in the fabric of American life that it's hard to generate much concern about its effects on kids. Most of us have fond memories of advertising: those Burma Shave signs whizzing by on the highway, Arthur Godfrey winking at us in black-and-white as he sipped his cup of Lipton Tea, Clara Peller growling "Where's the beef?" for Wendy's in the 1980s, and little Mikey gobbling up Life cereal to the amazement of his older siblings. We all have favorite commercials, and it's significant that many of these favorites are ads we remember from childhood.

That I'm both a parent and a psychologist contributes to my sense of urgency and personal outrage about the extent to which corporate interests subsume modern childhood. As the mother of a teenager whose growing up has coincided with an increasing intensity and sophistication of marketing efforts targeted at children, I struggle on a personal level to cope with its harmful effects. As a therapist working with young children, I see its impact on other people's children as well.

My concerns about kids and commercialism, the foundations of which date from my own childhood, have always influenced my professional choices. From the mid-1930s on, my parents were actively involved in struggles for social justice. My mother was a pioneer in the early childhood education movement. As an adult, carving out my own work with children, I took from her and her colleagues a sense of wonder about childhood— not a naive, romantic perception of blissful early years, but rather a recognition of the amazing possibilities inherent in each child. Creativity, originality, and integrity deserve to be nurtured, and all adults have an ongoing obligation to keep children's best interests at heart.

At the age of six I developed an admittedly eccentric, but enduring, fascination with ventriloquism that blossomed into a career. By my early twenties, I was earning my living with my puppets—through live and televised performances, by creating video programs about difficult issues for kids, and eventually as a puppet therapist at Boston Children's Hospital. Along the way, I earned a doctorate in psychology. I was fortunate to be able to work with the late Fred Rogers of *Mister Rogers' Neighborhood,* appearing on his program early in my career. With Family Communications, Inc., the company he founded, I have been writing and performing in video programs ranging in topics from helping children with cancer go back to school, to racism, prejudice, and diversity.

My stepson, Josh, was born in 1971. My daughter, Sasha, was born in 1987. Josh's daughter, Marley, was born in 2002. I can't help but contrast the commercial pressures affecting their experience of growing up. When Josh was a child, public television really was commercial-free. It is no longer. Nor did most of his friends have TVs in their rooms. While he did have to cope with sugar cereal ads on Saturday morning television, he did not have to deal with a barrage of soda and junk food marketing in school, unlike Sasha. And, when riding in a grocery cart neither Josh nor Sasha (unlike Marley) had to face aisle after aisle jammed with alluring, brightly colored packages containing edible, high-calorie renditions of his favorite cartoon characters, or candy in the shape of superheroes. The first video games came into being when Josh was a teenager, but the technological capacity for depicting media violence in graphic, gory detail did not develop until he was almost an adult. He listened to the radio, but while Sasha's music is interrupted with incessant ads for violent and sexually explicit television programs and movies, his was not.

As my daughter progressed through elementary school, the press of commercialism was escalating at breakneck speed. Like all parents, I was coping with the effects of marketing at home. In 1996, as part of my work, I began to track its escalation in a broader sense as well. As the associate director of the Media Center of the Judge Baker Children's Center in Boston, Massachusetts, my mission was and is to work with media to promote the health and well-being of children and to mitigate the media's negative effects. I began to assess the growing body of research and reports documenting the impact of marketing on children. I immersed myself in the myriad books, journals, and newspapers written for and by people responsible for creating commercials and advertising campaigns that target children. I began talking to parent groups—and to children—about the effect of marketing on their lives. In recent years, a significant portion of my time has also been devoted to writing, speaking, and advocating on behalf of children in the marketplace.

Most parents struggle in one way or another to keep corporate culture at bay. In doing so they often feel beleaguered and quite alone. But I see their stories in the context of a large, cohesive, and frightening picture. The most common complaints about marketing to children center on specific products such as violent media, alcohol, tobacco, and, most recently, junk food. Yet to focus only on products is to underestimate the magnitude of the problem. Of equal concern are the sheer volume of advertising to which children are exposed, the values embedded in the marketing messages, and the behaviors those messages inspire.

Children have been targets for some kinds of advertising for a long, long time—from carnival barkers hawking freak shows to ads in comic books and, since their early days, radio and television. But it's not the same today. Comparing the advertising of two or three decades ago to the commercialism that permeates our children's world is like comparing a BB gun to a smart bomb. The explosion of marketing aimed at kids today is precisely targeted, refined by scientific method, and honed by child psychologists—in short, it is more pervasive and intrusive than ever before.

Today's children are assaulted by advertising everywhere—at home, in school, on sports fields, in playgrounds, and on the street. They spend almost forty hours a week engaged with the media—radio, television, movies, magazines, the Internet—most of which are commercially driven.[10] The average child sees about about 40,000 commercials a year on television alone.[11] Many, if not most, children's television programs, including those produced by the Public Broadcasting System (PBS), are funded through licensing, a practice that allows companies to market toys, clothing, and accessories based on characters or logos associated with a program.

Children, including very young children, often watch television by themselves, meaning that no adult is present to help them process marketing messages.[12] Poor children, a population in which children of color are disproportionately represented, watch even more television than their middle- and upper-class counterparts.[13] However, regardless of class, African American and Latino children watch more TV than Caucasian children.[14]

While television remains the major medium through which advertisers target children, it's no longer the only medium. In the 1970s, people concerned about marketing to children worried mainly about the effects of TV commercials on Saturday mornings. Now the average American child lives in a home with three television sets, two CD players, three radios, a video game console, and a computer.[15] Two-thirds of children between the ages of eight and eighteen have televisions their bedrooms, as do 32 percent of two- to seven-year-olds,[16] and 26 percent of children under two.[17] Electronic media continues to proliferate while, as a nation, our willingness to embrace technology constantly outpaces our understanding of its cultural, social, and ethical implications.

The escalation of graphic violence in movies and television, for example, has occurred in part simply because the technology became available—just as the invention of the scroll saw enabled all that curlicue furniture of the Victorian era. It is now possible to graphically recreate a disembowelment or melt an eyeball on the screen—and so we do.

When the Reagan Administration deregulated advertising on children's television in 1984, programs could be created for the purpose of selling children toys. Within a year of deregulation, all ten of the bestselling toys were linked to media programs.[18] Meanwhile, laws that might prevent the formation of media conglomerations grow ever more lax,[19] and today, megacompanies such as Viacom, Disney, or Time Warner are likely to own several television stations, radio stations, Internet service providers, theme parks, record companies, and/or publishing houses—all of which cross-advertise each other as well as food, toys, books, clothing, and accessories.[20] A few giant corporations control much of what children eat, drink, wear, read, and play with each day.

Through endorsements and licensing agreements, cartoon characters, pop singers, sports heroes, and movie stars are now icons for junk food, toys, clothing, and every imaginable accessory. There's also the fast-growing phenomenon of product placement: embedding product ads as plot points, scenery, or props within the content of movies and TV programs.

Marketing to children is not limited to electronic media; even traditional venues for spreading what used to be legitimately called popular culture—word of mouth, for instance—have been co-opted by corporations. Corporations engage in "guerrilla" marketing: ads and posters now get plastered on buildings and bus stops in a kind of corporate graffiti. There's also "viral" marketing, a term originally used to describe what happens when marketers invade Internet chat rooms and pose as ordinary kids to promote their products. Viral marketing also applies to the practice of handing out free samples of products such as CDs, for instance, to kids identified by other kids as "cool." Marketing companies actually comb neighborhoods to find what they refer to as trendsetters, knowing that when a trendsetter uses a product, other kids will want to use it. Of course, there have always been trendsetters—what's new is that they don't have to create a new look or discover a new band themselves. Now, adults may do much of the creating for them, paying the kids to set the trends.

What my colleague, psychologist Allen Kanner, first dubbed "the commercialization of childhood" got a boost from the political climate of the 1980s, which saw the beginning of a steady erosion of government support for public institutions and a glorification of the marketplace as the solution to and/or a model for solving social ills.[21] Corporate support, however, usually comes with a price. Sometimes entire public and nonprofit institutions sell naming rights to corporations. If your child has had trouble in school, he or she might attend a Burger King Academy.[22] Children who used to delight in Philadelphia's Please Touch Museum now visit the Please Touch Museum Presented by McDonald's.[23] Also common are social campaigns born of odd marriages, such as the American Library Association's partnership with the World Wrestling Federation (now called World Wrestling Entertainment) to promote literacy.[24]

Public schools, particularly, were urged by the Reagan administration to look to corporate America for rescue.[25] Historically, public school budgets tend to increase over the years because of rising student populations,[26] although recent years seem to be the exception.[27] In any case, a large portion of any budget increase is designated to cover specific government-mandated programs from special education to competency-based testing.[28] School administrators therefore routinely cite inadequate funding for general operations as justification for buying into such corporate intrusions in education as sponsored newscasts beamed into classrooms and a host of other marketing schemes that exploit our mandatory schooling laws. No wonder Consumer Union called their wonderful treatise on commercialism in schools *Captive Kids!*

The 1990s continued the assault on public funding for public institutions. When the Corporation for Public Broadcasting survived the near-fatal attack on its funding by congressional Republicans in 1995, PBS officials, facing immediate cutbacks in federal funds and the likelihood of even less government funding in the future, decided to seek other sources of revenue.[29] They redefined corporate underwriting of programs to include the sale of actual commercial time for specific products, like Juicy Juice, as sponsors of children's programming. Now it's virtually impossible to get a children's television program produced on public television without licensing agreements. Without regard for children's health, programs like *Teletubbies*[30] and *Clifford the Big Red Dog*[31] engage in promotions with fast-food companies like Burger King, McDonald's, Wendy's, and Chuck E. Cheese.

My colleagues—health-care professionals, educators, and advocates for children—are also worried about the more generalized and insidious messages implicit in this deluge of advertising. "Ten years ago, when I asked kids how they saw their future, they talked about what kinds of professions they wanted to have," a psychologist from California told me. "But now when I ask them those questions I find myself listening to a litany of things that they want to own! It's like the substance of their lives has been replaced by the externals." As a character from the movie *High Fidelity* says, "What matters is what you like, not what you *are* like."

According to a recent poll, 90 percent of parents think that marketing in media contributes to their children becoming too materialistic.[32] A survey of parents conducted by the Center for a New American Dream showed that 63 percent believed that their children define their self-worth in terms of what they own; 78 percent thought that marketing puts too much pressure on children to buy things that are too expensive, unhealthy, or unnecessary; and 70 percent expressed the belief that commercialism has a negative effect on children's values and worldviews.[33]

Parents have cause for alarm. People who highly value material goods (an orientation reinforced by consumer marketing) are likely to be more unhappy and have a lower quality of life than those who value more internal or nonmaterial rewards such as creativity, competence, and contributing to the community.[34]

As corporations vie more and more aggressively for young consumers, popular culture—which traditionally evolves from creative self-expression that captures and informs shared experience—is being smothered by commercial culture relentlessly sold to children by people who value them for their consumption, not their creativity. Consumerism as a value is marketed to children even in their toys. For the 2003 holiday season, Mattel produced at least seven Barbie Play Sets with a shopping theme. In addition to the one featured on the cover of this book, Let's Grocery Shop! Barbie, were Toy Store Barbie, Sweet Shoppin' Barbie, Shop & Style Fashion Barbie, Beauty Parlor Barbie, Chic Shoe Store Barbie, and Donut Shop Barbie.[35]

In the long run, our children's immersion in this commercial culture has implications that go far beyond what they buy or don't buy. Marketing is designed to influence more than food preferences and choice of clothing. It aims to affect core values such as lifestyle choices: how we define happiness and how we measure our self-worth. Meanwhile, the very traits that today's marketing encourages—materialism, impulsivity, entitlement, and unexamined brand loyalty—are antithetical to those qualities necessary in a healthy democratic citizenry. Instead of being a mainstay of American life, intensive advertising to children may be eroding its foundations.

A reporter recently asked me what I see as the most destructive aspect or effect of marketing to children as practiced in the United States today. I responded that marketing succeeds by purposely exploiting children's

vulnerabilities. Therefore, what you see as its "worst" effect will depend on
your child's weaknesses or predilections. For example, if your child is vulnerable to overeating and poor nutrition habits, then marketing of unhealthy foods (linked to childhood obesity) seems the worst. If your child
is vulnerable to eating disorders, then body-image marketing is what gets
your attention. If your child is susceptible to violent messages, then you
might see marketing of violent media and toys (linked to violent behavior)
as the worst potential effect of marketing to children. The same is true for
materialism, decreased creativity, family stress, and so on. Is obesity worse
than bulimia? Is violence worse than preteen sexual precocity?

The advertising industry's spin is that parents—not corporations—are
responsible for preventing the negative effects of media offerings and media
marketing on children. Certainly there are things parents can do. For one
thing, we can take televisions and computers out of our children's bedrooms. We can turn the television off during meals. We can monitor our
own consumerism and talk with children about the meanings embedded in
marketing messages. But parents can't do it alone. One family is hard-
pressed to successfully combat a $15 billion industry. Parents and children
need our help—as citizens, professionals, advocates, and activists.

The impact of corporate marketing on children's lives is breathtaking
in its depth and reach and is expanding around the world virtually
unchecked. This summer I sat in a restaurant in Santiago, Chile, surrounded by both Chilean families and posters of Barbie saying "Welcome"
in a variety of languages. A few years ago, when my work took me to Tblisi,
in the Republic of Georgia, I arrived during the grand opening of their second McDonald's. In the course of my research, I've come across studies of
the buying habits of Chinese children and the impact of advertising on
kids in India. I receive daily e-mails from colleagues around the country
detailing marketing efforts ranging from the subtle (Coca Cola's million-
dollar grant to the American Academy of Pediatric Dentistry, for instance)[36] to the blatant (the summer "camp" program that Toys "R" Us
now runs in its stores).[37]

Because marketing to children is so pervasive and affects so many aspect of their lives, my major struggle in writing about it has been in selecting topics and, of necessity, eliminating others. While marketing to
children is an international problem, I have chosen to focus my attention
on its impact on children and families in the United States because that's
what I know best. Other books center specifically, and in detail, on single

topics such as commercialism in the schools, for instance, or selling violence to children, or the effects of advertising on young girls. Instead, I've chosen to write about marketing from the perspective of what early childhood educators call "whole child development," taking the position that children are multifaceted beings whose physical, psychological, social, emotional, and spiritual development are all threatened when their value as consumers trumps their value as people.

While trying to find a home for this book, I encountered a lot of initial interest that rapidly diminished. Most publishers wanted me to write a "how to" book for parents. They envisioned a book entitled something like *Empowering Families: A Twelve-Step Program for Raising Advertising-Resistant Children.* That was not the book I had in mind, and so it was a relief when André Schiffrin at The New Press called and said, "I'm concerned that your book proposal is a bit *too* prescriptive."

Given that, I recognize that it's unfair to describe in gory detail the depth and breadth of how marketing affects children without offering some specific suggestions for what to do about it in both the short and the long terms. There are steps we can take as parents, as members of a larger community, and as citizens to stop the commercial exploitation of children. I outline these in chapter 12. I've also included a list of resources for public action. Throughout, I refer to the people taking care of children at home as parents. I mean that term to include grandparents, guardians, and anyone who has primary responsibility for raising a child.

I've never heard anyone, aside from an occasional marketing executive, say that advertising to children is good for them. And there's mounting evidence that it's harmful. Its motivating force is greed, just as surely as greed is the motivation for those corporate executives who cannibalize their own companies, create sweatshops, and artificially inflate consumer energy costs.

While children and their parents are most immediately affected, the transformation of childhood into a marketing demographic affects us all. It's a fact of life but not immutable. I believe that working together across political leanings, disciplines, professions, race, and class is the key to stopping the commercial exploitation of children. It is in hopes of helping to build such a coalition that I've written this book.

1

Notes from the Underground: Thirty-Six Hours at a Marketing Conference

THE CONFERENCE ROOM WALLS in the Yale Club of New York are paneled in rich, highly polished wood. Combined with the university's good name, they provide a veneer of academic dignity to any proceedings conducted within their confines.

I am attending the fifth annual Advertising and Promoting to Kids (APK) conference, sponsored by Brunico, Inc., the company that owns *KidScreen* magazine, "an international trade magazine serving the information needs and interests of all those involved in reaching children through entertainment."[1] In the advertising industry, the phrases "reaching children" and "communicating with kids" are euphemisms for marketing to children.

APK is not the biggest conference on marketing to children in the United States. That honor goes to Kid Power, one of a series run by a company called the Kid Power Exchange. In case you're wondering, the "power" in "Kid Power" is economic, and does not refer to self-esteem, empowerment, or any other remotely pro-child meaning. In addition to its annual Kid Power conference, the Kid Power Exchange runs other, more focused meetings like Kid Power Food and Beverage, Tween Power, Kid Power Latin America, and Teen Power, all designed to help corporations and advertisers target various segments of the kid market.

It costs a lot of money to attend these marketing conferences. The 2004 Kid Power Food and Beverage Marketing conference costs $2,899 for the conference plus two workshops.[2] The 2002 APK conference that I'm attending is a bargain at $1,495 plus $400 per workshop. The registration fees do not include room and board.

APK has been on my radar screen for a long time. For the past five

years, this particular conference has hosted *KidScreen*'s Golden Marble
Awards—the advertising industry's celebration of marketing to children.
The awards, not unlike the Emmys or the Oscars, are given solely on the
basis of artistry and/or effectiveness. Whether the products advertised are
good for kids, whether the messages embedded in the advertisements are
beneficial, or whether it's ethical to market to children at all are not taken
into consideration. My response when I read about the awards was outraged astonishment. I couldn't believe that people actually get awards for
manipulating children for profit. My second response was, "Someone
ought to do something about this." I contacted my colleague, Diane Levin,
and we began organizing demonstrations and other actions targeting the
APK and the awards.[3]

Before leaving to attend the APK conference, I was a little confused
about how to behave there. Should I add what I assumed would be a dis-
senting voice to the proceedings? I turned to my boss, Dr. Alvin Poussaint.
A psychiatrist who is a veteran of the civil rights movement and many other
campaigns for children, he has been a long-time colleague and mentor.
"So," I asked, "exactly how should I be at this conference?" His answer
was succinct. "Quiet," he replied. "Just be quiet." It was good advice.

In reality, however, from the first minutes of the first workshop, "Successful Brand Building Through Licensing," I find that unobtrusive silence is not going to be easy. First, there are only fifteen of us in the room.
Second, we are immediately asked to introduce ourselves and describe
why we are there. Lying is not my strong suit, but I also know that it is not
politic to announce that I am essentially a mole. After some fast mental
gymnastics, I have a solution. "I'm Susan Linn," I say brightly. "I'm a psychologist, and I'm interested in marketing." After all, both of these statements are true.

Leading us through the intricacies of product licensing are Joanne
Loria, executive vice president of the Joester Loria Group, and Jane Krae-
mer, vice president of sales and account management for the same company. Joanne explains that licensing is the process by which other
companies get to produce goods bearing the logo or image of trademarked
characters or of a property your company owns. In other words, the endless supply of sheets, backpacks, action figures, T-shirts, Happy Meal toys,
candy, cereal, and so on, decorated with characters from *Spider-man, Star
Wars,* or the latest hit from Disney, Nickelodeon, or the Cartoon Network,
are the result of product licensing.

According to the company's web site, Joester Loria claims responsibility—through the development of a licensing campaign for the now-
defunct teen soap opera *Beverly Hills 90210*—for setting the standards for
"live-action television licensing."[4] Joester Loria also claims credit for es-
tablishing "the viability of teen-direct marketing and merchandising." Licensing partners for *Beverly Hills 90210* included Coca-Cola, Noxzema,
Mattel, and AT&T, and resulted in over $500 million in sales worldwide.[5]

The two Joester Loria presenters set a pattern for speakers that continues throughout the entire conference. They are articulate, snazzily
dressed, and dedicated to their work. They also make statements about
children that leave me in a state of shock and awe. The people I encounter
at this conference have enormous influence over the lives of millions of
children and families. Unlike my colleagues—pediatricians, psychiatrists,
psychologists, social workers, educators—they do not connect the phrase
"what's best for children" with what they do.

Joanne Loria takes personal credit for her role in the financial success
of *South Park*, a big—and controversial—animated hit for Comedy Central, rated MA (for Mature Audiences). According to the TV Parental
Guidelines Council, programs rated MA are "specifically designed to be
viewed by adults and therefore may be unsuitable for children under 17."[6]
We are told, however, that in thinking about licensing, it is important to
know our target audience. Despite its MA rating, the primary audience for
South Park includes teens (thirteen to nineteen) as well as young adults
(twenty to thirty-four). The show is another example of the media industry's violation of its own voluntary rating system, as the program is being
marketed to children younger than the designated rating. Joanne assures
us several times that she doesn't want *South Park* to be associated with
children's products, and that she has always turned down deals for toys or
candy. The reason? Selling such children's products could lead to "bad
press." On the other hand, *South Park* clothing and accessories are routinely sold in the Juniors department of major retailers, for instance. And
who frequents the Juniors department? Kids at least as young as eleven or
twelve, in addition to teens.

After lunch we begin our second workshop, which sports the eu-
phemistic title, "Getting the Most Effective Communications Solutions for
New Product Launches." Advertising agencies don't "advertise," they
help companies "communicate" with their target audiences. For instance,
one fact among others I learn over the next few days comes from an African

American advertising executive who informs the audience that, in an exciting new innovation, marketers are now "communicating" with African Americans in church.

Since we've been joined by some new people for the afternoon, we begin with another round of introductions. I launch into the "I'm a psychologist and I'm so interested" routine again, except this time, for variation, I change plain old "advertising" to "advertising to children." The workshop leader's eyes light up: "Oh! You could be very helpful today." Great.

This workshop is led by two staff members from the New York office of DDB Worldwide Communications—one of the biggest advertising agencies on the planet, with 206 offices in 96 countries. The company grossed well over $1 billion in 1998. DDB's contributions to our quality of life include getting a population of moms to associate deserving "a break today" with McDonald's and, more recently, the Budweiser beer campaign featuring the tag line "Whassup?"[7] Described in the marketing press as "The hottest ad campaign in America,"[8] it won the Grand Prix award for advertising at the Cannes Film Festival.[9] The phrase "Whassup?" has become so popular that reporter Scott Donaton, writing for *Advertising Age*, complained it was introduced to his three young children by Radio Disney. "With apologies to the mouse," he wrote, "I couldn't believe my ears. Here was a song consisting almost entirely of what sound like samples from actual 'Whas-sup' commercials set to the beat of MC Hammer's 'U Can't Touch This.' Not surprisingly, my kids immediately began to yell 'Whassup' to each other." It didn't take long for Donaton's kids to connect the phrase to Budweiser.[10]

Meanwhile, the duo at the front of the room is very young and very energetic. "At the end of the day," one of them enthuses, "we want kids to say, 'I need this product. I want this product. I love this product.' "

We are divided into teams. Each team is charged with creating an ad campaign (or at least a single ad) for a fictitious product called "Stuff," which is a line of shampoos and gels for girls. The campaign is to be targeted at six- to eleven-year-olds. We're assured that Stuff is not a real product. Everyone, including me, is relieved. Perhaps unfairly, I assume that most of the others are relieved that DDB is not going to steal their ideas for a real advertising campaign. For my part, I'm relieved that I'm not actually going to be in any way responsible for convincing six- to eleven-year-olds that they "need," "want," and "love" a particular kind of shampoo.

As I begin working with my team, I feel a lot like an older version of the secret agent in John LeCarré's *Little Drummer Girl*. What is my obligation to the other people in my group? I wonder. Don't I owe them my best shot? After all, the class is going to vote to determine which campaign is the best. My team members include a bubbly and extremely competent young woman executive from Nickelodeon, who immediately takes charge. The other two—a young man from a New Mexico production company and a young woman who has a media property she's trying to sell—are significantly less bubbly and less experienced. I am the fourth.

I have to bite my tongue. After all, the age range of six to eleven constitutes a huge developmental span, ranging from just post-preschool to just preteen. I see lots of questions that seem obvious to me but that no one else asks: Why would a six-year-old need her own shampoo? For that matter, why would an eleven-year-old? Is it beneficial to kids in this age range to want their own hair products? Is it beneficial to their families? How much is Stuff going to cost? What's in it?

No one—including me—asks any of these questions.

Each team is given what's called a "brief," which presents the characteristics of our "demographic." We're told that the children to whom Stuff is being marketed are "closet kids." They like to be all grown up (or at least like teenagers) with their friends, but then they might go home and play with their Barbies in private. (I wish I could substitute "doll" for "Barbie" in this account, but in fact, Barbie is the example used.) I find the notion of a six-year-old needing to be a "closet kid" a depressing thought. Again, no one seems to wonder about the source of this phenomenon.

The Nickelodeon executive takes charge—clearly she has done this before. Since workshop leaders in both sessions have repeatedly lauded Nickelodeon as the grand master of marketing to kids, the rest of us assume that she does it very, very well.

In fact, the process of creating an ad can be exciting, challenging, and creatively satisfying. It's a process with which I have some familiarity. For several years, I worked at creating public service announcements (PSAs) for children about subjects ranging from prejudice to drug abuse. Since PSAs—like commercials—are quite short, the challenge is to compress the essence of what ad companies call a "big idea" into a tiny, focused space of time in a way that is both compelling and clear to your target audience.

When I first started speaking out about my concerns about marketing to kids, people frequently asked me if I experience any conflict of interest

because of my work in these public service campaigns. I don't. The goal of
a public service announcement is to transmit positive values to children or
to provide them with models for prosocial behavior, while the goal of a
product ad is to sell that product. The first, by definition, has the good of
society and the well-being of children at heart. The second has as its first
priority the ensuring of product sales: whether or not the values transmitted in the ad, or the products being touted, are "good" for kids is secondary at best and often irrelevant.

Even with the best of intentions, it's not always easy to be mindful of
the unintentional messages that might be sent when any sort of promotion
is aimed at kids. When I was consulting to the Leadership Council Education Fund (the educational branch of the Leadership Council on Civil
Rights), the group was embarking on a massive public service campaign
targeted at children and designed to promote diversity and combat big-
otry. The ad agency it was working with created a spot that featured an
opening shot lingering lovingly on an obviously multicultural group of babies. Suddenly the mood changed and each baby was stamped with a racial
epithet—"kike," "dago," and so on. A deep, authoritative voice intoned,
"Life's too short. Stop the Hate."

That spot, on my advice and that of other consultants, was never aired.
The problem was that the most powerful moments of its thirty seconds
were the racial epithets. Because young children are concrete thinkers and
cannot engage in abstractions, they would not be able to make the leap
from the images to the intended message, which was something like "babies start out innocent and beautiful and isn't it awful that they get stamped
with racial slurs and stereotypes." Instead, for many young children, this
would be one of their first experiences with racial slurs, and it was a pretty
good bet that those words would be what they would take away from that
experience.

Of course, that's not the kind of insight any of us were being asked to
give in this particular marketing workshop. In the advertising world, a
"creative brief" is an outline that lays out parameters for creative efforts. By
the time a creative team actually starts creating, a great deal of background
work has already been done. The "tone" and "message" of the ad have already been identified, as have those characteristics of the target population
that are relevant to the "pitch." The brief my team receives describing the
target audience for Stuff reads exactly as follows:

Kids 6–11 with a bull's-eye of kids ages 7–9. These kids are at a crossroads, with one foot in the kid world and one in the adult world. They may still have Barbies in their closets, but can't wait to shop at the Limited Too. Because they are at the cusp of a new phase in life, and are, therefore, beginning to explore their identity [*sic*]. They are looking for ways to express their new sense of individuality and independence. They are beginning to care about fashion and are even creating their own styles.

At this point, my vow of silence begins to weigh heavy. A freshman psychology major handing in this description of six- to eleven-year-old girls in even the most basic child development class would probably receive a failing grade—and I'm not talking about its brevity or even its marketing orientation. Since when do six-year-olds have one foot, or even a baby toenail, in the adult world? Six-year-olds and eleven-year-olds might both be on the cusp of a new phase of life, but it's not the same cusp. Sure, children are individuals and develop at different rates, but in general the kids on either end of this age grouping don't have much in common developmentally.

Envision a first-grader named Alicia walking to school with her sister Karla, who's a "big kid"—in the sixth grade, about to graduate to middle school. Which one would you trust to cross a busy street alone? Which one might you be able to leave by herself for a few hours with a friend in the house? Which one is starting to do long-term projects at school? Which has begun to develop breasts? Which one can go out for lunch or to a movie with friends?

Alicia doesn't have the same capacity for making judgments as Karla. That's why Karla has more privileges and more independence. Alicia is making a transition from magical thinking (believing, for instance, that maybe wishes *can* make things come true). She knows that puppets don't really talk and that Mom or Dad is the tooth fairy, but she has trouble with abstractions like "might" or "maybe."

When both sisters hear a classic story, posed by researchers interested in moral development, about a poor man who steals medicine for his sick wife, Alicia is appalled and cannot believe that there are any circumstances in which it might be okay to steal. (She's recently changed her opinion about that; about a year ago she would have said that stealing was wrong because you might be caught.) Karla also thinks stealing is wrong, but she's beginning to wonder what she would do if someone she loved needed medicine and she couldn't afford it.

When the girls watch television, six-year-old Alicia easily identifies commercials as separate from the programs, but she has trouble understanding that the way things are presented in a commercial might not be true. Her older sister, on the other hand, is more inclined to be skeptical; she knows that if you're trying to sell a product you always present it in the best possible light.

Some of the girls in Karla's sixth-grade class are starting to get pimples, and most of them can't stand to get dirty or smelly; Alicia still argues with her mom about why she needs to take a bath. Karla is starting to wash her hair every day and is using a lot of shampoo. She worries a lot about being popular; Alicia isn't sure what "popular" means.

Eleven-year-olds may be considered preteens. Many of them (especially girls) are grappling with hormonal changes, and it's possible that they are already becoming immersed in complex questions of identity, but the classic adolescent identity struggle—Who am I in relation to my family and my peers?—involves choosing among differing points of view, beliefs, and values. In fact, teens' notorious self-consciousness about their appearance occurs in part because of their newfound awareness of themselves as individuals in relation to other people who may have different perspectives. Six-year-olds are just beginning to grapple with the idea that there *are* perspectives other than their own.

In the early 1990s, the Media Center at the Judge Baker Children's Center in Boston answered a call for proposals for programs specifically aimed at five- to seven-year-olds from the newly formed and briefly funded National Endowment for Children's Educational Television (NECET). After our initial proposal was funded and we had begun developing a pilot, we were asked to broaden our target audience to include six- to eleven-year-olds. From a demographic perspective, that probably made sense. It costs a lot of money to produce a television program, and the competition for audiences is intense; limiting the target age of a program to only two years narrows that program's reach and potential for both sustainability and benefit to children. From a developmental perspective, however, even if one's motives are pure, targeting such a wide range in age poses problems, including the possibility that six-year-olds might be exposed, and unintentionally harmed, by content and images they can't grasp.

If a six-year-old is part of the target demographic for a product like shampoo, it's likely that the commercial will appear during television shows broadcast on one of the big three networks, or shown on stations like Nickelodeon that are "all kid all the time." It's also likely that the product will be marketed as being "for her."

If she watches a lot of television and the campaign is well funded, a six-year-old like Alicia will be exposed to the ad repeatedly. If she's developmentally on target, she is also likely to have a tendency to believe what she sees and won't yet understand that the ad is purposely designed make her want the shampoo. Since the ad is designed to convince her that this particular shampoo is "just for her," she's liable to be persuaded that she does want it and to ask her mom to buy it for her. Also, because advertisers understand that kids tend to look up to and emulate children older than themselves, a basic principle in children's television shows and advertisements is to cast children slightly older than the target audience. Thus Alicia is further primed in this case because the girl swishing her hair and holding up the bottle is about twelve.

Once eleven-year-old Karla discovers that the shampoo "just for her" is the favorite of her six-year-old sister, she's likely to want to distance herself from it since now it seems babyish. Because she's on the cusp between childhood and adolescence, it's likely that Karla will turn to products advertised to teens, with correspondingly older models and ads that are often quite sexually provocative in nature. Since ads teach values and behavior as well as sell products, it's quite possible that both the eleven-year-old and her younger sister will emulate advertised behavior (wearing precociously sexualized clothing, for instance) and absorb values (that even very young girls should be sexualized objects) that they can't fully understand and that can be harmful to them.

Most eleven-year-olds are physically, psychologically, and socially worlds away from their six-year-old siblings. Yet the kind of flawed and self-serving view that lumps the age groups together for marketing purposes informs the creation of billions of dollars' worth of advertising. In the APK workshop, and throughout the whole conference, presenters continually repeat the mantra that six- to eleven-year-olds (called tweens in the marketing world) are neither kids nor teens and therefore need their own products.

Biting my tongue even harder, I join my team members in an effort to create a really snazzy commercial. I suggest that we think about the "closet kid" phenomenon. After all, a life of flip-flopping between Barbies and the

Limited Too sounds exhausting. It certainly involves an ongoing series of transformations. "What if we position Stuff as transformative?" I ask. My fellow creators are intrigued. I'm sorry to say that I'm secretly thrilled.

We decide to start shooting in black-and-white until the (decorous) shower scene; once we encounter our multicolored soap bubbles we will move to glorious color. We are creating the notion of shampoo as psyche-delic. We bandy about suggestions for possible spokespeople for the prod-uct—like Britney Spears. This time I can't restrain myself. I wonder aloud if Britney is a good choice. The Nickelodeon exec nods knowingly. "Oh, I understand. She *is* getting kind of outdated." Well, no, that's not exactly what I meant. It's that plastic sexuality I was wondering about.

While the others mull over the visuals—never my strong suit—I find myself thinking about tag lines. "How about this?" I ask tentatively: "Stuff—For a Change!" Is that transformative, or what?

My tag line is a big hit! Several people comment on it, including a dy-namic young man from the first group to present their ideas, who pro-claims it much better than theirs. As we wind up, the woman from Nickelodeon smiles at me. "Great tag line," she says.

I'm delighted.

The next morning, the main conference begins in the Yale Club ball-room. Registration and schmoozing start at 7:45, and the formal program starts an hour later. To avoid conversation—after all, I'm not looking for a job, and I'm trying to keep quiet—I arrive pretty close to 8:45. I avoid con-tact with my fellow workshop attendees, who, to be honest, are not seeking me out either. After plopping my program book down on one of the round banquet tables I wander over to the breakfast buffet, where it becomes clear that I have not arrived late enough. As I pour my coffee I'm ap-proached by a tall, slim man with thinning hair, a rather sad smile, and a faint Canadian accent. "Are you from the Judge Baker Children's Center?" he asks. I can feel a rush of adrenaline—my second day at APK is not going to go according to plan either, and to calm myself down I silently chant my mantra: "Be quiet. Be quiet. Be quiet." Still, I'm not about to deny my affil-iation.

"Yes, I am," I answer, smiling politely.

"I'm from Brunico," the man offers. In fact, he's the company's presi-dent. A well-trained spy would probably have walked away at this point or contrived to spill her coffee. I, on the other hand, am cursed with a perverse sense of the absurd. I'm dying to see what's going to happen next. So I wait.

"How did you find yesterday's workshops?" he asks. I know the right answer to that one. "They were very interesting," I reply, offering silent thanks to whoever invented the word "interesting," which has seen me through years of difficult "what did you think of" challenges. But Mr. Brunico, as I have come to think of him, is not going to let me off easy. "In a positive way?" he asks. "Or a negative way?" I've been outed.

I stare at him blankly for a moment. Clearly, there's not much point in pretending any longer. "Well," I answer, "we have some serious philosophical differences." He nods. "You know," I continue, "this is the only conference about children that I've ever been to where nobody questions whether the work they are doing is good for kids or not." For better or worse, this comment is a conversation stopper.

Perhaps Mr. Brunico is thinking that it's not the job of advertisers or marketers to think about the welfare of the children they target. If so, we disagree. Shouldn't we all be concerned about children's welfare? Aren't they our hope for the future? Instead of responding to my comment, after what I remember as a very long pause, he mentions that his own children are doing fine. This time it's my turn to be silent. He's not the first person I've heard point to their own well-functioning children as icons of why it's okay to market to kids. It's a comment I find puzzling. What about how other people's kids are doing? Is he suggesting that his children are immune to advertising, and, by extension, that advertising doesn't work? As I struggle in silence over whether to ask any of these questions, he departs with a courtly nod. A few hours later, at lunchtime, he stops by my table to ask if I'm "gathering good ammunition."

"Actually, I am," I reply.

For the next two days, this conference continues to trouble me with its loud absence of a moral/ethical context for marketing to children. At least, there is no public expression of such a context.

During a break, I chat with an elegantly dressed young woman. After a while, she shares some of her concerns about her work. "I draw the line at schools," she says. "I don't think we should market in schools. We had a project in a school, and I was really uncomfortable." But she loves her job. "I love kids," she says. "Where else would I get to play with kids all day? I talk to my friends who've gone on to clinical psychology programs, and they say that most of their work is managing—or working with parents. I get to play all day. Sometimes I think I should be doing something that's more useful. Maybe this is a rationalization, but, you know, I did a project with McDonald's—not about selling hamburgers, but about Ronald Mc-Donald. And Ronald McDonald is about having fun and making kids happy. He doesn't sell anything." Her voice trails off and she looks at me sideways. "Maybe that's a rationalization."

Roshan Ahuja, a professor of marketing ethics at Xavier University, has been writing about what the world of business ethics calls the "Pontius Pilate Plight,"[11, 12] which characterizes the experience of a schism between the ethics of your trade or profession and your own personal ethics. During my three days among the marketing experts, waiting foolishly and in vain for moral/ethical issues to be raised, I found myself thinking about that condition. Are there emotional costs to living with such a split?

One of the first speakers to address the whole conference (his talk is entitled "The End of Marketing As We Know It") reiterates, like some kind of uplifting religious chant, "The purpose of advertising is to sell more stuff, to more people, more of the time." Having recently left a position with Matchbox Cars, he speaks with pride about the work he did there on product licensing. "Truth be told," he says, "there is so much money to be made off licensing that it kind of competes with your core business. Licensing is like printing money." He then explains that licensing creates a connection to consumers so that a kid will think, "I'm a Matchbox kid and Matchbox surrounds my life."

To beef up sales, Matchbox turned to McDonald's. Inspired by the U.S. Mint's release of the state quarters series—which are evidently "hot" collectibles for children—they launched a fifty-car collection of Match-boxes, each featuring a state license plate and the date that state was admit-ted to the Union. The catch was that six of these vehicles were found at only McDonald's as part of a Happy Meal. In other words, to complete the collection, kids had to go to McDonald's.

From a marketing standpoint, this promotion is a great idea. It com-bines children's inclination to collect, young boys' interest in cars, and parents' inclinations to promote prosocial and educational activities. However, I wonder if I'm the only person listening who's also thinking about how unfair it is to hold a kid's car collection (and a kid's parent) hostage to McDonald's. After all, we're not talking about just one Happy

Meal purchase but at least six, and probably more, since it's part of the fun that you never know which toy from a series will turn up in *your* burger box.

Of course, in theory, all parents have to do is refuse to take their children to McDonald's—and endure their disappointment at not being able to complete an educational, prosocial, fun collection. But, as is made abundantly clear in another presentation, it's difficult for parents and children to resist McDonald's wide-ranging, well-funded, multipronged, neverending, and virtually inescapable marketing campaigns. For younger children, the touchstone of the campaigns is Ronald McDonald, the jolly clown with the red hair and big, big smile whom *Advertising Age* named second only to the Marlboro Man on its list of the top ten advertising icons of the twentieth century.[13]

The discussion of Ronald occurs at this conference in the context of child development. As in past years, APK offers a developmental/psychological snapshot of children for the purpose of helping attendees learn more about how to target their campaigns toward various age groups. Previously, this slot had been taken by Ph.D. psychologists. This time, however, the honor goes to a young woman from the Leo Burnett ad agency who does not have an advanced degree in psychology.

I don't know the reason for this switch, but I like to think that it has something to do with a growing public concern about psychologists and their role in marketing to children. In 1999 Gary Ruskin, of the advocacy group Commercial Alert, and psychologist Allen Kanner wrote a letter to the American Psychological Association signed by sixty psychologists urging the APA to take a stand regarding psychologists who use their professional expertise to help corporations target children with marketing. The letter generated a great deal of press and, as a result, the APA assigned a task force to look into this matter and into marketing to children in general.

The 1992 Ethical Principles of the American Psychological Association include one titled "Social Responsibility," which stated, among other things, that psychologists should "apply and make public their knowledge of psychology in order to contribute to human welfare."[14] I was dismayed, however, to discover that that in the new version of the principles, effective June 2003, the APA eliminated that sentence—and the entire Social Responsibility Principle—from the document.[15] Unfortunately, there are many from the ranks of our profession who help companies market successfully to children by routinely employing the principles and practices of child psychology—from developmental theory to diagnostic techniques.

Developmental psychology—the study of how children develop and change over time—has traditionally provided the underpinnings for community practices and public policy designed to protect children and to promote their well-being. Jean Piaget's studies of how children's understanding of the world evolves are the cornerstone of countless school programs and teaching methods, which are also informed by Lawrence Kohlberg's work on moral development. Erik Erikson's constructs of psychosocial "tasks"—and the consequences of failure to successfully navigate those maturational milestones—provide the foundation for parent education, especially about early childhood education, and are used to help therapists understand their clients' needs. What commercial interests have taken from their work, however, also serves as the foundation of what the advertising industry calls market segmentation, or target marketing. In *What Kids Buy and Why: The Psychology of Marketing to Kids,* for instance, principal author Dan Acuff, president of a market research company called Youth Market Systems, has this to say about the relevance of child development to marketing and product development:

> We have divided or segmented the youth target . . . in accordance with a wide
> variety of scientific research such as that of Piaget, Erikson, and Kohlberg. . . .
> It is an in-depth understanding of the child consumer that provides the only real
> access to approximating a "winning formula" for the development of products
> and programs that succeed with kids.[16]

Both Erikson and Piaget write about children with such care and respect that it seems the height of cynicism—not unlike that displayed by the commercial that features the image of Gandhi to sell Apple computers—to use their work to hone marketing techniques for what advertisers frequently call the "kid market." For many marketing experts, however, it's just another strategy in a cutthroat competition for "share of mind."[17]

The marketing industry, with the help of psychologists, targets its campaigns to hook children by exploiting their developmental vulnerabilities—the ways that their cognitive, social, emotional, and physical development influence decision making, likes, dislikes, interests, and activities. "Playing off teen insecurities is a proven strategy," writes the author of a piece on teen marketing in a 1997 issue of *Marketing Tools.* "But even that won't get you very far if you're using a stale campaign and yesterday's slang."[18]

In the industry newsletter *Selling to Kids,* a 1998 article on selling prom-related items, written by Rachel Geller of the Geppetto Group, a company specializing in marketing to children, provides tips for retailers based on "intensive work with psychologists," encouraging them to exploit teenage vulnerabilities. "There's no end to teen narcissism: focus on the fantasy," is one bit of advice offered, along with the following:

> Teens are more difficult because they are an oppositional subculture, interested in shutting out the adult world. However, there are enormous opportunities for the marketer who is able to understand both the reality and fantasy of teen life.[19]

That same year, the global marketing company Saatchi and Saatchi hired a team of psychologists and anthropologists to do a study on Generation Y, or today's tweens. The following excerpt from a 1999 issue of *Selling to Kids* reported the group's findings to the industry and urged companies to market to these children's need to belong and to establish a group identity:

> Generation Y also has a strong need for community. In order to win these consumers, children's business retailers should change their goal to selling a community experience, instead of selling a product. The retailer must move to a "community" mentality where the Generation Y consumer becomes empowered, and they get involved. . . . These findings, the result of an exhaustive study conducted by ad agency giant Saatchi & Saatchi over a six-month period, have particularly significant implications for children's business retailers: change your goal from selling a product to creating a hip, community experience . . . and you'll win the loyalty of what Saatchi & Saatchi calls today's "connexity" kids.[20]

Anyone who works with teens and preteens—or who reflects on his or her own experiences at that stage of life—is aware that adolescence is a time of confusion, insecurity, and even rebellion. The challenge for the caretakers of those who are making this passage is to help them safely navigate the turbulence. But for marketers, adolescent vulnerabilities provide grist for the profit mill.

Marketing agencies are as relentless in their quest for knowledge about children as any academic institution—and they are certainly better funded than most universities. In fact, to the dismay of many in the traditional bastions of the social sciences, a great deal of the research currently being conducted on the lives of children is being done by and for the corporate world; as Paul Kurnit, president of an agency specializing in marketing to children, states, "We've probably done more recent original research on kids, life stages and recognition of brands than anybody."[21] What's missing, however, in reports of data collected for market research, or how those data are used, are the questions that should be central to all psychological research conducted with children: Am I using this information to make children's lives better? How will this application of developmental psychology benefit children?

None of the articles quoted earlier questions the ethics, let alone the psychosocial impact, of inundating teens and preteens with images and messages designed to foster insecurity as the primary motivation for action, nor do most of the hundreds of articles and books I've read in the course of my research. It seems that no one in the advertising industry, whatever their private concerns might be, publicly questions either the ethics or the effects of marketing messages that play to a child's vulnerabilities. In fact, for years most marketers have maintained that public concern about the impact of marketing on children is overblown. In a 1997 article in *Business Week*, Tom Kalinske, former chief executive officer of Sega of America and Mattel, Inc., said, "I have a high regard for the intelligence of kids." The article went on to explain that "Kalinske and others in the industry believe that kids today are more sophisticated consumers than the generations that preceded them, well able to recognize hype and impervious to crude manipulation."[22] Mr. Kurnit expanded on this point of view in *KidScreen*, explaining that "It's a point of fact that today's child is more savvy than ever before about what it's like to live in a commercial society. . . . And what parents are telling us is that kids are requesting brands and are brand-aware almost as soon as their verbal skills set in."[23]

By championing children's "intelligence" and "sophistication" as a rationale for the escalating onslaught of child-targeted commercials, marketing experts reveal that their love affair with psychology is as superficial and deceptive as the ads they create.

Children's alleged sophistication about media and marketing is also used as justification for product placement—the growing trend of embedding products as props and backgrounds in movies, television shows, and video games. Product placement has even led to such spin-offs as books for babies that look just like a Froot Loops box or a package of M&Ms. Commenting on the latter, Julie Halpin, CEO of the Geppetto Group, portrays such books as a marketing tactic with benefits for all: "For the marketer it's creating affinity for the brand. For parents, the kid is learning to count. There's no downside." [24]

Really? When childhood obesity is a major public health problem,[25] it's hard to see that inculcating babies with an affection for candy, or sugared cereal, is so benign. And while there are laws prohibiting product placement on television programs directly targeted to children, there are no similar laws regarding films for young audiences, which is why, for example, the popular 2001 film *Spy Kids* contained an advertisement for McDonald's disguised as a plot point.

One key aspect of the problem is that the industry confuses—or pretends to confuse—the trappings of sophistication with maturation. That babies and toddlers request or recognize brands in no way reflects that they are "savvy" about marketing, which would imply a capacity to decode and resist advertising messages. It does suggest that very young children are highly susceptible to many forms of suggestion, including marketing—a fact that is borne out by academic research.[26]

The marketing industry's embrace of the notion that children are leapfrogging through development at breakneck speed is simplistic at best, potentially harmful, and certainly self-serving. While evidence suggests that girls are entering puberty at an earlier age than did their mothers and grandmothers,[27] and that both boys and girls are beginning to abuse drugs, alcohol, and tobacco at younger ages,[28] I have not seen evidence that children's emotional development is keeping pace with their behavior—and we don't know what meaning kids make of their early exposure to the trappings of maturation through the media. How does a seven-year-old understand the plastic sexuality of Britney Spears? How do ten-year-olds cope with the pressure to dress and act in sexually provocative ways, to swagger, and to rebel as a matter of style?

According to the toy manufacturers, proof of children's increasing sophistication lies in statistics showing that they are leaving traditional toys behind at a younger age, trading them in for video games and pop-culture icons. Their response is to market toys that are representations of media culture, solving sales problems on several levels since media-based toys are a gold mine for both toy companies and media conglomerates. However, we don't know much about the impact that dolls based on sexy pop stars have on the emotional/social development of young girls, or about the effect of the macho images of wrestlers or super heroes on young boys. We can't discount the likelihood that targeting even young children with marketing campaigns for "sophisticated" toys like video games contributes to their apparent disinterest in the more traditional playthings that give them latitude to imagine and create.

Here we encounter a collision between the concept of market segmentation and the desire of advertisers to expand their consumer base at least expense to themselves. For instance, the industry's tendency to group six- to eleven-year-olds together (or eight- to twelve-year-olds, as in the quote earlier) as a one-size-fits-all target audience for everything from food to clothing and toys to MTV is in part based on the traditional delineations for audience demographics in children's television programming.

Back to the APK conference and Ronald McDonald. The session on developmental psychology is called "How Kids Grow: Marketing to Kids at Different Stages." Like the young woman I spoke to earlier, the presenter is young, energetic, well-dressed, and wildly enthusiastic about children. Given that she has only thirty minutes to cover the psychological, social, emotional, and cognitive development of children aged two to twelve, she does a pretty good job; if much of what she says is simplistic, it's at least in the ballpark in terms of accuracy. She neatly demonstrates the relevance of child development theory to marketing by presenting ads created by her agency that illustrate exactly how the insights she's offered can be translated into a commercial.

The first commercial she shows is one designed to elevate Ronald McDonald's ratings among two- to five-year-olds, ratings that evidently began to slip a few years ago. The presenter repeats the same self-deluded claim I heard twenty-four hours ago—that Ronald McDonald doesn't sell anything. He's instead about fun, trust, happiness, and other warm, fuzzy feelings.

It's true that Ronald McDonald doesn't actually tell kids to eat hamburgers, but the reality is that he does a great job of inculcating positive feelings in children all over the world, all in the service of selling fast food. In 1990, research with eight-year-olds showed that when children were asked, "Who would you like to take you out for a treat?" fathers, teachers, and grandparents all ranked behind Ronald McDonald and General

Mills's Tony the Tiger.[29] Over half of the nine- and ten-year-olds surveyed in an Australian poll thought that Ronald McDonald knew best what's good for children to eat.[30]

When Ronald's popularity was on the wane with preschoolers, Leo Burnett was hired to shore it up again. The commercial our presenter shows features a group of somber little kids tiptoeing in an anxious fashion into a museum. At the front desk they encounter a stern, white-haired woman who tells them in no uncertain terms that they must be quiet. The children are cowed. But suddenly—Ronald appears! The kids burst into smiles, the music switches from somber to joyful, and he leads them, frolicking happily, out of the museum and over to McDonald's—rather like a clown-faced Pied Piper.

It's hard to understand how anyone can believe—except in the narrowest sense—that Ronald McDonald isn't selling anything. It's true that he never actually says, "Buy a Happy Meal," but in another spot I've seen, he asks a group of bored-looking kids if they want to "race to McDonald's." In yet another, young musicians having a boring time playing classical music stop and rush to follow Ronald to the restaurant; in the closing shot he's holding a box of McDonald's French fries.

Actually, the rat catcher of Hamlin Town provides a pretty good metaphor for Ronald McDonald. He looked harmless and his music was irresistible to children, but the children who followed him were lost. We don't know where the children of Hamlin Town ended up after following the piper, but a growing number of the kids enticed by Ronald McDonald (or Tony the Tiger, the Keebler Elves, or any of the other fast or junk food cartoon icons) end up in obesity clinics or hospitalized for type 2 diabetes.

And the emotional messages in these commercials are so troubling. Aside from the message that museums and classical music are boring, children are also getting the seductive, developmentally targeted, and life-threatening message that eating fast food will make them happy. Combine that with hooks like the Matchbox cars that are available only at McDonald's, or tie-ins featuring favorite movie and television characters (and the fact that McDonald's is only one company targeting children in this way), and it becomes clear why it's difficult for parents to "just say no."

The presentations I hear at the APK conference over the course of seventy-two hours are detailed, loving descriptions of individual assaults on children and families that, taken together, amount to an all-out war. They also take on a kind of Orwellian cast in their "War Is Peace" style of language. I hear the president of Toys "R" Us say that his company no longer has customers; instead, the mega toy store chain has "guests." I hear the Matchbox guy present an interesting spin on a phenomenon known in the marketing-to-kids world as "getting older younger." In the toy industry this translates into the profit-deflating notion that children appear to be outgrowing playthings such as dolls and toy cars more quickly, which means that companies have to work more aggressively to market products to young children because the life span of children's interest in each toy is getting shorter. "The window for cool" is smaller, he says. Companies have to either sell more toys to a narrower age group (hence promoting collections) or broaden the reach of their product, which often involves some kind of Internet site.

The presentations are upbeat—the speakers are charismatic. I realize, as speaker after speaker recounts success stories, that a side benefit of presenting at conferences like these, of course, is that it's an opportunity for marketers to market themselves and their companies. But one crack appears in the Matchbox guy's veneer—when he suddenly says that he doesn't want his young son to know anything about *Digimon,* a wildly popular television program on Fox featuring violent monsters. He shrugs and says, as if it were self-evident, "I don't want him to grow up too fast."

2

A Consumer in the Family:
The Nag Factor and Other Nightmares

"I already fight with my fifth grader about R-rated movies and watching wrestling on TV. Now he's listening to the most disgusting music on the radio. Every other word is 'bitch,' or 'fuck.' I know it's not good for him. My parents hated my music too, but somehow this feels different."

"I can't believe that I actually bought my daughter a Barbie [says a longtime feminist]. She kept begging me for one and I finally gave in. I just got worn down, and I'm already so strict with her about other things."

"Last time we went to the grocery store, my four-year-old had a meltdown in the cereal aisle. He kept pestering me to buy some sugar cereal or another. When I said no, he had a huge tantrum right then and there. The thing is, I don't *want* him to eat a lot of sugar. But maybe I shouldn't be so strict about it."

I don't absolve parents of responsibility for their children's well being in a commercially driven world, but most of the parents I talk to are doing their best in what often feels like an unending and overwhelming struggle. In the face of well-funded, brilliantly strategized, and relentless commercial assaults on their children, parents are expected to be unyielding gatekeepers and their children's sole protectors.

"I think it's all the parents' fault," an older woman comments during a call-in radio show about marketing to kids. "They are too indulgent these days. They need to learn to say no." I often hear comments like this when I talk about children and the marketplace. I don't agree. After years of exploring advertising and advertising practices as they affect children, I've come to the conclusion that telling parents to "just say no" to every marketing-related request that they feel is unsafe, unaffordable, unreasonable,

or contrary to family values is about as simplistic as telling a drug addict to
"just say no" to drugs.

The phrase "It takes a village to raise a child" may have been overused
during the past decade, but it's still an evocative metaphor for the argument that caring for our children is a collective effort that has to extend beyond the immediate family. It also reminds us that children's experiences
beyond their own households—in the neighborhood, in school, or in the
larger community—can have a powerful impact on their growth and development.

As I listen to parents and think about my own experiences, I am reminded of a conversation I had with a colleague of mine who works with
families in a neighborhood saturated with gangs. He talked about the an-
guish of parents who find that—despite their best efforts—they can't compete with the seductive offerings of a toxic street culture. The culture of
marketing that pervades all our communities, from the poorest to the rich-
est, is similar in that it competes with parental values for children's hearts,
minds, and souls. These days, the village raising our children has been
transformed by electronic media, a ubiquitous, commercially driven force
in all our lives. What this means is that children are bombarded from
morning to night by messages designed not to make their lives better but to
sell them something.

Most of the studies on media marketing to children have focused
on the products advertised, not the *process* of the marketing or the consequences of that process. But there are consequences, and among
the most insidious of these is marketing's effect on family life. Parents may
hold the line and refuse to buy, they may overindulge children by acquiesc-
ing to every request, or they may strain their finances by buying more
than they can really afford. Conflict about stuff marketed to kids is a cause
of stress in families,[1] and marketers are well aware of that fact.[2] Advertising
clearly influences the things children ask for—if it didn't, of course, companies wouldn't be spending so much money doing it.

A 1999 article in *Advertising Age* begins, "Mothers are known for in-
structing children not to play with their food. But increasingly marketers
are encouraging them to."[3] On grocery and toy store shelves, this has
translated into a rash of such nutritional "necessities" as green catsup,
chocolate-flavored French fries, and battery-operated lollipop holders that
twirl around by themselves. In chapter 6, I discuss marketing's impact on
nutrition, obesity, and eating disorders; here I want to explore the attitudes

and philosophies behind the creation of such products and the campaigns to sell them, as well as the impact of those attitudes and philosophies on families.

Starting with the simple example cited from *Advertising Age,* it's certainly true that children like to play with food. For babies, being able to eat with their fingers and explore the textures of food is a valuable tactile experience, but the fact that children *like* playing with food is not enough justification for encouraging them to continue to do so long after babyhood and against their parents' wishes.

Our job as parents, in addition to nurturing and protecting our children, is to help them learn to live in a civil society by transmitting positive values and standards of behavior. One of the more relentless aspects of this task is to sort out, sometimes on a daily or hourly basis, those things that are harmless or even beneficial to children from those things they like to do that may cause them harm, cause harm to others, or cross our own personal threshold for irritating behavior.

In the grand scheme of things, playing with food against a parent's wishes seems like a small transgression. In and of itself, it is, though that's not the point. By targeting children with ads designed to entice them to play with food, marketers are willfully encouraging children to do something that they acknowledge is contrary to most parents' expectations and values. In fact, the marketing industry purposely comes between children and parents in many instances, potentially wreaking all sorts of havoc in family life. One of the most egregious examples of evidence that they do this comes from a 1998 study on nagging. Conducted not to help parents prevent nagging but rather to help retailers exploit nagging to boost sales, the study, called "The Nag Factor," was conducted by Western Media International (now Initiative Media Worldwide) and Lieberman Research Worldwide.[4]

According to a press release from Western Media International headlined "The Fine Art of Whining: Why Nagging Is a Kid's Best Friend," the study identifies which kinds of parents are most likely to give in to nagging. Not surprisingly, divorced parents and those with teenagers or very young children ranked highest. The study identifies some things children often nag for, estimating for each how often nagging was successful: in four out of ten trips to "entertainment establishments like the Discovery Zone and Chuck E. Cheese," in one out of every three trips to a fast-food restaurant, and in three out of every ten home video sales.[5]

Since research conducted by marketing companies is proprietary, which means that researchers' methods are not usually made available to the public, these firms sell their reports for a great deal of money. I don't know how much the Nag Factor study sold for, but in 2003, for instance, a publication called *The U.S. Market for Infant, Toddler and Preschool Products: Vols. 1–3,* second edition, cost $6,000.[6]

Perhaps because it found that "the impact of children's nagging is assessed as up to 46 percent of sales in key business that target children,"[7] the Nag Factor study attracted a great deal of attention in the marketing world, and several publications described the study and how it was conducted in various amounts of detail. In a story headlined "The Old Nagging Game Can Pay Off for Marketers," *Selling to Kids* (a marketing newsletter, not an advocacy group) reported that in the study, researchers asked 150 mothers of children aged three to eight to keep a diary recording their kids' purchase requests over a period of two weeks. The moms reported a total of 10,000 nags—an average of about 66 nags per mother, or about 4.7 nags per day. The study identified two different kinds of nagging. The first was "persistence nagging," or repeated requests for a product. The second was "importance nagging," when kids gave a reason for why they wanted a product.[8] To use the example cited by Western Media executives: "Mommy, I need the Barbie Dreamhouse so Barbie and Ken can live together and have children and have their own family."[9]

The persistence with which children nag seems to increase as they get older. A recent survey of 750 kids between the ages of twelve and seventeen produced the finding that, on average, they may ask nine times before their parents give in and let them have what they want. Nagging seems to peak in early adolescence. Of the twelve- and thirteen-year-olds surveyed, 11 percent reported nagging parents more than fifty times for one specific product or another—and all of these were products they had seen advertised.[10]

To help corporations fine-tune their strategies for encouraging nagging, the researchers at Western International Media divided parents into different categories:

- "Indulgers" are parents who basically give in to their kids' every whim.
- "Kids' Pals" are parents who want to have fun, too, just like their kids.

- "Conflicted" describes single and/or divorced parents, whose purchasing behavior is often influenced by guilt.
- "Bare Necessities" are parents who seem able to fend off their kids' pleas and ultimately make all of the purchasing decisions on their own.

"Marketers need to understand," the *Selling to Kids* article reminds them, *"that a single marketing or advertising message may not resonate with different kinds of families."*[11] (I've added the italics.)

And who are the "Bare Necessities," the parents who cope so well with nagging? According to the people who did the survey, they are the parents whose lives are the least stressed—they are the most affluent and the least likely to have babies or toddlers in the house.

We might hope that "The Nag Factor" was an aberration. It's alarming to think that people would actually want to wreak havoc in families just to make a buck, but exploiting the nag factor—or "pester power," as it is also called in the industry—continues to be a perfectly acceptable tool from the marketers' point of view. Kelly Stitt, senior brands manager for Heinz's catsup division, had this to say in the *Wall Street Journal:* "All our advertising is targeted to kids. You want that nag factor so that seven-year-old Sarah is nagging Mom in the grocery store to buy Funky Purple. We're not sure Mom would reach out for it on her own."[12]

It's distressing that someone can be so matter-of-fact about a highly researched and effective assault on the fabric of family life. Yet, within the advertising industry, Stitt's attitude is not unusual. If advertising executives have any doubts about "pester power," these seem to center only on whether it's effective, not whether it's ethical. A recent story in the industry journal *Brand Strategy* raised a naive modicum of hope in my mind. The headline read, "Kids' Brands Must Exercise Pest Control." "Wow," I thought. "They certainly should!" However, rather than taking the moral high ground, the author, Linda Neville, a research consultant at the "strategic marketing and consumer insight" agency New Solutions, merely questions whether encouraging kids to nag is effective over the long haul. "The concept of 'pester power' is easily understood and widely used as a rationale for marketing initiatives, but how helpful is it for brand strategies?" she asks.[13]

Neville urges companies to dig deeper into parent-child relationships

for a more effective long-term marketing strategy. Pester power is fine at
the "point of sale" (in family life, that translates into those arguments at the
grocery store about sugar cereals or fruit roll-ups), she says, but over the
long haul, companies should focus on *styles* of parent-child negotiations.
She urges companies to engage in "relationship mining," which she describes as "an overall description of the method for understanding family
forces. Mining refers to the process of uncovering the motivations of different family members and the reasons for particular outcomes when con-
flicting needs occur." She suggests that "sensitive qualitative research is
needed. Interviewing child and adult pairs, both separately and together, is
particularly useful." [14]

     Sensitive to whom, one wonders.

     For those of us who free-associate, the metaphor of "mining" family re-
lationships is particularly and painfully evocative. Families are perceived
as a repository (the mine) containing valuables that are there for the ex-
tracting—and exploiting. I often wonder whether the 150 mothers who
participated in the "whining" study, or those who might have participated
in a company's "mining" surveys, are made aware of what the research is
actually for.

     Academic research is regulated by something called a human subjects
review, which requires informing subjects about the research, especially
about any risks that they might be harmed by it. Market research, at least in
the United States, is subject to no such regulation. Suppose a researcher
approached you and said, "I'm conducting research whose results will
make your life more stressful because your children will be better able to
nag you to buy them things," or, "I want to mine your family relationships
to better understand how to get you to agree to buy your kids things you
don't really want to buy them." Would you participate?

     One of the product campaigns Neville holds up as a wonderful exam-
ple of the benefits of family relationship mining is for Kraft Lunchables, an
item that "balances the needs of parents and children." She goes on to explain: "It's a fun brand that gives [children] a feeling of control (in the way
it allows kids to assemble their own lunch) and makes them feel good in
front of their friends. Although parents moan about the cost and excess
packaging, they buy Lunchables because [the product] meets their over-
riding need to ensure their child eats a nourishing lunch. The added benefits of convenience and freshness are also strong benefits." [15]

     Given that there are lots of nourishing foods for children to eat, and given the expense of this line of products, I'd say that Lunchables don't really meet any pressing need other than convenience. While Neville skims lightly over parents' objections about the cost and packaging, the environmental advocacy group MASSPIRG (the Massachusetts Public Interest Research Group) awarded Lunchables a Lifetime Wastemaker Achievement Award in 2001. MASSPIRG describes the product this way:

> Small "Lunchable" servings of food are packaged in a segment[ed] plastic tray covered with plastic wrap and an outer cardboard shell. This repeat Wastemaker won this award in both 1990 and 1992. Instead of cutting down on the packaging, they've added a new line of "Pizza Swirls." In addition to being overpackaged, two thirds of this product's calories come from fat and sugar.[16]

Toward the end of Neville's article is a sentence that seems to be tossed off casually but is, in fact, something of a smoking gun (once again, I've added the italics):

> Parents do not fully approve—they would rather their child ate a more traditional lunch—*but this adds to the brand's appeal among children because it reinforces their need to feel in control.*[17]

Twice in this article Neville acknowledges that parents object to Lunchables, yet having a product that parents object to is spun as a good thing—it adds to the product's appeal to children. Neville never questions whether it's in children's best interest to exercise their need to be in control by choosing a high-priced lunch loaded with fat and sugar and calories that is ensconced in packaging excessive enough, even in an age of excess packaging, to be singled out for a Lifetime Wastemaker award. Her article is important not because it's so unusual but because it is emblematic of two things: the advertising industry's blatant disregard for the plight of parents, and its exploitation of children's developmental vulnerabilities.

Marketing products by feeding into children's "need to be in control" exacerbates an ongoing, normal tension in family life that arises as children move from the total dependence of infancy to the independence of adulthood. In the world of child psychology, we call this a need for "autonomy." How parents and children navigate this constantly changing terrain depends on factors such as the child's temperament, the cast of characters in the immediate and extended family, and parents' own temperament, class, religion, and values. The advice that parenting experts from Dr. Spock to Penelope Leach give parents usually includes the admonishment: "Pick your battles." This used to be good advice, but now that children are subjected to hordes of finely honed marketing campaigns for everything from candy to violent movies, it's almost impossible for parents to know which battles to pick.

When my daughter was eleven, I went to a conference on children and the Internet where I was lectured for eight hours on the importance of monitoring her on-line activities. When I picked her up that evening, I dutifully had yet another discussion with her about Internet safety. Then she turned on the car radio and found her favorite music station. The DJ was talking gleefully to a young woman on the phone:

"You hit him with a baseball bat?"

"Yeah, they was doin' it in my living room, and I hit him with a baseball bat."

"You hit your boyfriend with a baseball bat?"

I turned off the radio.

So which battle should we pick? Should we pick the violence battle? Or the language battle? The candy battle? The sugar cereal battle? The Lunchables battle? The sexualized clothing battle? The World Wrestling Federation battle? Should we fight the hours-watching-television battle or the television content battle? Is it okay for children to watch one hour of television a day if it's a particularly violent hour? What about the video game battle? The Internet battle? Or the radio battle? If we refuse to let children go to R-rated movies when most of their friends seem to have that privilege, should we also limit their access to radio stations that play music that rates a "parental advisory" label in the store? If we refuse to buy children clothes emblazoned with corporate logos, should we also deprive them of Barbies, Pokémon, or the latest toy craze?

The problem is that while parents are trying to set limits, marketing executives are working day and night to undermine their authority. For parents raising children who are innately more impulsive, or more likely to take risks, the stakes are even higher. These are the children who are eager to explore the world and who are more likely to test limits—which means that adhering to the advice to "pick your battles" is difficult even under normal circumstances.

The industry spin is that it's up to parents to protect children from the marketing onslaught. When Kenn Viselman, head of itsy bitsy Entertainment (the company responsible for licensing *Teletubbies* products in the United States), was asked in an interview for *KidScreen* about the program's ties to Burger King and McDonald's in the light of concern about childhood obesity, he said: "The reason that there's childhood obesity is because caregivers don't have enough time to spend with their children. So what they're doing is giving their kids eight hours of TV a day." [18]

The same article contained a comment from Peter Reynolds, then CEO of the Wisconsin-based Brio Corporation, the American subsidiary of a Swedish toy company: "Parents aren't losing control, they're giving it up," he stated flatly. "If your child nags you to let him play in the middle of the freeway, do you do that? The responsibility of the purchase always lies with the adult. Yeah, 72 times a day you're going to be asked: 'Can I have that toy? Can I have that toy?' But if the answer is no 72 times a day for three or four weeks, then they stop asking." [19]

The prospect of spending a month saying no 2,160 times to a child you love is enough to drive any parent crazy. Suppose some of your child's requests are reasonable? Is our goal to cure children of asking for what they want? By encouraging children to nag, and by bombarding them with messages that material goods are the key to happiness, the marketing industry is taking advantage of parents' innate desire for their children to be happy.

Marketing experts and others point to single-parent families, two-career families, lack of adequate day care, and all sorts of other reasons for stress between parents and children. I agree that many of these issues are major concerns. I also believe that the marketing industry (or anyone else) has no right to take advantage of children whose parents are unable to provide them with ideal care.

At least some people in the marketing industry don't agree. When Lucy Hughes, director of initiative and strategy for Initiative Media, was interviewed in a film called *The Corporation,* she justified the Nag Factor study this way: "If we understand what motivates a parent to buy a product . . . if we could develop a creative commercial—you know, a thirty-second commercial that encourages the child to whine . . . that the child understands and is able to reiterate to the parents, then we're successful." [20]

As for the ethics of such tactics, she said, "Is it ethical? I don't know. But . . . our role at Initiative is to move products. And if we know you move products with a certain creative execution placed in a certain type of media vehicle then we've done our job." [21]

3

Branded Babies:
From Cradle to Consumer

On September 1, 1998, in maternity wards all around the country, newborns got a jump-start on their lives as media consumers and marketing targets. PBS Kids, along with Ragdoll Productions, itsy bitsy Entertainment, and Warner Home Video, celebrated the release of a series of *Teletubbies* videos by making "Teletubby Gift Packs" available to babies born on that day. Hospitals distributed the packs—including copies of two videos, *Here Come the Teletubbies* and *Dance With the Teletubbies,* and a mini-Teletubby plush toy from Hasbro—free of charge.[1]

Teletubbies, in case you don't know, are small humanoid creatures with television sets embedded in their tummies. Their heads are topped by antennae, which in their incarnation as stuffed toys are conveniently sized to fit in a baby's grasp, like a plush rattle. On their television program, the Teletubbies babble unintelligibly in a language sounding a lot like toddler talk as they frolic in a lush, fairy-tale landscape. Under the watchful eyes of a blue-eyed, giggling baby ensconced in a glowing sun, they interact with things of great interest to young children—a butterfly, a giant ball, a toaster. One of the program's main characters is a vacuum cleaner. The Teletubbies' TV tummies show films of real toddlers and caring adults engaged in such activities as playing games or fixing bicycles. Periodically a speaker set on a tall pole calls the Teletubbies to assemble at an appointed place: "Teletubbies, come here!"

As a television series, *Teletubbies* first appeared on BBC (British Broadcasting Corporation). It debuted in the United States on the Public Broadcasting Service in 1998, accompanied by a slew of toys and accessories. It is the first television series ever marketed as educational for children as young as one.

Whenever I think about the recent explosion of marketing to "under twos," I find myself face to face with *Teletubbies*. The program may seem like old news—it exists only in reruns today—but the success of this particular series and its spin-offs raises several important and very current issues all at once. These include the efforts of marketers to promote brand recognition even before a baby can talk, the connection between marketing and decreased government funding for public and cultural projects, the commercialization of previously public space, as well as the effects of increased exposure to screen media on the very young.

By the 1990s, it was inevitable that babies and toddlers would be included in the deluge of child-targeted marketing. As an article published in *KidScreen* explains, "When it comes to building kids [*sic*] brands, executives speak in terms of growing with a child from cradle to university. Yet when it comes to building a kid property's product offering, often the only way to grow is 'backward' "[2]—that is, to cultivate an ever younger demographic.

As they mature, children often discard playthings or clothing or other items that they associate with their younger selves—"But that's for babies," a new kindergartner might announce about a toy he played with the previous summer. Therefore, from the sole perspective of profit, it makes perfect sense to try to reach one step further back and market that product to the babies themselves.

When it comes to products specifically designed for children, "cradle to university" may be the most one can hope for, but many manufacturers are looking for brand loyalty to last from cradle to the grave.[3] James McNeal, a psychologist who has written extensively about how and why companies should market to children, estimates that a lifetime customer could be worth $100,000 to an individual retailer.[4] Babies are a once and future gold mine for marketers, which helps explain why companies such as Ralph Lauren and Harley Davidson are now targeting infants and toddlers by putting out items like tiny T-shirts and sweatshirts with their logos on them.[5]

But wait a minute. Aren't such infant and toddler products really marketed to parents? Well, yes—and no. Infants certainly can't ask for brands. Remember, however, that according to industry research, toddlers are requesting brands as soon as they can speak.[6] This would suggest that children may develop positive feelings about logos or licensed characters *before* they have words to ask for the products associated with them. As any parent can attest, even before a child has language, a tiny pointing finger accompanied by excited noises is enough to indicate "I want that." By marketing nursery linens, mobiles, and crib toys decorated with brand logos or images of licensed characters, marketers are doing what they can to ensure that babies will recognize and request similarly adorned products ranging from cereal to stuffed toys as their verbal skills evolve.

Whenever I see crib sheets emblazoned with Looney Tunes characters, or the Sesame Street "First Years Elmo" two-in-one bathtub, which positions a large portrait of the famed Muppet character to face the bathing baby, I can't help thinking of what I learned in undergraduate psychology classes about what the Nobel Prize–winning behavioral scientist Konrad Lorenz called imprinting. In a well-known series of papers published on the eve of World War II, Lorenz documented a phenomenon he had first observed when he himself was a boy—that baby geese who are exposed to a human being rather than to their mother at a certain time just after hatching will (presumably for the rest of their goslinghood) follow that human being around as if he or she were their parent. The human image becomes "imprinted" in their brains as "Mother."

It's always risky to extrapolate from animals to humans without research to prove specific parallels, but for what other reason would companies *make* baby paraphernalia adorned with media characters and corporate logos? They might be marketing to parents and grandparents attracted to a particular familiar brand, but they also believe it provides a jump-start on brand loyalty that could last through preschool and early elementary school, if not, for companies like Ralph Lauren, for life.

I suppose the kind of positive link between an image and a product that marketers hope to foster is based on building an association through what social scientists call "conditioning" rather than on imprinting. If the baby who snuggles in Sesame Street sheets and drinks from a Bugs Bunny bottle is also regularly plopped in front of a television to watch programs featuring the same characters she sees on her crib, clothes, mobile, and toys, her familiarity with those characters means (perhaps even before she's fully verbal) that trips to the grocery store will be characterized by squeals of joy every time she sees them on cereal boxes and cries of disappointment if the cereal doesn't land in the grocery cart.

The *Teletubbies* gift package for newborns looks a lot like the kind of preemptive strike that corporations have often used to establish brand loyalty among purchasers of products for infants and toddlers—and eventually among the children themselves. But why would a television network ostensibly devoted to the public interest engage in such a promotion?

When PBS survived the 1995 congressional assault on its funding, fans of educational, noncommercial television heaved a sigh of relief. PBS officials, however, facing immediate cutbacks in federal funds and the likelihood of even less government funding in the future, decided they had to seek other sources of revenue. Eight years later, PBS, actually a consortium of local public television stations, seems to be flourishing. But at what cost? The effects of diminished and ever-threatened government funding are taking their toll on PBS as a noncommercial entity, and are affecting its educational mission as well.

Since its inception in 1967, PBS's struggles for funding have made it continually vulnerable to commercial exploitation. When the Carnegie Commission on Educational Television drafted what became the blueprint for the Corporation for Public Broadcasting (CPB—the conduit through which federal funds flow to PBS), Congress rejected the commission's suggestions that a substantial source of federal funds be established to support the new public corporation in the future. As a result, PBS has always walked a fine line regarding corporate underwriting. By the mid-1970s, public television was receiving over $7 million a year from oil companies alone.

During this time, although PBS had its critics on both the right and the left, it did a good job building a reputation for providing thoughtful, high-quality, noncommercial television. Its children's programming—including educational innovations for children aged three and older, such as *Mister Rogers' Neighborhood, Sesame Street,* and *Reading Rainbow*—was justifiably lauded by parents and educators as a trusted oasis in a desert of commercial hype.

Unlike the offerings of cable stations—which provide a wide range of options for viewers, including programs designed to be educational—PBS programming is available to homes regardless of income. As a result, and contrary to charges by those who would destroy public television, its audience is broad and diverse, especially in children's programming. Young children who live in communities with high concentrations of poverty are almost as likely to be viewers of PBS programming as preschoolers and kindergartners living in more affluent areas.[7] Given that poor children watch more television than middle-class children and are more likely to use it as a primary means of learning about the world,[8] access to this important source of free educational programming can often be a powerful positive influence in their lives.

After the 1995 cutbacks in government funding, PBS officials (of necessity, they have argued) hopped on a fast track toward reinventing the Public Broadcasting Service as a kinder, gentler version of its commercial siblings. Exactly a year later, the consortium announced that *Masterpiece Theatre,* the acclaimed drama series, would be called *Mobil Masterpiece Theatre.*[9] At the same time, promotional spots that looked an awful lot like commercials began to appear at the beginning and end of programs.

In addition, PBS, which had already begun forming partnerships with for-profit companies, intensified its efforts in that direction. Microsoft,[10] Devillier Donegan Enterprises and Buena Vista Television (both subsidiaries of Disney/ABC Television), and Turner Home Video are a few of the companies working with PBS.[11] In a 1998 memo to station managers, PBS notified personnel that the term "corporate sponsorship provided by" could, in some cases, be an acceptable acknowledgment for major corporate underwriters.[12]

PBS executives now refer to the Public Broadcasting Service as "the new PBS." Their 1998 annual report, with the theme "Doing good while doing well," reflects an organization that has become ever more prone to defining itself in terms of the language of the marketplace. Potential corporate investors are pitched the concept of PBS as a "brand," while PBS officials continue to encourage the American public to think of the consortium as a purveyor of noncommercial broadcasting.

In a painful irony, even as PBS continues to market itself simultaneously as "commercial free" and as a "brand," it represents a potential gold mine for all sorts of commercial interests, and this is especially evident with regard to children's programming. To cite but one telling example, the network recently announced a deal with the Mills Corporation, a real estate investment firm that develops shopping malls and has trademarked the term "Shoppertainment."[13] According to the *New York Times,* PBS Kids Pavilions at Mills Corporation malls are being designed to target the "sippy-cup-and-stroller set" and feature television kiosks with PBS programming, guest appearances from PBS stars, and licensed PBS Kids merchandise and T-shirts.[14]

A spokesperson for PBS announced that this partnership is "about reaching the viewers, about keeping us relevant and having more points of impact,"[15] but of course for the Mills Corporation, it's about having "a financial benefit in the long term by enabling us to lease at the best economic terms to tenants who want to be near mall attractions like this."[16] The first PBS Kids Pavilion opened at the Mills mall in St. Louis in 2003. It's described in the Mills Corporation's initial press release heralding its partnership with PBS as a "kid-friendly area [that includes] retailers, courtyards, exhibition space, restaurants and learn-and-play areas in [sic] a very grand scale, acting as a high-profile regional attraction designed for both parents and kids to enjoy." A month or so before its opening, the pavilion transformed into the "PBS Kids Neighborhood." It is situated across from the Children's Palace Outlet clothing store and adjacent to "a lounge area equipped with 24 plasma-screen televisions broadcasting Mills TV, which will include, among other items, sports highlights, news and mall advertising."[17]

According to the PBS vice president for business and development, "The Mills Corporation is a wonderful partner for PBS Kids, sharing our vision of delivering high-quality educational experiences to our broad family audience. . . . This is an important vehicle to extend our brand at a grassroots level while growing our relationships with our local stations and sponsors. Kids will learn and play with characters they watch each day at a place where families already spend time."[18]

"Our brand"? "Growing our relationships"? This is the language of marketers, not believers in a public mission. Other things about this statement trouble me as well, not the least of which is the use of "grass roots," a term that the *Oxford English Dictionary* defines as "the fundamental level; the source of origin."

According to the *American Heritage Dictionary*, the term refers to "people or society at a local level rather than at the center of major political activity." My own understanding of the term combines both definitions. It is most often used to describe political activity generated by people attending to their own interests rather than by government officials or higher ups in any power structure attending to theirs. If the people of St. Louis had come together and lobbied the St. Louis Mills mall developers for a PBS pavilion, the term "grass roots" might apply. To my knowledge, however, that's not how it happened.

It's also troubling that the implication of the PBS presentation of the partnership seems to be that since kids are already at the mall, we might as well expose them to "our brand." This seems to me either naive or duplicitous. The Mills Corporation's own publicity presents PBS as an "attraction," which suggests that they are using the PBS Kids Pavilion to attract customers and to persuade prospective retailers and restaurants to rent space in their mall. According to various news reports and press releases, most of PBS's revenues from this venture will come from royalties on Mills Corporation's use of the PBS Kids name and logo and creative design elements. PBS will split the profits fifty-fifty with local affiliates.[19] Their own share will go "straight into more quality kids' programming."[20] Quality? Absolutely. The PBS lineup still features wonderful children's programming. But it is *not* commercial-free.

A joint report from PBS and the Markle Foundation dated April 17, 2002, evaluates the new PBS Kids brand and makes recommendations for the future of children's programming on public television. The report includes suggestions on a range of topics, but of particular interest are its recommendations on commercialism, which include the following statement: "Marketing value lies principally with public broadcasting's content and character sub-brands. This allows PBS Kids to maintain some distance from merchandising and sustain its 'we're not selling anything but learning' message."[21] In other words, as long as it's only the programs selling the products, PBS itself is still technically noncommercial.

In a hairsplitting sense, that distinction may be meaningful. For parents fielding pleas for Chicken Dance Elmo and trips to Chuck E. Cheese (thanks to the PBS program *Clifford the Big Red Dog*),[22] there's not much difference. In any case, public television's partnership with the Mills Corporation violates even that minimal requirement, since revenues for PBS will come from the Mills Corporation's use of the PBS logo and related design elements.

The truth is that at a time when public funds for after-school programs or maintenance for public parks and playgrounds is waning, what PBS is "partnering in" is an increased blurring of the distinction between commercial and public space. A shopping mall is not a playground. Playgrounds exist solely for the purpose of providing space for children to play. A commercial mall is not a nursery school, a public library, or a museum, all of which share the purpose of enriching and educating. First and foremost, the purpose of a shopping mall is to generate profit by leasing space to tenants whose goal, in turn, is to generate profit by selling goods. One can argue that parents could just take their children to the PBS Pavilion and go home without buying anything. A few may be able to do it. But if the pavilion is proximate to fast-food restaurants and toy stores, and if—as the advertising industry suggests—kids are requesting brands as soon as they can talk, it's not going to be easy.

PBS officials take the position that loosening restrictions on corporate underwriting, actively seeking corporate funding, and engaging in commercial, revenue-generating partnerships is the only way PBS can survive in a climate of diminished government support, escalating production costs, and a cutthroat media marketplace. They may be right. Traditionally, most proponents of public television have felt that corporate underwriting messages at the end of programs are a small price to pay for the quality broadcasting they have come to expect from PBS. It can even be argued that some revenue-producing tie-ins do have educational merit. However, the pace of what we might call "commercial creep" is accelerating and its range is expanding to include the very young.

For marketers, commercial partnerships with media programmers whose offerings are designed for children—including PBS—represent a gold mine, not because of the programs themselves, but because of the profits from product spin-offs. Sales of toys, clothing, and accessories bearing images licensed from entertainment totaled about $20 billion in 1999–2000.[23] A trip through any major toy store or the infant and toddler section of any department store shows that it takes increasing effort to find items for young children that are not linked to any media product.

Together, PBS's acquisition of *Teletubbies* and its embrace of the attendant spin-offs and marketing campaigns represent a major programming decision that extended this trend toward commercialization, a decision that also carries the potential to negatively affect the lives of young children in another important way—by encouraging parents and other caretakers to expose children as young as nine months old to ever-increasing doses of television and other screen media. Meanwhile, in 2001, executives at itsy bitsy Entertainment, the program's distributor for North and South America, estimated that the program was reaching one billion toddlers worldwide.[24]

Teletubbies achieved brief notoriety when the Reverend Jerry Falwell insisted that Tinky Winky, the purple Tubby with a triangle-shaped antenna who frequently carries a purse, was damaging children's morals by modeling a gay lifestyle. Unfortunately, Falwell's preposterous homophobic attack fueled the wrong controversy. In fact, the real problem with *Teletubbies* has nothing to do with its content, which is no better or worse than any other program on PBS. The real problem has to do with whether it's good for one- and two-year-olds, or even nine-month-old babies, to be watching television at all.

Teletubbies' producers and promoters argue that children under two will see television anyway, and that it's better for them to have a program created especially for them. It may be that one-year-olds spend time in front of the television, and they may sometimes even be engaged by it. But babies are not turning on the tube themselves out of some inherent need. Nor are they likely to be clamoring for a favorite program. Babies, unlike older children, are not subject to peer pressure to buy into popular culture. Even if all of their day-care buddies are watching TV, one-year-olds don't discuss programs around the juice table. In fact, the first two years of life are about the only time that parents can easily avoid struggles with their children about television watching and tie-in toys.

Meanwhile, one-year-olds are subjected to television because their parents, day-care providers, or older siblings turn it on in their presence. Before *Teletubbies,* this happened when siblings were watching after school or on weekends, when parents were watching the news or other adult programming, or when harried parents used TV as a way of taking a break. If a baby's exposure to television were limited to one half-hour program a day, it's unlikely that the experience would be harmful. But now that one-year-olds have a program "designed especially for them,"[25] it's likely that they will be exposed to it in addition to, not instead of, whatever they were exposed to before. And because, as PBS publicity materials state, parents trust PBS to provide age-appropriate educational programming, it is very possible that many parents—who don't realize that age-appropriate television for one-year-olds might well be an oxymoron—are now actively encouraging their youngest children to watch it.

Current research shows that, on average, parents are placing babies in front of videos at about six months of age and that they begin exposing them to television at about nine months. Babies between one and twenty-three months watch more television (an average of 1.12 hours) than videos (0.41 hours). They are in front of a screen for more than 90 minutes each day.[26] According to a report from the Kaiser Family Foundation, on a typical day, almost 60 percent of children under two watch television.[27]

Teletubbies spawned a spate of research about babies' comprehension of television. At least one researcher I spoke to thought it was possible that a TV producer could produce something that was beneficial to babies as young as nine months old because researchers are finding that babies can imitate some of what they see on television. But Dan Anderson, a professor of psychology at the University of Massachusetts in Amherst who has devoted a great deal of his professional life to researching the impact of television on children, notes, "We still don't know very much at all about how babies and toddlers understand television, and at this point, there's still little reason for children under 24 months to watch television. They learn more from real life, and TV takes away from real world contact and stimulation."[28]

There is still little research on babies and television, and there was even less when *Teletubbies* was in active production. Conducting studies about comprehension and learning with preverbal children is extremely difficult because they can't tell you what they know. There is some evidence that babies pay attention, at least intermittently, to television.[29] There are some data suggesting that they can imitate vocalizations they hear on television[30] and imitate simple actions that they see on the screen— although not as readily as they can from real life.[31]

Recently, research from the Georgetown Early Learning Project suggests that babies as young as fifteen months old can imitate simple actions seen on television and are more likely to imitate them with increased viewing. Twelve-month-olds also showed some capacity to imitate very simple actions shown on television. However, the study confirms that they seemed to learn more quickly from real life experiences.[32] In fact, even children as old as two, unlike their three-year-old counterparts, still have difficulty applying information they receive from television to real life.[33]

The Early Learning Project's researchers suggest that their study has practical implications for television producers: "As producers develop children's educational programming, it is beneficial for them to know that repetition of actions and episodes may enhance learning. This may guide them as they aim to create programs that supplement learning inside and outside of the home."[34]

Even if babies imitate behaviors they see on TV, is watching television good for them? Given the fact that children's programming in the United States is funded largely by corporate sponsorship and partnership, the information provided by these studies is also valuable to advertisers making the commercials for products associated with those programs.

There's also evidence that babies may pick up emotional cues from television. The implications of one recent study conducted at Tufts University seem particularly disturbing. After watching a televised segment of an adult actress with a toy, babies as young as twelve months old will choose or reject the real toy depending on the emotions she expresses toward the toy. Using the same words but changing her facial expressions and voice tone, the actress expressed enthusiasm or fear and the babies responded in kind. They could interpret that response while viewing a twenty-second segment.[35] The researchers suggest that parents might want to be careful about what kinds of television programs they let their babies watch. Violent programs, or programs where actors display strong negative emotions, could be disturbing for very young viewers.

Parents might also think about commercials or programs designed to sell toys. If, as this research indicates, one-year-olds respond to positive and negative emotions on television, they are prime targets for manipulation, especially because they don't have the cognitive capacity to mediate their emotional responses.

There are all sorts of reasons why advertisers choose to target our emotions rather than our intellect. Psychologist David Walsh, president of the National Center on Media and the Family, summed it up best: "Emotion focuses attention, determines what we remember, shapes attitudes, motivates, and moves us to act. It should not come as a surprise, therefore, that the emotional centers of the brain become the primary target for marketers and advertisers. This list of the roles that emotions play could easily be mistaken for an advertiser's wish list. What advertiser would not want to capture a customer's attention, implant the message in his memory, shape his attitudes, motivate him and change his behavior."[36]

Advertising works best if it can evoke from its target audience a strong and positive emotional response. Advertisers have the best chance of evoking an emotional response strong enough to influence viewers when people don't know they're being influenced, or if they have a limited capacity for critical judgment. That describes very young children to a tee! Have you ever met a baby, or even a toddler, with even remotely adequate critical judgment?

What we're learning from new technologies such as brain imaging, combined with the news that babies seem to respond emotionally to displays on television, makes me feel more strongly than ever that it's best for babies to be kept away from television. We now know that babies are born with billions of neurons that continue to make connections as they grow and mature. Because young children's neural networks are forming at such a rapid rate, they are readily influenced. The connections that are forming include those that affect emotions and attitudes.[37]

If, as the study from Tufts suggests, babies are affected by emotion displayed on television, it's possible that watching positive or negative emotions displayed toward a product on the tube can affect their attitudes about that product not just in the short term but in the longer term as well. In other words, advertisers may be right. Brand loyalty can begin in the cradle.

When it comes to cognitive development, much of neuroscience research today supports the conclusions of Jean Piaget, the Swiss psychologist who used meticulous observation and clever experiments to produce an outline of how children's intellectual understanding grows as they mature, and who identified infancy as a stage of "sensory motor development." Babies, he concluded, learn through touch and taste as much if not more than through sight and sound, and they need opportunities, when they are ready, to move around and explore the environment and their own capacities. In other words, they need to engage actively with the physical world.

Piaget's work and the work of his followers, along with advances in neuroscience, have implications for a wide range of educational and health policies as they relate to children's development. For instance, literacy experts recommend that parents read to babies and talk to them over the course of a normal day as a means of helping them develop preliteracy and language skills. Unfortunately, the idea that the environment affects brain development also translates into a slew of media programs and media products hyped through unsubstantiated claims that they will have a positive impact on children's intelligence.

By contract, *Teletubbies* will continue to run until 2008. Until then, at the very least, its presence on public television will continue to lend credence to the program's unsubstantiated claims that it enhances children's social and intellectual development. It also continues to provide a rationale for a new generation of "educational" electronic video and computer products designed for infants and toddlers.

Early on in their tenure with PBS, the producers of *Teletubbies* collaborated with Microsoft to develop software and interactive toys that relate to the television program, using their link to PBS to encourage parents to think that it's "educational" for babies to use computers when there is no research to support such claims.[38] Few electronic media programs of this kind existed before 1997, the year the series debuted on BBC, but the financial success of *Teletubbies* helped usher in the transformation of babies into a viable market for videos and computer software. For harried parents, the program's educational patina also justifies a questionable impulse to use televisions and computers as electronic babysitters for their youngest children.

Of course, the advent of *Teletubbies* isn't the sole reason for this increase in "educational" media products for babies. We can blame some of it on Mozart. In 1993, results were published from a study conducted at the University of California at Irvine, claiming that listening to Mozart improved students' performance on a standardized test;[39] a few years later another study claimed that preschool children who learned to play a keyboard showed increased IQs.[40] Neither of these studies have been successfully replicated, but the so-called "Mozart Effect" is still reverberating in the baby and toddler media market.[41]

In 1998, the governor of Georgia introduced a recording called *Build Your Baby's Brain Power Through the Power of Music,* containing works by Mozart, Beethoven, Handel, Bach, and others. The tapes and CDs were to be given to parents of every baby born each year in Georgia.[42] It was a nice thought, and probably preferable to giving newborns videotapes of *Teletubbies* or any other program; most early childhood experts believe that listening to all kinds of music from classical to jazz is probably beneficial to babies, and most babies seem to enjoy music. However, although I'm not a neuroscientist, I suspect that playing classical music to babies who are not getting proper nurturing, attention, or positive stimulation of all kinds is not going to do much for their brains.

If the impact of the Mozart Effect—unproven as it is[43]—was limited to audio recordings, I wouldn't be writing about it in this book. But the late 1990s saw a boom of allegedly brain-boosting videos for under-twos. Adorned with titles such as *Baby Einstein, Brainy Baby,* and *Baby Genius,* they all seem to have been designed to evoke guilt and anxiety in parents who—hearing the latest sound bite about brain development—want to do the right thing for their children. The pressure such "educational" videos place on parents was evident to me recently when a young colleague and mother bought a *Baby Einstein* video for her eight-month-old. "I know it's probably ridiculous," she sighed, "but I couldn't help myself. Suppose it does make a difference?"

The message that parents are getting is that what they might normally do with their babies—cuddle, play, sing, talk, and read to them—is not enough. Instead, they should be propping them in front of the television, which, according to the American Academy of Pediatrics, is probably one kind of stimulation babies don't need.[44]

My most recent discovery in the world of baby videos is a series called *Baby Gourmet.* According to a press release, these videos, targeted to the four-month- to four-year-old market, provide "a multi-sensory experience for children designed to introduce little ones to beautiful fruits and vegetables, the artistry of foods and holidays in a gentle and amusing way that stimulates both the left and right hemispheres. Highlights include the Mozart Effect, vocabulary and language, word/picture association, sequencing and logic, colors, textures and shape, as well as creativity."[45]

The language in this press release includes virtually every buzzword marketers have invented for touting their products for babies as "educational," but until someone invents smell-a-vision, taste-a-vision, and touch-a-vision, the "multi-sensory" experience *Baby Gourmet* provides is really limited to sight and sound, just like that of any television program. Since we still don't know how babies understand television, it's hard to see how the makers of a video program can claim it stimulates their brains at all—let alone determine whether it's the right or the left hemisphere that's being stimulated.

Baby Gourmet seems to have been created out of the best of intentions. If its creators had limited their marketing to twos and up, this would be—at worst—just one more unnecessary children's video series on the market. At best, it might be beneficial to kids. But until we know how babies respond to television, it's irresponsible, and potentially harmful, to create video programming aimed specifically at them.

The same is true for computer software, which is now a booming market that capitalizes on parents' fears that their children might be left behind if they don't have computer experience early on in life. From 1997 to 1999, sales of educational computer software for preschoolers rose from $45.2 million to $67.8 million nationwide.[46] *Baby Einstein,* which was recently sold to Disney Interactive, now also comes as "lap ware"—that is, computer software designed for babies and toddlers who need to sit on their parents' laps in order to use the computer.

In addition to "brain-building" software, babies are also targets for software derived from television programs or movies, including such offerings as *Sesame Street Baby* (for ages one to three years) and Disney's *Winnie the Pooh Baby* (ages nine to fourteen months). Yet developmental psychologists and early childhood educators from around the country have raised questions about the value of computer play for young children. Some suggest that it may even be harmful, in that it takes babies and toddlers away from the active, multisensory exploration of the world that is so important to their healthy development.[47]

This chapter is not the place to engage in the complicated debate over the pros and cons of computer technology and children, but in my experience, most children find computers compelling and need no encouragement to spend hours at a time playing computer games or using the Internet. They also pick up computer skills quite quickly. The hours children spend in front of a computer are not replacing the time they spend watching television: these new technologies, including handheld computer games, are expanding children's total screen time,[48] thereby reducing the amount of time they spend engaging in physical activities and interacting with other people.

Alvin Poussaint and I have written extensively on the marketing of *Teletubbies* because we feel that PBS has done the public a great disservice by packaging the program as educational for babies.[49] Babies and toddlers need, most of all, to make close, trusting connections with people they love and to make sense of the world through active exploration using all of their senses. The last thing they need to be doing is watching television. We're not alone in holding this view. Not long after *Teletubbies* premiered in the United States, the American Academy of Pediatrics, citing the long-term effects of our earliest experiences on brain development, the lack of research about television's impact on babies, and the potential negative effects of television in general, issued a strong recommendation that children under two should not watch the tube.[50]

We are only beginning to understand what television really means to the very young. Because we don't know what, if anything, very young children gain from viewing television, and because it has been demonstrated that watching television can be habituating, Dr. Poussaint and I and many others have argued that it is irresponsible for the creators and promoters of *Teletubbies*—or any other television program—to encourage parents to expose their children to it at such an early age. Yet Teletubbies remains on PBS, positioned as an educational program.

When *Teletubbies* first appeared in the United States, its producers

and distributors made elaborate claims regarding the series' educational
value for its target audience, including babies—claims that do not stand up
to close scrutiny:

> *Teletubbies* offers a new generation of television viewers—the youngest and
> most impressionable—the opportunity to feel safe in and enjoy the ever-
> changing world.
>
> —PBS[51]

> We're especially excited about the *Teletubbies* web site because the television se-
> ries is designed to help young children become comfortable with technology.
>   —Alice Cahn, then director of children's programming at PBS[52]

> [Children watching *Teletubbies*] . . . will feel more confident, I think, to play,
> and more reassured to play.
>   —Anne Wood, creator of *Teletubbies*[53]

These statements are reminiscent of that most basic and manipulative
advertising technique of convincing potential buyers that they have a de-
fect that can be cured by buying a product. In this case, each claim implies
that children begin life with a deficit—a deficit that, in fact, doesn't exist.

There is no evidence that children raised with adequate parenting do
not feel safe in a changing, evolving world. There is no evidence to show
that children raised in a technological world are uncomfortable with technology. Nor is there evidence that these same children do not feel "confi-
dent to play." In fact, as I'll discuss at length in chapter 4, play comes
naturally to children as their form of exploration and learning about the
world. The capacity to play can be squelched by a child's environment, or
it can be reinforced, but it does not have to be taught.

Kenn Viselman, the head of itsy bitsy Entertainment, has also declared
that *Teletubbies* was designed to recognize and provide programming for
an underserved audience of very young children.[54] To say that one-year-
olds are "underserved," a term usually associated with people needing and
not getting adequate health care or social services, implies that *Teletubbies*
is serving a need—that babies *need* to watch television. "The idea of creating an extension of the viewing experience for the child is very important,"
Viselman told the *Los Angeles Times*. "When you don't put out any prod-

uct at all, you're doing as great a disservice to your audience as putting too much product out into the market."[55]

Carrying this missionary zeal into the arena of product licensing, Viselman waxed enthusiastic about the predicted popularity of *Teletubbies* merchandise: "You're looking at a major multimillion-dollar property," he told *Time* magazine.[56] Meanwhile, Alice Cahn of PBS was quoted in the *Christian Science Monitor* as saying, "Merchandising was never, ever a consideration in choosing that show. Educational content was always first and foremost in our minds.[57] This statement is puzzling, given the proven commercial track record of *Teletubbies* in Great Britain and the lack of research about the program's educational value.

It's true that after *Teletubbies* was already ensconced in its Ready to Learn programming line-up, PBS commissioned a company called Applied Research and Consulting (ARC) to conduct research on the program, but the study did not look at whether *Teletubbies* was fulfilling its educational goals. Instead, it consisted of observations about how parents used *Teletubbies* in the morning, and how children responded to the show. In a conversation with ARC staff, I learned that the only concrete information they had found regarding babies' responses to the program was that a significant number laughed at a particular image—the large image of a baby's laughing face inside a rising sun.

I then asked the researchers at ARC to comment on the specific claims *Teletubbies'* creators and promoters make about the ways it enriches learning experiences for the younger members of its target audience. In virtually every instance, no data existed to back up the claims. For instance, *Teletubbies* is supposed to "promote affection." Materials put out by the itsy bitsy Entertainment company service claim that "children are able to enjoy the *Teletubbies* while continuing to discover who they are and how their relationships work."[58] There is no data to support the claim that babies can do this, or even how they do this, with or without *Teletubbies*.

Teletubbies is also supposed to "celebrate individuality." By watching the show, "children are taught to see that it's acceptable to be different and have separate interests from the crowd." Such a message would certainly be beneficial for older kids, but there is absolutely no evidence that one-year-olds need to be protected from peer pressure, nor is there any way to measure whether or not they understand that message.

Teletubbies teaches through repetition, it is claimed: "Children are given time to make predictions, which is essential in the development of their thinking skills." At this point, there is no way to tell whether twelve-month-olds are making predictions or not. In a telephone conversation, one executive at itsy bitsy Entertainment pointed out to me that parents who watch the program with their babies can use the time to verbalize predictions, but the researchers at ARC found that parents watched *Teletubbies* with their children only intermittently.

While its educational merit has proven to be questionable at best, there's no doubt that *Teletubbies* has been a commercial success for PBS. While we don't know how much funding PBS receives from *Teletubbies* merchandising, we do know that the program and its products have generated well over $137 million for the BBC.[59] Alan Hassenfeld, the former chairman and chief executive of the Hasbro toy company, estimated in 2000 that the dolls alone produced between $30 million to $50 million in annual sales.[60]

From my point of view and from that of other critics, *Teletubbies* and its PBS partner have been shameless in their commercial exploitation of young children. Consider their tie-in toy promotions with both McDonald's and Burger King. In 1998, Kenn Viselman made the following statement about product development for *Teletubbies:* "The whole purpose is to do what's right for children." According to a New Jersey newspaper, Mr. Viselman explained that "Giving a one-year-old who loves the televised *Teletubbies* a *Teletubbies* doll to hug and talk to is a natural extension of the educational and play value of the show. . . . Making deals to sell *Teletubbies* T-shirts for teenagers, to put Teletubbies in Happy Meals, and to arrange a 'Teletubbies on Ice' tour are not, and that's why no such deals are in the works."[61] By 1999, however, although Teletubbies were not yet in Happy Meals, they were being given away at Burger King, and by the year 2000 *Teletubbies* had in fact switched to McDonald's. According to Viselman, the change was attributed to "a desire to work with the largest fast-food chain."[62]

Given the rise of childhood obesity in the United States, it is unconscionable for any PBS children's program to partner with a fast-food company. In a telephone interview, a spokesperson for itsy bitsy Entertainment expressed the opinion that it was a good thing for McDonald's to be directing parents to support good-quality television programs. She went on to say that parents have to be responsible for their children's nutrition, and that if they felt McDonald's offerings were unhealthful, they could buy the Happy Meals toys without buying the food.

In 2003, at a McDonald's in Brookline, Massachusetts, the toys promoted in Happy Meals cost $1.77 when sold separately. The meals themselves cost $2.72. Since one of the biggest attractions of McDonald's to families with low incomes is that their food is inexpensive, it is naive to believe that most families would go into a McDonald's and spend $1.77 for a toy they could get for "free" with a meal costing only 95¢ more.

In response to my questions about *Teletubbies'* fast-food promotions, itsy bitsy Entertainment sent a *Teletubbies* exercise video that is distributed in day-care centers and nursery schools around the country. The program was originally broadcast on PBS as part of a campaign called "Teletubbies Get Up and Go! First Annual Exercise Day." To publicize its effort, itsy bitsy Entertainment issued a press release headed, "Teletubbies Stand Up to Obesity in Kids." The release claimed that "the *Teletubbies* are taking the lead in the fight against obesity in children." Later in the release, Kenn Viselman is quoted as saying, "Children look up to the *Teletubbies,* so it is our responsibility to promote health and fitness—that starts early and may last a lifetime—through them."

Certainly the notion of an exercise video for toddlers, whose whole *raison d'être* is movement, is ludicrous, as is the idea that one exercise video can undo the damage caused by McDonald's use of beloved children's icons to sell kids food that is not good for them. It is naive at best, and hypocritical at worst, for itsy bitsy Entertainment to help McDonald's and Burger King sell fast food to babies and toddlers while positioning itself at the forefront of fighting childhood obesity, and the fact that PBS is supporting them in their efforts is a betrayal of everything the Public Broadcasting Service claims to stand for.

I've focused on PBS and *Teletubbies* because the history of this partnership tells us something about how commercial interests and the logic and language of the marketplace can come to overwhelm the more altruistic motives of an ostensibly public enterprise. This one case is intended only as an example. In nearly all realms of our society, the marketers' emphasis on selling and consuming as opposed to creating and contributing to the public good seems to be reaching further and further into our lives and the lives of our children.

I started this chapter with a story about marketing to newborns. I'm going to end it with one about prenatal marketing. When my daughter-in-law was pregnant, she was browsing in a bookstore and came upon a book adorned with beloved Dr. Seuss characters that was designed for parents to read to their babies *in utero*. Intrigued, she began leafing through it, only to discover that it was essentially an advertisement that consisted entirely of informing her unborn baby, in Seussish rhymes, about all of the Dr. Seuss books he or she would encounter after leaving the womb.[63] I'm guessing that *Oh Baby, the Places You'll Go! A Book to be Read In Utero* is an early warning sign that marketers are no longer satisfied with marketing to children in the cradle. Does it herald a new and industry-wide competition for brand loyalty from *conception* to the grave?

4

Endangered Species:
Play and Creativity

FOUR-YEAR-OLD SEAN bounced around the office I use at the day-care center, searching the toy shelves for something interesting to do. He rejected the dollhouse, the board games, the blocks and puzzles. Finally he picked up a stuffed dog and stared at it in puzzlement. "What does it *do?*" he asked. "You can make him talk," I suggested. "But how?" he wondered, looking for a button or string. "Like this," I answered, picking up a stuffed cat and talking through it in a funny voice. Sean was enchanted.

I am passionate about play. Aside from love and friendship, it's what I value most about being a person. Preserving and nurturing children's capacity to play is essential to all aspects of their mental, social, and emotional development. Play is a fundamental component of a healthy childhood and linked inextricably to creativity. The ability to play is central to our capacity to take risks, to experiment, to think critically, to act rather than react, to differentiate ourselves from our environment, and to make life meaningful.

Play has always been central to my professional life. Before I became a psychologist, I earned my living as a ventriloquist. It's not surprising, therefore, that I place marketing's impact on children's toys and play among the most dire consequences of commercial culture. In some ways, it's also the most frustrating to talk about.

At first glance, worries about the erosion of children's play may seem trivial, especially when placed next to concerns about whether current marketing promotes violence, unsafe sexual practices, and childhood obesity, which most people agree are not good for children. Grasping the importance of play requires more thought. Until people understand and

acknowledge the importance of play, it's hard to get anyone excited about
threats to its existence.

Although most of us play, it's easy to take for granted and hard to describe. The best description comes from D.W. Winnicott, a brilliant pediatrician and psychoanalyst who practiced in the mid-twentieth century.
"In playing," Winnicott wrote, "the child manipulates external phenomena in the service of the dream and invests chosen external phenomena
with dream meaning and feeling." [1] In plainer language, we play when we
actively use objects and ideas to express our own, unique inner lives, fantasies, and feelings.

Play comes naturally to children. They play—often without knowing
they are doing so—to express themselves and to gain a sense of control
over their world. But play is continually devalued and stunted by the loud
voice of commerce. Play thrives in environments that provide children
with safe boundaries but do not impinge on their ability to think and act
spontaneously. It is nurtured with opportunities for silence. For children
who are flooded continually with stimuli and commands to react, the cost
is high. They have fewer opportunities to learn to initiate action or to influence the world they inhabit, and less chance to exercise the essential
human trait of creativity.

Given the current confluence of sophisticated electronic media technology and the glorification of consumerism, it's becoming increasingly
difficult to provide children with an environment that encourages creativity or original thinking. They are assaulted with the noise from advertising
and the things it sells from the moment they wake up until bedtime. The
time and space available for their own ideas and their own images, for un-
hurried interactions with print or pictures, shrinks with every blockbuster
children's film or television program—inevitably accompanied by a flood
of "tie-in" toys, books, videos, and clothing.

The ongoing saga of *Harry Potter* is a good example. [2] What was most
amazing about the initial hoopla surrounding Harry is that it was for something hopelessly old-fashioned: a series of well-written books. At a time
when purveyors of children's culture insist that kids have no attention
span, children were mesmerized by 300-page books with no pictures. As
advertisers market sex and cynicism to world-weary tweens, nine- to
twelve-year-olds were losing themselves completely in a magical struggle
of good against evil. While media executives insist that even babies need
electronic bells and whistles to hold their interest, millions of children ex-

perienced the world of Harry Potter essentially in silence, the stillness broken only by the rustle of pages turning or the quiet murmur of someone reading aloud.

We can no longer take the silence of reading and the integrity of books for granted. The precious initial quiet around *Harry Potter* was irrevocably shattered by the click of e-commerce and the jingle of cash registers. Harry is now a brand. We not only have the film series, we have Harry Potter school products, toys, and food as well. As a result, fans of the books relinquish not just money, but a piece of themselves to Time Warner, owner of the licensing rights. The images we see on the screen are not ours. They belong to Chris Columbus, director of the mega-hit *Home Alone,* who directed the first two *Harry Potter* films and to whoever directs the sequels. Six-figure production budgets guarantee lots of nifty special effects, and nothing is left to the viewer's imagination.

The experience of seeing a favorite book character look wrong on the screen is as old as film itself. Children's movies have been accompanied by a few products at least since the 1950s—I remember spending hours putting together a punch-out Captain Hook's pirate ship. What's changed is the scale.[3] From the first, Warner Brothers has been spinning *Harry Potter* films into products, products, and more products: puzzles, board games, dolls, and other toys from Mattel; computer games from Electronic Arts; construction games from Lego. Then there's candy, costumes, socks, shirts, boxer shorts, backpacks, calendars, duffel bags, and rolling luggage. With each new film release, we and our children can expect to see images of Harry, his friends, and his enemies everywhere—in magazines, on television, and, until their exclusive rights run out, in Warner Brothers Studio Stores all over the world.

Before author J.K. Rowling sold the licensing rights to Warner Brothers for a mere $500,000,[4] her books were a respite from a culture saturated by commercial and electronic media. Children got to exercise their own creativity as they interacted with Rowling's imaginary world. They didn't need products to enjoy the story; all they needed was themselves and a book.

Now, children reading *Harry Potter* for the first time will know what his world looks like before they even open a book. They will be deprived of a chance to conjure their own visions of the Hogwarts School for Wizards and its occupants. Once they see the films, children will no longer assign their own cadence and movement to their favorite characters.

These lost opportunities wouldn't matter so much if other books were achieving this magnitude of popularity. But they aren't. For many kids, *Harry Potter* was an oasis of silence in a barrage of corporate noise. As we bombard our children with images, words, and sounds that leave nothing to be imagined, we are transforming them from creators to reactors.

I'm not meaning this to be a wholesale criticism of children's films—or of the *Harry Potter* films in particular. Watching a film can be a creative experience for children, especially if it serves as a springboard for creative play. However, a film that serves as a marketing tool for zillions of products—many of which dictate how kids will process the film or play about it—robs children of creative experience.

Marketing campaigns built on licensed products send a message to children that whatever they generate is not good enough. Embedded in any marketing campaign is the message that consumers *need* the product being advertised (remember "importance nagging"?). For children, "needing" the Harry Potter toys and accessories licensed by Warner Brothers means that they can't imagine playing without a store-bought costume instead of a homemade one, a battery-operated vibrating quidditch broom instead of the one used to sweep the kitchen floor, or an official Harry Potter wand instead of a stick they can pick up outside.

D.W. Winnicott, whose work I mentioned earlier, died in 1971, long before personal computers, cross-marketing, and video games came into being. Linking creativity to mental health, Winnicott believed that children thrive in environments with safe boundaries but that do not impinge on their ability to think and act spontaneously. Writing at a time when the divisions in most families related to fathers working and mothers taking care of the children, he called such delicately balanced environments "good-enough" mothering. These days, people writing about the phenomenon he described refer to it as "good-enough parenting."

A good-enough parent holds a baby tightly enough for the baby to feel secure, but loosely enough for the baby to gesture. As the baby's gesture brings responses—a coo, a smile, a laugh from a parent—she learns the difference between what comes from her and what comes from others. As her spontaneous gestures and sounds generate warmth and approval from her parents, she learns that she is capable of evoking a response and of making good things happen. For children whose parents hold them too tightly, or who flood them continually with stimuli and commands to react, the cost is high. The children never learn to initiate action or to affect the world they inhabit. They never experience creativity.

I imagine that it's not easy to resist the siren song of fame, power, and fabulous wealth. When she sold her first book, Rowling was an unemployed single mother. Still, some artists do hold out. Bill Watterson, creator of the wildly popular comic strip *Calvin and Hobbes,* is one example. Even after he stopped creating the strip, Watterson refused to sell the licensing rights. Somehow he's managed to resist the lure of an estimated $10 million a year from product sales. We should all be grateful to him. The world Watterson created is still unfettered by greeting cards, pillowcases, and ceramic mugs. We enter it unencumbered by interpretations from producers, directors, actors, and art departments.

J.K. Rowling spent her tween and teen years isolated from the excesses of popular culture. When she was nine, her family moved near the Welsh border, close to Britain's Forest of Dean—rural, wild, and beautiful, rife with legends, and relatively isolated from popular culture. In interviews, she speculates that the setting and the lack of things to do stimulated her imagination. I wish that Rowling's insight into the source of her own creativity had enabled her to turn down the Time Warner millions. Harry Potter did not evolve from exposure to television, movies, and the products they sell. His roots are in the silence J.K. Rowling found in the Forest of Dean. He grew in a space she was allowed to fill with her own visions. He grew in the glorious experience—endangered now more than ever—of listening intently to voices no one else has heard.

Of course, Harry Potter is not the only literary character whose image is used to sell a plethora of products to children. He joins the ranks of Winnie-the-Pooh, Clifford the Big Red Dog, the Cat in the Hat, Madeline, and a host of others. According to a feature in *Publishers Weekly* with the lower-case moniker "Licensing Hotline," Target Stores has launched a new brand called "Sunny Patch" based on the *Miss Spider* books. David Kirk, author and illustrator of the series, has designed all one hundred Sunny Patch products, including but not limited to clothing, gift cards, and home furnishings. As part of the launch, Nickelodeon aired a computer-animated Sunny Patch special—sponsored by Target, of course.[5] Nicholas Callaway, Kirk's partner in an entertainment company called Kirk & Callaway, had this to say about the concept: "It's a little bit deeper than the licensing model. . . . Our approach was to create a children's lifestyle brand in which every product tells a story." [6] Six new Sunny Patch brand books will be sold exclusively by Target for six months before they are available elsewhere.

The lines between publishing children's books and marketing to kids are so blurred that Scholastic, Inc., publisher of *Harry Potter* and the *Miss Spider* series, and which for years has had a stellar reputation in children's publishing, was the focus of a national letter-writing protest when the company co-sponsored the Advertising and Promoting to Kids conference in 2001.[7]

The market (and our children) are so flooded with images of media characters that even marketing executives are taking notice. Warren Kornblum, chief marketing officer at Toys "R" Us, described the phenomenon in *Brandweek* as "sort of a runaway train."[8]

Conformity, impulse buying, defining self-worth by what you own, and seeking happiness through the acquisition of material goods are traits that marketing inculcates in consumers. All of these are antithetical to creativity, which draws sustenance from inner resources rather than external dictates, fads, fancies, or rewards. Creativity is characterized by originality, the capacity for critical thinking, and the ability both to recognize the difficulty in a problem and to search for solutions. It's not in marketers' best interest for consumers to think too much, too well, or too critically about their products. In chapter 10, I will talk about marketing's impact on creativity again, this time in the context of preserving democracy. But for now, let's go back to play.

Children play for fun, but—often without knowing it—children play for lots of other important reasons as well. When a four-year-old climbs up a jungle gym, she's practicing gross motor skills, learning about balance, and about risks. When she builds with blocks, she's exploring properties of gravity and design. When her older brother paints or draws, he's improving his fine motor skills and engaging in self-expression.

When kids play house, or space explorers, or engage in any kind of dramatic play, they are expressing feelings and trying out relationships and roles. They are also learning important skills such as sharing, taking turns, compromising, and building consensus. Because expressive play simultaneously provides a window into children's experience, allows for self-expression, and offers an opportunity to make meaning of the world, play is central to children's psychological well-being. In therapy, when children play out themes of divorce, hospitalization, or other traumas, they are gaining mastery over these difficult issues and the emotions they produce.

Play requires physical and/or mental activity. The impetus for play comes from within children. It is their way of learning about the world. It is inherently satisfying in and of itself and requires no goal. Once a goal is more important than the activity, that activity is no longer play. In competitive sports, for instance, once winning becomes more important than the process of playing, the games or matches cease to be play. The ability to play and be playful is a sign of health.[9]

Once we acknowledge the importance of play, it makes sense that toys—the things children play with—are also of critical importance. There's some unintentional irony in the fact that so many toys today are labeled "educational." The best toys are inherently educational in that they serve as tools for helping children actively explore, understand, and/or gain mastery over the world. Even if they have multiple parts, they are simple enough to be put to many different uses, and to become different things in a child's imagination.

The recent proliferation of computer chips that enable toys to move or make sounds on their own renders children passive observers rather than active participants in play. Because children are attracted to glitz and because these are the toys being marketed to them, they may desperately want stuffed animals or dolls or action figures that walk and talk independently, or toys that whiz, bang, whistle, and hoot at the press of a button. However, because they discourage active, imaginative play, toys that do only one thing soon become boring; children use them a few times and then are ready for a new toy that does something else. Perhaps it's no accident that such toys bring to mind the phenomenon of "planned obsolescence"—the design, production, and sale of products, like panty hose, that break or wear out almost immediately or are quickly outdated. The problem is that if profit is the primary motivation for creating and marketing, then how children play with the toy is irrelevant. All that matters is that they keep buying more toys from the same company.

Take a look at the Pokémon empire, which generated more than $1 billion between 1998 and 2001. Pokémon is not just a trading-card game; it's also a popular TV cartoon, a series of Nintendo games, a movie (movies, actually; the first installment was titled *Pokémon: The First Movie*), a line of stuffed animals, a Radio City Music Hall extravaganza, a line of Halloween costumes, and even a set of cake decorations—perfect for your child's birthday party, at which he or she will no doubt also receive many of the aforementioned Pokémon toys and games as presents.

If nothing else, Pokémon represents a brilliant marketing ploy. The theme song of the TV program features a pulsing chorus of "Gotta catch 'em all." Winning—good triumphing over evil—can only be achieved by capturing all of the Pokémon characters. For children, that means collecting all of the Pokémon cards. These days, mega toy stores like Toys "R" Us are filled with placards urging kids to "collect them all." Everything comes in a series. The message is that kids should not be satisfied with one of anything.

Pokémon may be on the wane, but 4Kids Entertainment, its American distributor, has acquired Yu Gi Oh, another blockbuster franchise complete with cards, videos, computer games, and a television series. The company, whose chief executive is Al Kahn, the man behind the Cabbage Patch Doll craze in the 1980s, has entered into a four-year, $100-billion deal with Fox to create programming for their Saturday morning slot. Fox is gearing that slot toward young boys, who are the biggest market for action figures.[10] According to an article in *Crain's New York Business,* "Television gives 4Kids a vehicle to expose the products for which it has the licensing rights to potential young customers." In the same article, Mr. Kahn elaborates, "We can launch our own concepts and give them the time to seed. . . . 'Fox Box' is a platform for us."[11] In other words, Fox and 4Kids will be broadcasting commercials all Saturday morning, every Saturday morning.

Because children use play to understand the world, the toys we provide for them serve as lessons and reflections of society's values. That's why it's legitimate to ask questions about the impact of Barbie dolls on girls' expectations about their lives or feelings about their bodies, or about the impact of excessively and explicitly violent toys on children's attitudes and behavior. It's also important to question the *nature* of a child's experience playing with a particular toy, as well as the toy's actual form or content. Do we want our kids to be inundated with toys that train them to react, rather than toys that encourage them to think and generate action?

In 2002, the Jewish Museum in New York City mounted an extremely controversial show called "Mirroring Evil: Nazi Imagery/Recent Art." One of the most controversial pieces was Zbigniew Libera's "Lego Concentration Camp Set." At first glance, the classic, brightly colored box and the block construction beside it evoke endless hours of creative fun. Consistent with modern-day Legos, it's clear that the set is designed as a kit rather than as a free-form collection of blocks. The picture on the box, which is carefully replicated in the construction beside it, suggests that the pieces enclosed make a particular construction which appears at first to be some kind of a fort or modern army encampment. Closer examination shows that in fact this apparently harmless children's toy contains the building blocks for a Nazi death camp—including skeleton-like figures that serve as the emaciated inmates.

Reviews of the show complained that it was an outrage to depict a death camp as a child's plaything. Certainly the notion of children building a model death camp for fun *is* horrifying. A modern example might be a toy that would enable children to play at blowing up the World Trade Center. Unthinkable? In 1996—five years before the attacks on September 11, 2001, but well after the blasts there in 1993—Trendmaster marketed exactly such a toy. Called the "Independence Day Defend N.Y. City Micro Battle Play Set," it included miniature models of the World Trade Center, the Statue of Liberty, and the Empire State Building to blow up. It is no longer on the market.

As I'll discuss in the chapter on marketing violence, acts of destruction and terrorism are routinely marketed to children in the guise of entertainment. War toys, guns, torture chambers, and toys that glorify battles past and future are all grist for the lucrative toy market. And these don't include graphically violent video games. An actual children's toy designed to encourage children to build a miniature death camp *would* trivialize the horrific meaning of the Holocaust. There would be nothing positive to be gained from it. But where do we draw the line? Perhaps the North Vietnamese would draw it at the GI Joe Green Beret action heroes, so popular during the Vietnam war. Native Americans probably draw the line at plastic celebrations of their ancestors' destruction such as a model Fort Apache, which has recently been reissued by Marx Toys, Inc.[12] I'm sure that Lego would never produce a concentration camp construction set, but where on the continuum do we place other toys that glorify human destruction?

Apologists for marketing violent toys, and for exposing children to violent media, argue that these products tap into a preexisting dark side of childhood and allow children to gain mastery over their violent fears and fantasies.[13] Anyone who has ever experienced the rageful cries of a baby, comforted a child after a nightmare, or confronted a preschooler who has been treated unjustly, has no doubt that children experience a whole range of powerful, negative feelings and fears. It's also true that playing out children's angry or even violent fantasies is a good way to help them gain some insight into, and control over, life's more difficult moments. But it's important to remember that the explicitly violent video games, movies, or toys so popular today are not generated by children. Each gory detail is created by an adult.

Some reviewers accused Libera of "contaminating" an excellent toy. In fact, I noticed a disclaimer from the manufacturer exhibited next to the doctored packaging. It's true that building with Legos has been a wonderful creative experience for children over the years, but the concentration camp piece reminds me of a disturbing trend in commercial children's toys away from nurturing creative play to fostering a more constricted experience. Legos, like other creative construction toys, now tend to be packaged as kits rather than as free-form collections of blocks. The brightly colored boxes, and the instructions within, provide a compelling argument for a "right" way to put the blocks together. I often see this with the children I treat.

As I am sitting on the floor of a hospital playroom with Annie, who has just turned seven, she reaches for a box of Lincoln Logs and dumps them out on the floor. In addition to the logs themselves, the set contains one plastic roof, one doorway, three window frames, and a set of instructions detailing exactly how to build three different structures. The original Lincoln Logs sets, from the 1930s, contained only logs—novice builders just left openings for the windows and doors. At that point the kits did not come with preconstructed accoutrements, so children could place the openings anywhere. Like modern versions of Legos, today's Lincoln Logs offerings come with instructions rather than a few suggestive pictures of multiple possibilities.

Keeping a rather anxious eye on the pictures, Annie tries to duplicate one of the detailed models on the page. Before she has it exactly right she places a plastic roof on top. It doesn't fit. We have not built the structure exactly to specification. Dismissing my suggestion that we build something of our own, she tries again to get it right. In fact, it's not clear to me that we could have created a structure much different from the three models. A building set that allows for creativity should contain lots of different-sized pieces: this kit contains only enough logs in just the right numbers to build only those structures depicted in the instructions.

Tiring of the logs, Annie pulls out a plastic container of dinosaurs. These come with plastic palm trees, rocks, and even a volcano. They also come with a plastic floor plan showing exactly where every tree and rock should go. "The trees go there," she says, pointing to the palm fronds depicted on the plastic. I place a tree on an unmarked piece of land. "No," she says, moving it. "They have to go here." The volcano and even the rocks have to go on their designated spots.

She takes out a dinosaur and hands me another one. "These have to fight," she says. I begin making my dinosaur talk. "No!" she insists. "They can't talk." "Why can't they talk?" I asked, puzzled. "It's like the movie," she explains impatiently. "You know! They fight and they can't talk!"

That old standby Play-Doh, another creative toy, is also now marketed primarily in kits, many of them designed in partnership with companies interested in selling other products. Consider, for instance, a Play-Doh Mc-Donald's kit, which features molds designed solely for the purpose of enabling children to make Play-Doh French fries, Big Macs, Chicken Mc-Nuggets, milkshakes, and other foods sold at the ubiquitous fast-food franchise. Even putting aside the fact that such a toy is a blatant device for marketing fattening, unhealthy foods, the children who encountered it in my office at the day-care center invariably used that Play-Doh set only to make the products they were "supposed" to make. Each spent one session extruding French fries and stamping out burgers, then lost interest.

Even those few commercial toys unadorned with electronic bells and whistles sometimes do more to squelch creativity than to promote it, especially if they are tied to media characters. When my daughter was three, I took her along to a local television station where I was working on some public service announcements. She trotted into the lobby dangling a stuffed frog from one arm. She loved stuffed animals and had a lot of fun creating voices and personalities for them. "Who's your frog?" asked the receptionist. "Kermit?" We walked a little further and met a producer. "Who's your frog?" he asked. "Kermit?" This exact scenario was repeated with three other people. By the time we left there was no doubt as to the identity of her frog. It was, from that time on, Kermit and Kermit only. The imaginative possibilities of a rather unspecific frog had been supplanted by someone else's creation.

It's impossible to talk about the impact of marketing on children's imaginations without talking about media. These days, board games and stuffed animals, dolls and action figures are likely to be products licensed from films, TV programs, and even video games. A stuffed dog is not just any mutt a child might use to call a new character into being, but a specific dog with a specific media-implanted personality, voice, and life history. Action figures—already controversial because they are often equipped with weapons—are not generic soldiers, or cowboys and Indians (and, after all, many kids of all kinds of backgrounds identified with the Indians), but detailed characters tied to specific films or TV series.

In and of itself, television seems to put a damper on children's imaginative play. Ready-made visual images and story lines require less work from viewers. When children play with a toy based on a particular television character, they play less creatively, especially right after they have watched a program.[14]

When I play puppets with children, I am careful to give them puppets that cannot be identified with media programs. Under these circumstances, the children are free to imbue them with any personality traits that might be relevant to their own lives. When the children bring media characters to our play (even such a benign personality as Kermit), they stick rigidly to that character's television persona and try to reproduce the character's voice. Surprisingly, this is also true of adults. When I teach workshops for teachers or therapists, each participant picks a puppet from my extensive and rather motley collection. Most of these are entities devoid of media associations, but somewhere along the line I picked up a Cookie Monster puppet. As we go around the room, the teachers or student therapists (with some embarrassment) spontaneously create all sorts of characters. Whoever has the Cookie Monster invariably gets locked into a rigid representation of that specific, predetermined character, which, however endearing it might be, discourages any creative input.

Another toy at the day-care center is a memory game based on the wonderful PBS series *Arthur*. Called "Arthur's Library," the game involves tiny cards representing books. But the only books in Arthur's library are Arthur books. Therefore, every game we play is a sales pitch for the Arthur books (and the videos, television program, toys, and clothes associated with the character) and those alone. The game itself is fun, but the reality is that the game would be just as much fun if it were played with an unbranded deck of cards, or with characters unrelated to any other context.

Increasingly, we are depriving children of the invaluable challenge of populating their own fantasy worlds with characters of their own creation. It's true that books, films, and television programs have long been fodder for children's imaginative play. For better or worse they've always generated toys as well. But it has been only since 1984, when the Federal Trade

Commission deregulated children's television, that licensed products have dominated the market so completely.[15] Before deregulation, partnerships designed to use television programming to sell products, such as the one I described earlier between 4Kids and Fox Television, were prohibited by law.

Deregulation has had a profound and worrisome effect on children's toys and, by extension, on their creative play.[16] In 2002, nine of the ten bestselling toys were de facto advertisements for television programs, movies, and videos.[17] The top seller, Barbie as Rapunzel, refers also to a movie starring, thanks to modern media technology, Barbie herself (and Anjelica Huston).

My daughter was lucky enough to attend a wonderful preschool called the Corner Co-op. It was exactly what Winnicott would have described as a holding environment—a place designed for children to engage in the kind of creative play that enables healthy growth and development. The Corner Co-op is still in existence. It's not a fancy school, nor is it jam-packed with toys. Mostly the kids are gloriously busy with art supplies, balls, blocks, and discarded finery in the dress-up corner. They walk to a local park to play on swings and a jungle gym.

I found myself thinking about the Corner Co-op recently when I came upon news that American Greetings, which owns the licensing rights for the Care Bears—a children's brand and television program marketed in the 1980s—was distributing free Care Bear educational materials to 25,000 preschools around the country. The materials are supposed to promote prosocial behavior and to teach children "to care." In fact, during "National Care Week," a corporate invention designed to take place during the campaign, parents and children will be given a certificate to sign declaring that they in fact do care. It looks like American Greetings expects them to care a lot: the Care Bears marketing plan called for sales to top $203 million in 2003.[18]

American Greetings paid the marketing firm Youth Marketing International a six-figure fee to create the teaching materials. It can't hurt that Joel Erlich, a former teacher and the president of Youth Marketing, was recently named Kid Marketer of the Year by *Brandweek*.[19] A film, DVDs, and videos are part of the campaign.

The rationale marketers use for marketing in preschools is that kids are more likely to engage if the materials used in the curriculum are based on familiar characters. The problem with that argument is that its very premise—that preschool children are easier to engage when teachers use familiar characters to engage them—denies the natural curiosity and delight in discovery inherent in young children.

Recently, a reporter called me about marketing in preschools; she told me that she had talked to a preschool teacher using a corporate-based curriculum on handwashing. I was taken aback. Most of the preschool children with whom I work love to wash their hands—not because they are clean freaks, but because they like to play in water and they get an extra kick making bubbles with soap. Getting them to wash their hands isn't a problem—sometimes they get so lost in playing with soap bubbles that it's a problem to get them to *stop* washing—yet the marketing industry is doing such a good job of convincing adults that children need licensed products in order to grow and develop that, for example, Scholastic is selling preschool teachers a "Clifford's Kit for Personal and Social Development." According to Scholastic's web site, Clifford the Big Red Dog inspires "Children to become Great Big People."[20] The kit teaches kids to, among other things, be truthful, responsible, have respect, work together, and play fair.[21] These are all admirable qualities, but early childhood educators have been fostering these traits in children for years—without help from Clifford, the Care Bears, or any other media-based character.

Psychologist Selma Fraiberg called her classic book on early childhood *The Magic Years* for a good reason. The title refers in part to a period in children's cognitive development that is prelogical and based on an egocentricity that places them at the center of a wonderful and terrifying universe where monsters are real and wishes make things happen. However, it also refers to the magic of a young child's capacity for originality, honest self expression, and delight in exploration. As kids get older, these qualities provide the foundation for critical thinking and rigorous academic exploration. The problem is that these are the same qualities we've placed in jeopardy by letting the marketplace encroach on our children's fantasy lives—allowing the bottom line to dictate how and with what they are allowed to play.

5

Students for Sale:
Who Profits from Marketing in Schools?

WHEN MY DAUGHTER was in third grade, her school's annual spring concert—usually a mix of jazz, folk, classical, or even rock music—was a program titled "An Evening of Disney." I was appalled. Instead of expanding their horizons even a little, my daughter and her schoolmates were devoting their year to learning the one body of music every eight-year-old in America is sold on a daily basis. Now it's being marketed to them in schools, along with videos and little mouse ears. I couldn't see how spending school time on Disney music expanded children's learning or enriched their musical lives. When I complained to the music teacher, she responded, "But the kids like it."

I didn't know it then, but the Disneyfication of my daughter's musical education was just a small sign of the times. It occurred only a year or so before Ed Winter, an enthusiast for marketing in schools who would have a profound effect on its nature, told *Business Week*, "Marketers have come to realize that all roads eventually lead to the schools." [1]

In-school advertising began escalating in earnest in 1990. It now includes (but isn't limited to) corporate-sponsored newscasts, field trips, classroom materials, vending machines, gymnasiums, walls, and whole buildings. Have you visited your child's school lately? Perhaps she's learning about energy production and consumption through the lens of companies like Exxon Mobil[2] or professional associations like the American Coal Foundation ("Unlocking Coal's Potential through Education").[3] Her inspiration for reading may be coming from Pizza Hut—complete with coupons to be redeemed at your local franchise.[4] She may be attending mandatory assemblies where she can learn about job interviewing from McDonalds.[5] If she lives in Washington, D.C., and wants to go into the hotel business, she might be attending the Marriott Hospitality Charter

School.[6] If she's a kid in trouble, she could attend a Burger King Academy.[7]

If she's on a school athletic team, her shoes may come from Nike or Adidas.[8] Her school's scoreboard could owe its presence to the countless bottles of Coke or Pepsi she's bought from school vending machines and sport a company logo.[9] Access to her opinions and ideas might have been sold to a market research company.[10,11] Her only exposure to current events might be brought to her courtesy of the aforementioned Ed Winter. He's the guy who thought of Channel One, the twelve-minute news program that includes two minutes of commercials that her school is obligated to show daily for 90 percent of the school days each year.[12]

Public schools have been venues for at least some corporate marketing since their inception. In fact, a 1929 report from the National Education Association published a treatise warning teachers about "free" corporate handouts, suggesting that corporate materials belonged in the classroom only if they were essential to a child's education.[13] In the 1930s schools became a battleground between corporations and the nascent consumer movement.[14] Students in the 1950s routinely saw corporate-sponsored "educational" films. By 1954, over 3.5 million students watched about 60,000 showings of films from the National Association of Manufacturers. By 1959, one in five corporations reported sponsoring educational materials.[15]

In the early 1990s the scope of commercialization of schools began escalating at an unprecedented rate. At the Commercialism in Education Research Unit at Arizona State University, Professor Alex Molnar has been tracking media mentions of school commercialism since the start of that decade. In 2002, he found 4,631—in contrast to the 991 found twelve years earlier.[16] As one marketing expert explained, "'Ten years ago, schools were more or less acting as gatekeepers. . . . They were suspicious of manufacturers coming into schools to do business."[17] In 2000, a federal government report from the General Accounting Office (GAO) called marketing in schools a growth industry.[18]

Just as corporations and the free market are currently seen as models for solving health-care or other social problems,[19] they are also viewed as a solution for troubled public schools and school systems. To paraphrase the old corporate maxim, "If it's good for General Motors, it's good for education."

We are in the middle of a nationwide thrust to turn schools over to for-profit companies and Education Management Organizations (EMOs) such as Edison Schools, Inc. Even when cities and towns stop short of actually turning their children's education over to the business world, corporations have become models for running school systems.

Are corporations such great models? It seems like a bad joke to me that even as the heads of corporations like Enron, Worldcom, and Tyco are charged with cannibalizing their companies, the heads of major school systems, including those in Chicago and Philadelphia, are now called CEOs rather than superintendents.[20] The school department in the town of Brooklawn, New Jersey, even has a director of corporate development.[21] Though they are ultimately responsible for the *education* of millions of school children, many of the newest administrative appointees—whether they are called CEOs or superintendents—are not, and have never been, educators. The New York City schools are run by Joel Klein, the former American CEO of the German media conglomerate Bertelsmann.[22] In Seattle, an army general was replaced as superintendent by an investment banker[23] who recently resigned amid news that under his tenure the district overspent its budget by tens of millions of dollars.[24] In Philadelphia, the new CEO is the former city budget director for the city of Chicago and the former CEO of the Chicago Public Schools.[25] It has become the norm to measure a school's success only by its students' scores on standardized tests, just as a corporation is judged by its profits.

I've briefly mentioned the ongoing debates about restructuring public school management, school vouchers, and for-profit schools because such discussion is critical to the health of public schools. The push for school vouchers—which allocate to parents a certain amount of tuition dollars to spend wherever they want—applies the economics of the free market to education. However, these issues go way beyond the scope of this chapter. Since whole books have been devoted to them, I'll limit my discussion to more direct forms of advertising in schools—why it's happening, what forms it takes, and why it is a problem.

For corporations, of course, there is no downside. Because they are "contributing" to education, they look like good corporate citizens. They get to place their brand in the faces of students who, because of mandatory schooling laws, can't escape from it. To quote Joel Babbit, former president of Channel One, the commercially based news program mentioned earlier, "The advertiser gets kids who cannot go to the bathroom, cannot change the station, who cannot listen to their mother yell in the background, who cannot be playing Nintendo."[26]

The notion that marketing in schools is a reflection of good corporate citizenship is debatable. Since when do acts of good citizenship necessitate a *quid pro quo?* If you believe, as I do, that all of us—including corporate executives—benefit from a well-educated populace, the following questions come to mind: Why should your child's education be tied to someone else's monetary gain? Don't we all have an obligation to support public schools?

Those in the education trenches who allow, if not embrace, corporate marketing in their schools—superintendents, principals, teachers, and school board members—don't justify it on philosophical, political, or educational grounds, nor do they suggest that it is in the best interest of children to use school as a marketplace. For them, it comes down to money.

In 2003, my own state of Massachusetts cut its school budget for the first time in a decade.[27] Last year, legislators raised the school budget only 1 percent as opposed to the annual increase of 10 percent that had become common.[28] During the same legislative session in which this minuscule increase was passed, legislators also passed a law allowing schools to sell the sides of school buses to advertisers. According to one legislator, "We saw it as a way of getting a few more dollars in the door."[29] Massachusetts is not an exception. When school personnel look to commercialize their students' school experience, they almost always plead poverty.

In 2001, when the Brooklawn, New Jersey, high school announced that it would call its new school gymnasium "Shop Rite" after the local supermarket chain agreed to put up $100,000 ($5,000 a year for twenty years) to help pay for it, the school board hadn't asked for a tax increase for thirty years. Almost half of Brooklawn residents are senior citizens. "We don't want to bankrupt our seniors," the school board president explained, but the school superintendent added, "It's the privatization of public responsibility. . . . We'll be the first school district to be branded with a corporate logo. You hope children can become sophisticated enough to deal with it."[30]

Groundwork for the current iteration of corporate involvement in schools was laid in the Reagan years. Under Ronald Reagan, the federal government began to cut back the money states received for public programs, and the privatization of public services began to be seen as a solution for everything from prisons to garbage collection. In 1982, Reagan's Education Task force put out a treatise called *A Nation at Risk*, a rallying cry to business to get involved in schools.[31] At the same time, the federal government began to cut back on money for state programs, including those for education. These days, the federal government is responsible for only about 6 percent of school funding. But states and local communities have always borne the brunt of paying for educating their children. At its height, the federal government was responsible for only 10 percent of school costs.[32]

It's true that, at least until 2003, even taking inflation into account, school budgets have been rising over the past two decades. Even so, over the past fifteen years—which have seen a great escalation in school commercialization—they have not kept pace with growing populations.[33] Nor have budgets risen in proportion to the costs of federally mandated programs for which local school systems are responsible. Schools are obligated by law to meet the costs of special education programs and, more recently, to meet standards for achievement in certain subjects. In 2002, the Association of School Administrators estimated that testing mandates would cost states more than $7 billion over the next seven years[34]—at a time when forty states faced budget deficits.[35]

Before the current cuts, money that might have gone for equipment, maintenance, and classroom materials was already being spent for other things. Now the situation is even more dire. Wealthier communities might pass tax overrides to raise money for school buildings or to maintain certain programs. But poorer communities, or wealthy communities that don't make education a priority, are in a terrible bind. Schools with poorer students already receive less state and local aid than other schools.[36]

For corporations competing to sell children products, the current budget crunch is a gift. "Tight budgets opened doors," enthused a writer for *Promo* this year. Quoting an executive from the youth division of Alloy—a teen clothing catalogue-cum-web portal/magazine publisher— the article explained that administrators "are becoming more open to commercialism and thinking about how they can reduce budgetary problems." As a result, "brands are learning to create curriculum-based programs when possible or appropriate, bring mobile tours to schools, infiltrate locker rooms and sports fields, and sample, sample, sample."[37]

So what's the problem? How is marketing to children in schools harming them? If, as I'm arguing in this book, it's harmful in their leisure time, it's certainly harmful during the hours they spend in school. Worries about advertising's impact on childhood obesity and nutrition, for instance, which I discuss in the next chapter, apply in any venue. But when products are advertised in school, there is an implicit message to students that the school supports that product. Whatever feelings children have about school—whether it is a positive or a negative force in their lives—there is an expectation that what they are learning there is good for them, in the same way that eating vegetables is good for them. At the very least, children believe that the adults involved in schools believe that what's happening there is good for kids.

We cannot expect kids to separate the message from the messenger. So when, as a mother reported recently, her fifth-grade daughter was handed a deodorant sample during health class, it carried a stamp of official approval. When a teacher in a local junior high decorated his wall with a poster of World Wrestling stars exhorting the joys of reading, he was endorsing violence as well as literacy. When a cafeteria in an elementary school in Superior, Wisconsin, featured a life-size cutout of teen pop star Britney Spears (who shills for Pepsico) as a "Got Milk" promotion (complete with information about how to get her latest CD), the school simultaneously endorsed milk, Pepsi, the teen singer, and whatever values she promotes in her music.

Dorothy Wolden, whose seven-year-old daughter attended the school at the time, was furious about the cutout and has this to say about her attempts to get it removed:

> In the cardboard stand-up, she [Britney] is wearing a short black t-shirt and
> black leather pants with studs, exposing about 3 or 4 inches of her tum. Be-
> tween her feet, below the "Got Milk?" and her "signature," is an ad with a pic-
> ture of her then-latest CD cover that says "Get Britney's new album 'Oops I Did
> It Again' on Jive CDs and tapes IN STORES NOW. The same ad was on the 3
> by 3 poster of Britney on the cafeteria wall.
>
> One of the silliest stories about the whole thing was that someone decided
> my problem must be Britney's tummy and pasted a hand-lettered sign over her
> skin that said "Drink Milk!" (but left the album ad exposed). The superintend-
> ent in a phone conversation wondered if my issue was with the leather or the
> studs if not the skin. He told me, "Some schools are coloring in that stomach
> area with black marker; would that satisfy you?"[38]

The implicit endorsement of products and of commercialism itself is concerning, but marketing in schools raises other major worries. Critics believe that it interferes with the fabric of the public school system and, most important, with learning. In 1929, the National Education Association's position that corporate-sponsored classroom materials undermined democratic control of school curriculum was based on the fact that presentation of such material bypassed review by the school board members elected from the community.[39] More recently, others have expressed, and continue to express, concerns about content.

The only goal for creating classroom materials should be furthering the education of students using that material. Once a goal becomes imprinting brands into students' consciousness, or creating a positive association to a product, education is likely to take a back seat.[40] Is, for instance, a corporation likely to be unbiased in its presentation of subjects in which it has a vested interest? According to Consumer Union's 1995 review of seventy-seven corporate-sponsored classroom kits that claimed to be educational, the answer is "no." Nearly 80 percent were found to be biased or incomplete, "promoting a viewpoint that favors consumption of the sponsor's product or service or a position that favors the company or its economic agenda. A few contained significant inaccuracies."[41] Materials from energy companies and professional organizations such as Exxon (now Exxon Mobil) or the American Coal Foundation, for instance, were found to be biased in their presentations of the pros and cons of reliance on fossil fuel. Through the American Petroleum Institute, the oil and gas industries produce classroom materials about energy. These can be downloaded at a site called classroom-energy.org.[42] In addition to the Institute's own materials, the site includes links to science lessons produced by oil and gas companies.

Why do teachers use corporate-sponsored materials? For one thing, schools have cut back on the amount of funding available for classroom materials.[43] Not only that, corporate materials are often slick-looking, with interesting graphics. Many teachers I know complain about using dreary out-of-date textbooks. However, even if teachers don't reject materials because they are dotted with corporate logos, the materials they use in the classroom should be vetted for bias or inaccuracies by curriculum specialists.

In recent years, much of the public outrage about marketing in schools has focused primarily on Channel One, which is a daily video program consisting of ten minutes of news interspersed with two minutes of commercials designed specifically for schools.

Channel One came into being in 1989 under the auspices of Tennessee entrepreneur Chris Whittle, who was the first to take advantage of the development of cable and satellite technology for the purpose of marketing to children in school. According to Channel One's web site, the program is fed to 12,000 middle, junior, and high schools around the country, and is viewed by more than eight million students.[44] Schools that sign on with Channel One contract to show the broadcast on 90 percent of school days and in 80 percent of their classrooms.[45] Teachers are required to show the program in its entirety, including the commercials.

What do schools get in exchange for broadcasting Channel One? For the duration of their relationship, the company provides every school with a color television monitor for every twenty-three students, VCRs as part of a central control unit, blank video tapes, a fixed satellite dish on the school roof, and free installation of cable wiring.[46] The value of this equipment has been estimated variously at $25,000[47] to $50,000.[48] Except for the wiring, all of the equipment is removed when Channel One's contract is terminated. The catch is, this equipment isn't really free. In the course of a school year, students spend the equivalent of five instructional days watching Channel One. The teaching time lost to the ads alone is equivalent to one entire school day per year.[49] The school time lost to Channel One costs tax payers $1.8 billion dollars per year, and $300 million pays for time spent watching commercials. Advertising space on Channel One currently sells for roughly $200,000 per day for a thirty-second spot.[50]

A study examining which kinds of schools tend to use Channel One found that schools in poor neighborhoods are more likely to have it. These are the schools that frequently spend less money on their students. In fact, schools that spend the least amount on teaching materials are three times as likely to have Channel One than schools that spend more. The study's author concluded that in schools with scarce resources, Channel One is often used instead of "traditional" kinds of instructional materials—like books.[51]

People frequently ask about the quality of the news on Channel One. Is it educational? The reviews are mixed. There are studies showing that students who have Channel One know slightly more about current events than students who don't have the program.[52] Others show no difference.[53] While students watching Channel One may have a better recollection of current events than their nonviewing peers, they don't seem to have an increased understanding of the events they remember.[54] I don't know of any studies that measure the educational value of Channel One against twelve minutes of current events taught by a good teacher, or against twelve minutes spent reading a credible newspaper each day, or, for that matter, twelve minutes spent watching a noncommercial newscast.

In his eloquent essay, "How to Be Stupid: The Lessons of Channel One," New York University professor Mark Crispin Miller makes the point that the news as seen on Channel One is "even more compressed and superficial than the stuff the networks give us: big accidents and major snowstorms, non-stories about the Super Bowl, horse-race coverage of domestic politics, bloody images of foreign terrorism, the occasional nerve-wracking and largely unenlightening visit to some scary place like Haiti or Tibet, and features—either grim or inspirational—on teens suffering from various high-profile torments (cancer, AIDS, addiction)."[55]

A 1997 study analyzed thirty-six Channel One programs and found that only 20 percent of the program featured stories about recent political, social, or cultural events. The other 80 percent was devoted to sports, weather, natural disasters, features and profiles, and self-promotion of Channel One.[56] In 1998, Channel One hired an education director.[57] A review in the *Columbia Journalism Review* two years later suggested that the news quality had improved somewhat.[58] At this point, there is no education director listed on the company's web site,[59] and when I called the company, the person I spoke to said that there was no such position.

In any case, discussions about the quality of Channel One's news are distracting. Even aside from the commercials, Channel One represents a corporate intrusion into the lives of children—taking a total of five instructional days' worth of school time over the course of the year—in which one corporation dictates the content of "lessons" for eight million students without review from their teachers, principals, superintendents, or school boards. Teachers are allowed to preview programs and can opt not to show them—but the number of programs they can reject is limited to 10 percent of the whole.

While the effectiveness of the news content is debatable, the commercials seem to be a great success. To quote Dr. Miller again:

The ads on Channel One would seem to be especially powerful, however, because they thrive by contrast not just with the news before and after them, but with the whole boring, regimented context of the school itself. . . . Imagine, or remember, what it's like to have to sit there at your desk, listening to your teacher droning on, with hours to go until you can get out of there, your mind rebelling and your hormones raging. It must be a relief when Channel One takes over, so you can lose yourself in its really cool graphics and its tantalizing bursts of rock music—and in the advertisers' mind-blowing little fantasies of power: power through Pepsi, Taco Bell, McDonald's, Fruit-A-Burst and/or Gatorade ("Life Is a Sport. Drink It Up!"), power through Head 'n' Shoulders, Oxy-10 and/or Pantene Pro-V Mousse (" . . . a stronger sense of style!"), power through Donkey Kong and/or Killer Instinct ("PLAY IT LOUD!") and/or power through Reebok ("This is my planet!").[60]

The effectiveness of advertising on Channel One has been documented in qualitative[61] and quantitative studies.[62] When University of Missouri communications professor Ray Fox studied 200 students who viewed the Channel One newscast on a daily basis, he found, not surprisingly, that students clearly remembered the ads. He also found that the ads entered the fabric of their lives. Students incorporated Channel One into their creative writing and even reported dreaming about some of the ads.[63]

A study that compared two schools that were matched in every way except for the presence of Channel One found that kids who watched Channel One in school showed more of a preference for products on it than kids in schools that didn't show the program. Of even more concern is that students exposed to Channel One showed more inclination toward materialistic values than those who weren't exposed. The study found that regular viewers of Channel One were more likely to agree that: money is everything; a nice car is more important than school; designer labels make a difference; wealthy people are happier than poor people.[64]

These findings run counter to the argument of proponents of Channel One, and of any marketing in schools, that in-school advertising has little impact on children because they are exposed to advertising in all aspects of their lives. This study suggests that the ads on Channel One (and presumably other advertising in schools) have more of an impact—not just on brand preferences but also on students' values—because they are seen in the classroom at the behest of school officials and are integrated into the whole gestalt of "school" and what is taught there.

Running neck and neck with Channel One in arousing public ire is the phenomenon of "pouring-rights" contracts, in which a major beverage company, usually Coca Cola or Pepsico, buys the exclusive right to market their products within a school or school system. Since increased soda consumption is linked to the growing epidemic of childhood obesity, pouring-rights contracts have been coming under increasing scrutiny in recent years.

When Kelly Brownell, director of the Center for Eating and Weight Disorders at Yale and an outspoken critic of selling soda or any kind of junk food in schools, visited his son's public high school, he counted thirteen soft-drink machines—providing students with a total of 170 options to buy a beverage. Only one of those buttons yielded a container of 100-percent juice. Eleven were for water. The other 158 choices were for soft drinks. Describing the contents of a vending machine dominated by a big Minute Maid juice logo, Brownell reports in his book, *Food Fight,* that the buttons on that particular machine yielded no containers of 100-percent juice and that four of the buttons were for Yoohoo, a sweetened chocolate drink.[65]

A look at some facts about soda consumption lends credibility to the concerns of health-care providers:

- Per capita, Americans are consuming almost five times as much soda pop as they were fifty years ago.[66]

- According to a study at Boston Children's Hospital conducted with children aged seven to eleven, the odds of becoming obese increase for each additional can of sugar-sweetened drink consumed each day, as does BMI (Body Mass Index), which measures weight in proportion to height.[67]

- A twenty-ounce bottle of soda contains 260 calories.[68]

- For people already meeting their caloric needs, one twenty-ounce soda a day for a year could increase their weight twenty-seven pounds.

- A healthy teenager weighing 120 pounds, who exercises regularly, would have to walk at a moderate pace for two hours to burn off one twenty-ounce bottle of soda.[69]

The U.S. General Accounting Office's report identified beverage contracts as the most lucrative of all marketing done in schools.[70] It's certainly profitable for the beverage companies, who are also building brand loyalty. The amount of money schools get for selling these rights, and what they give away to get that money, varies from district to district and sometimes from school to school. It seems to depend on the bargaining acumen of whoever is negotiating the contract. Often, but not always, the amount schools get is tied to commissions on the amount that students drink.

For instance, the West Ashley School in Charleston, South Carolina, gets $ 0.40 for every dollar plunked in a vending machine.[71] The school, which has about 2,100 students, now has approximately one vending machine per fifty students[72] and is realizing about $3,000 per month.[73] Figuring a nine-month school year, they are gaining about $13.00 per student. Per person, students spend about $3.57 each month in those vending machines, or about $32.00 per year. In other words, the students are paying almost $32.00 for $13.00 worth of whatever the school buys with their "extra" money.

The argument is that kids would be buying soda anyway, so they might as well spend that money in school. That may be, but if schools had no vending machines, the inconvenience of obtaining soda during school might enable students to cut down on their consumption. The fact that the vending machines are tied to school funds makes using them that much more attractive. The covert message is "Drink soda and support your school." Sometimes the message isn't all that covert. Some contracts even include quotas—the students are required to drink a certain amount each year. A Colorado Springs superintendent gained notoriety a few years ago when someone leaked a memo he wrote suggesting that students weren't buying enough cola. In order to receive payments ranging from $5,000 to $25,000 per school, the district had to meet a quota of 70,000 cases a year.[74]

A report published by the California Endowment provides insight into pouring-rights contracts. Of five districts involved, commissions ranged from 39 to 56 percent from vending machine sales. Districts received one-time bonuses ranging from $25,000 to $1,000,000. One district signing an exclusive contract also agreed that the corporation's logo could appear on all fountain cups used throughout the district. Those cups had to be purchased from the company. In addition, the company's advertisements would appear on all scoreboards, marquees, and in gymnasiums, and the company had exclusive advertising rights at any events held throughout the school district.

Another contract gave the beverage company "the exclusive right to make beverages available for sale and distribution on campus, including rights to install and operate all equipment that dispenses beverages from any location, to offer fruit drinks, packaged waters and other products in the cafeteria lines of all schools, and to provide all beverages sold at athletic contests, booster club activities and all other special events conducted at any location on the campus."[75] In this contract, "campus" referred to "every school and facility owned or operated by the School District, now or in the future, including all elementary, middle, high and alternative schools, athletic facilities, and concession stands, and, for each building, the grounds, parking lots, dining facilities, food service outlets and vending areas."[76]

The number of vending machines placed in schools almost always increases. In Edison, New Jersey, most schools didn't have soda machines (and those that did had only two) until they signed their exclusive agreement with Coke. After the agreement, all of the high schools had four, most junior highs had three, and most elementary schools had one.[77]

The problem with sending all of these vending machines to school is nicely summed up in a 2001 U.S. Department of Agriculture report to Congress titled, "Food Sold in Competition with USDA Meal Programs." The report says, "When children are taught in the classroom about good nutrition and the value of healthy food choices but are surrounded by vending machines, snack bars, school stores, and a la carte sales offering low nutrient-density options, they receive the message that good nutrition is merely an academic exercise that is not supported by the school administration and is therefore not important to their health or education."[78]

In 2001, Coca Cola announced that it was responding to public concern about obesity and changing its exclusive contracts with some schools.[79] However, Coke has continued to negotiate exclusive deals with schools.[80] Bolstering Coke's presence in the public education system, the company's biggest bottler, Coca Cola Enterprises, is now an official sponsor of the national Parent-Teacher Association. One of its executives sits on the PTA's board of directors.[81]

Candy and other snacks are also sold to students in vending machines. Legislation that would authorize the Department of Agriculture to prohibit sales of foods like soda and candy in schools have been proposed repeatedly to Congress. It's not surprising that the bills have been blocked by lobbyists from the soft drink and sugar industries. What's sad, however, is that they have been joined by the National School Boards Association and the National Association of Secondary School Principals, who say that the loss of funds to schools would do more harm than the costs to children's health.[82] How are children going to thrive when educators are pitted against health-care professionals and nutritionists, forcing us to choose between their health and their education?

Pouring-rights contracts can also have an impact on aspects of children's lives other than obesity. I recently received the following e-mail from an understandably irate father whose daughter was prevented by Pepsico from embarking on a fund-raising endeavor that involved selling bottled water named after her school teams:

> My name is Gary K. Boyes Sr. I am the Father of Andrea Boyes, the cheerleader whose fund-raising intentions with custom labeled bottled water have been banned from the public school grounds by Pepsi. We are in Salem, Oregon. She is allowed to market her Titan water anywhere but where it was designed for. . . .
>
> My daughter was asked for a fund-raising idea. She worked out almost the whole thing herself. She chose a healthy consumable as the product for repeat sales. She designed the label and made all arrangements for production of the new West Salem Titan water. All I did was pick up the first order when completed. She essentially set up a small business to continually provide funding. In addition to this planned legacy from the first cheerleading squad at the new school, she had an as yet unpublished private goal that she kept under wraps until seeing the sales rates. She was hopeful that it could support a scholarship program so that a student that wanted to be a cheerleader could try out without regard to their parents' ability to cover the high cost of making the squad. Many are forced to forgo even trying, and she wanted it to become possible for everyone based on their skills. At 15, she worked one day a week through the summer as an office manager for a local construction company and paid all of her cheerleading costs herself. She didn't have to, she wanted to.
>
> I have been getting a quick education on what I was generally apathetic about before. I can tell you I'm pretty ticked off with what I've found out.

The Salem Keiser school district where Mr. Boyes's daughter is a student has an exclusive ten-year, $5-million contract with Pepsi. The district also has exclusive contracts with food service, furniture, athletic equipment, and computer dealers.[84]

Both Channel One and beverage contracts are major commercial intrusions into the educational lives of children, but they are by no means the only culprits. Less well known but equally pernicious is the degree to

which—often under pressure from administrators to turn more profit—
school food services have been selling fast food to their students during
lunch.[85] The presence of fast food and fast-food chains is most common in
high schools,[86] but by the mid-1990s, Pizza Hut, Taco Bell, and Domino
Pizza were gaining popularity in elementary schools as well.[87] A school in
San Lorenzo, California, has a student-staffed Burger King right on its
campus.[88]

What's troubling is that many nutritionists, including those within
public education systems, seem to accept and even embrace food marketing in schools. A survey of nutrition professionals showed that while most
of the respondents agreed that a product should have nutritional value to
be marketed in schools, they did not feel that the underlying goal of food
marketing—to create customers—is incompatible with the public-service
aspect of their profession.[89]

Meanwhile, food marketing in schools abounds: Kellogg's has created
nutrition education kits that promote Pop Tarts. General Mills has the "Big
G Box Tops for Education" program that encourages sale of their products
by donating money based on the number of product box tops the kids collect. Branded snacks are sold by students for fund-raisers. The Sampling
Corporation of America helps companies distribute and promote products
in elementary schools. Cafeteria posters may celebrate candy.[90]

A school principal sent me an "educational" poster about nutrition
put out by the Frito-Lay company. A rather small representation of the
USDA food pyramid is almost dwarfed by Frito-Lay products (as well as
an enormous image of Pokémon characters). The poster exhorts kids to
"Snack for Power, Snack for Fun!" "Did you know," the poster says,
"Cheetos, Doritos and other Frito-Lay snacks give you the bread/brain
power that the food guide pyramid says you need? That means that you
can include Frito-Lay snacks along with toast, spaghetti, rice and crackers
as part of a nutritious diet!" A picture depicts a bag of Doritos and a glass of
milk with the caption, "That's some powerful snack."

The poster arrived at the school accompanied by the following note:

> Dear Cafeteria Manager:
> Frito-Lay is tapping into the popularity of Pokémon for its latest promotion,
> and we want you to benefit from it. Enclosed you'll find a colorful poster
> for your cafeteria—with a nutrition message for kids about the Food Guide
> Pyramid.

The poster uses the Pokémon characters to capture kids' attention, and then lets them know that Frito-Lay products can be an important part of snacking right—as in the familiar Food Pyramid—because Frito-Lay snacks can help them meet their daily Bread/Grain requirements.

Display this poster in your cafeteria. It'll make the lunchroom a more fun and interesting place for your students, tell a story about nutrition and help build your cafeteria sales.

Given growing concern about childhood obesity, the more optimistic among us can hope that the days of junk-food lunches and vending machines littering schools are on the wane. Thanks to the hard work of parents and advocacy groups, districts across the country are beginning to cut back on the ways the food industry can market to kids in schools. Both the outcry and the decline, however, seem to be focused on marketing unhealthy food, not on marketing per se. Those young children who manage to avoid marketing in their preschools are likely to be hit with some kind of advertising from the moment they start kindergarten. Here's one mother's experience:

I am the mother of three children, aged 18 months, 3 years and 5 years. My oldest child is currently enrolled in kindergarten, so I am at the beginning of an 18 year (at least!) relationship with our town's public school system.

Last month my son came home with his "Scholastic Book Fair order form," to be completed and sent back in with a check for total amount purchased. I recall filling these out as a child and bringing them back to school (after my mother made each of us erase the joke/riddle book choices and choose a "real" book instead—ha-ha). I was informed that the children would be bringing the orders to the library at school and would bring the books home that same afternoon.

While I was annoyed that a child who may not be able to afford a purchase would be singled out in front of his peers, my irritation was soon twofold. My son told me about a book that he wished he had purchased because he knew it was very funny. When I asked how he knew, he told me that "it was in the movie we saw." Upon further investigation, I have since found out that each class sits through a 5-10-minute "movie" (i.e., commercial) which highlights the Scholastic books available for purchase, during library class time.

While I am irate, I am discomforted at the prospect of charging into the administration office and causing a stir during my son's first three months of school. . . . [91]

Ordering books from Scholastic and Scholastic Book Fairs are time-honored traditions in many schools. While these practices certainly are a form of marketing, many people concerned about advertising in schools have looked the other way because they seemed like a harmless way to get books into children's hands. Now, however, Scholastic sends out a video highlighting some of the books available to schools planning a fair. As this e-mail illustrates, the videos are extremely effective in convincing the kids who watch them to select certain books. Children's book choices are not guided by teachers, or by what looks interesting to them as they peruse selections at the fair, but by commercials. They are buying what the corporation wants to sell at that time.

A few months ago, I got a call from a television producer who was doing a story on the Field Trip Factory, a company that links schools with corporations who "donate" field trips to their stores or factories. For instance, the mega pet-store chain Petco sends students to their store, where an employee shows them various kinds of pets. The kids go home with coupons for goldfish and Petco stickers for their notebooks, all in a giant Petco bag.[92] For a "Fitness and Safety in Sports" trip, kids get to go to a Sports Authority store. The trademarked "Be a Sports Authority" trip is described as a "Free 60- to 90-minute trip through the aisles of the Sports Authority." The web site even shows how teachers can meet national education standards in physical education.[93] The children also go home with a goody bag—including a store coupon worth five dollars.[94]

These field trips are a slippery slope. Growing up in Detroit, I have fond memories of going to the Wonder Bread factory and the Vernors soda pop plant. But I also remember field trips to the zoo, the historical museum and the Detroit Symphony youth concerts. Field trips are often among the first casualties in a budget crunch.[95] Schools participating in Field Trip Factory trips seem to do so because they are free; it may be their only chance to get students out of the classroom. That means that they are taking students to Petco, for instance, *instead* of to the zoo.

Trips to the Sports Authority are positioned as taking the place of physical education classes, which are no longer routinely offered in schools. According to a Sports Authority vice president, "Children today need more initiatives to get out and play. . . . If the Sports Authority can provide that, especially considering the cutbacks in P.E., I think it is appropriate for companies to take up the slack. And what better organization to do this but a sporting goods store?"[96]

In addition to bringing companies together with schools, the Field Trip Factory provides scripts for store personnel charged with handling the trips. However, they can't script every interaction, so when a reporter from National Public Radio's *Marketplace* accompanied a class on one of the Sports Authority trips, an employee ended the trip with the following speech, "There's a little lunch bag in here and a coupon for you to give to your parents to bring them back in here, so they can buy all of the stuff that we talked about today. How's that sound? You like shopping here, right?"[97]

The Field Trip Factory describes its mission as providing free field trips to "cash-strapped schools." Since the most impoverished schools are usually attended by impoverished children, I can't help but wonder what kind of family stress is fomented when children come home with coupons and urge their parents to go back and buy "all the stuff" they talked about on the field trip. One parent, quoted in the *Washington Post,* felt his daughter's class trip to Petco was positive, but called it "cruel and unusual punishment for parents." He added, "We'll have to deal with the fallout. . . . She'll be wanting to buy cats [and] parakeets for the next two weeks."[98]

In answer to concerns about promoting commercialism, a Field Trip Factory executive claimed that the trips helped kids become educated consumers.[99] However, when reached by phone, she explained that the trips to grocery stores helped children become educated consumers because they taught children to look at different prices within the store. When I asked if the trips ever talked about comparison shopping at other grocery stores as part of learning to be educated consumers, she said that they did not. The executive emphasized that the trips were designed to educate, not to sell products. She mentioned a trip to a Saturn dealership as an example through which children learned about automobile safety. She explained that her company did not tell kids to go home and talk to their parents about products. That message does not seem to be getting through to employees of at least some of the Field Trip Factory destinations. A spokesperson for a Saturn dealership in Illinois was quoted as saying, "We get to market to local areas, to local schools. This becomes, you know, dinner conversation. 'What did you do today?' 'Well, we went to Saturn. . . .' "[100]

As de facto funding for public schools continues to decrease, it's likely that, without more public outcry, corporations will continue to be more than willing to leap into the breach—at a cost. Instructional time, access to accurate information, and the chance to develop critical thinking skills may all be lost as corporations take an increasing role in public education. The most concrete cost to children and to the pocketbooks of American taxpayers is the contribution marketing in schools makes to childhood obesity, but marketing anything to children in public schools compromises their education. Advertising soda and junk food in schools, however, is particularly cruel, putting children at risk by pitting educators struggling to fund their education against health-care professionals fighting for their lives. Not by a long shot, however, is marketing in schools the only way that food companies target children. They are inundated with food marketing all day long.

6

Through Thick and Thin: The Weighty Problem of Food Marketing

I WORK EACH WEEK in a day-care center and after-school program in Boston. We rely heavily on donations for equipment, and I never know what I'm going to find in the office that I use there. One afternoon, looking through a collection of CD-ROMs with one of the boys, I was surprised to see one from the Hershey corporation. We put it into the computer and spent some time playing various games designed completely around candy. After only a few minutes of images of Hershey bars and foil-wrapped Kisses whizzing by on the screen, I was dying for chocolate. On another occasion, one of the kids noticed a McDonald's Play-Doh set on the shelf. We spent an hour making molds of hamburgers and extruding French fries from a special machine. The same thing happened—I started craving fries and burgers, and I *never* eat at McDonald's.

When asked to name a life-threatening behavior inculcated by media, people inevitably think of violence, but childhood obesity and its flip-side counterparts, anorexia nervosa and bulimia, are escalating public health problems that are exacerbated by media and media marketing.

McDonald's spent over $1.3 billion on advertising in 2002 in the United States alone, making Burger King's $650 million seem paltry by comparison. Pepsico spent more than $1.1 billion, outspending Coca-Cola by about $544,000.[1] Kraft Foods (owned, incidentally, by tobacco giant Phillip Morris—now called Altria Group), maker of Kraft Macaroni and Cheese, Oreos, and Kool-Aid, spent about $465 million in 2001.[2] The year before, Burger King spent $80 million just on advertising to children,[3] and Quaker Oats spent $15 million pitching Cap'n Crunch.[4] When it comes to food, children are targets for everything from edible checkers to battery-operated lollipops. No wonder 25 percent of American children

are overweight, obese, or at risk for obesity.[5] Obese children are more likely
than other kids to become obese adults.

As we all know, obesity is not simply a cosmetic issue. It's associated
with heart disease, stroke, and other weight-related health problems. According to the Centers for Disease Control, "Among overweight children
between 5 and 10 years of age, 60 percent already have at least one cardio-
vascular disease risk factor, such as elevated blood lipids, blood pressure,
or insulin levels that can lead to atherosclerosis, hypertension, and diabetes in adulthood."[6] Recent years have seen an increase in the number of
children diagnosed with type 2 diabetes, usually found in adults.[7] The
amount of time children spend watching television (and, more recently,
playing computer games, being on-line, and watching videos) is usually
cited as a prime factor in the escalation of childhood obesity. Data that im-
plicate the tube are piling up.

Over the past twenty years, studies by researchers have found the following:

- The incidence of obesity is highest among children who watch four
  or more hours of television a day and lowest among children watching an hour or less a day.[8]

- Preschoolers who have televisions in their rooms are more likely to
  have weight problems than those who don't.[9]

- More than 60 percent of the incidence of being overweight in children aged ten to fifteen may be due to excessive television viewing.[10]

- Among teenagers, the incidence of obesity increases by 2 percent
  for every additional hour of television watched.[11]

- For many children, reducing television viewing reduces weight.[12]

It's more comfortable, at least from the standpoint of corporate interests, to blame lack of exercise for the obesity/television connection. If only
kids would be more active, people say, the problem would be solved. That
argument, of course, takes the onus off the people responsible for marketing high-calorie, high-fat, high-sugar food to children.

The problem is not just that kids are sedentary couch potatoes. Their
lives are awash in food marketing. Along with toy ads, food ads account
for most of the marketing that targets kids.[13] In 2002, Burger King, Mc-
Donald's, and Yum Brands (Pizza Hut, Taco Bell, A&W, Long John

Silver's, and Kentucky Fried Chicken) spent a combined total of almost $1.4 billion on television advertising.[14] Nestle, Hershey, and Mars, Inc., account for another $708.2 million.[15] Some of this advertising is probably targeted to adults, but a lot of it is reaching children.

I recently taped six hours of programming on Nickelodeon one Sunday afternoon. Reviewing the tapes, I counted forty food commercials, or about one every nine minutes. According to one study, kids watching Saturday morning television are exposed to one food commercial every five minutes. Almost all of these are for foods high in calories, fat, salt, and/or sugar.[16] Most of the movies and many of the TV programs children watch are marketed with off-screen food promotions. Once a program is associated with a particular brand, the program itself becomes an ad for that food. Visit any supermarket and you'll find shelves filled with examples of these links between the media and food manufacturers.

Take Nickelodeon's hit *Rugrats*—Chucky, Angelica, and the other *Rugrats* tykes now grace packages of Kraft Macaroni and Cheese as well as Farley's Fruit Rolls, a peanut-butter-and-jelly-flavored Good Humor ice cream sandwich, and Amurol bubble gum with comics printed on the gum itself ("view and chew"). Nickelodeon itself has its own line of fruit snacks featuring Nicktoons characters.[17]

Tie-ins like these are designed to lure children into selecting foods associated with favorite movie or TV characters. They are also designed to keep children continually reminded of products. As one marketing expert says, corporations are "trying to establish a situation where kids are exposed to their brand in as many different places as possible throughout the course of the day or the week, or almost anywhere they turn in the course of their daily rituals."[18]

Children's introduction to TV-linked calories often begins in earnest with juice. According to beverage industry writer Lisa Rant, "The beverage aisle is brimming with brews for babies, and mom can take her pick from a plethora of multi- and single-serve solutions with products packaged specifically for the pediatric set. Apple & Eve travels down Sesame Street with Elmo's Punch, Big Bird's Apple, Grover's Grape, and Bert & Ernie's Berry juices. . . ."[19]

Sesame Street isn't the only children's program to cash in on juice boxes for the littlest children. Libby's offers juice boxes adorned with *Arthur* characters, and, says Rant, "Since toddlers are naturally drawn to colorful graphics and familiar characters, Mott's made its move with juice boxes that have featured Nickelodeon's Rugrats and, more recently, [characters from] PBS's *Dragon Tales*. The innovative *Dragon Tales* promotion ran for six months, with changes in graphics every forty-five days to 'refresh' the campaign."[20]

Leaving aside for a moment the question of whether juice is good for children,[21] from a juice company's point of view—and that of many parents—little juice boxes or containers make sense: they're small enough for a young child to handle (both physically and with regard to appetite) and relatively unspillable. As a Julie Halpin, CEO of the Gepetto Group, explained, "Companies often find it difficult to generate enough volume with a product designed only for infants and toddlers. . . . Because this is a relatively short life-stage, the product needs to encourage enough purchase frequency to make sense as a business proposition. If the line of products can be broad and appropriate for different times of day and drinking occasions, a brand for this consumer can work."[22] One way it works is to boost sales by reaching around adult purchasers with packaging designed to appeal to children directly.

It's true that parents can "just say no" to a toddler's grocery-aisle requests. But it's also true that toddlers, going through the developmental phase of differentiating themselves from their parents, are prone to do that by actively and tenaciously asserting their voice, needs, and wants. For media- or brand-saturated little ones and their parents—even for families who restrict television viewing to PBS—a trip to the grocery store, which can often be fun, may turn into a struggle.

Food advertising works.[23] Children's requests for food products, misperceptions about nutrition, and increased caloric intake have been shown to be linked to television advertising. So have parental purchases.[24] One thirty-second food commercial can affect the brand choices of children as young as two, and repeated exposure has even more impact.[25]

The food and media industries' solution to childhood obesity is exercise. Kraft Foods touts its "Helping to get kids moving!" campaign on its corporate web site.[26] The General Mills web site promotes the president's challenge for physical fitness.[27] It's not that I have anything against exercise—I'm all for it—but I find it hard to believe that exhorting kids to be more active while drowning them in ads convincing them that food will make them happy is going to cure children of overeating or of obesity. A grown woman would have to bicycle for two and a half hours to work off the 665 calories in one super-size fries from Burger King.[28] Therefore, I was not particularly encouraged when, in the summer of 2002, I came across the Centers for Disease Control's plan to spend $125 million over one year (and more the next) to combat childhood obesity through an ad campaign designed to "sell" children on exercise.

The CDC's initial goal was, according to a rather oddly headlined Associated Press story ("Federal Government Starts Ad Campaign to Try to Teach Kids to Play"): "Seeding brand loyalty for physical activity just like corporations seed loyalty for hamburgers and video games is marketing exercise like a brand."[29] A brand? *USA Today* elaborated on that theme: "This is selling a product, but the product isn't something on the shelf in the grocery store. . . . The product is an invitation to kids to be social and try all kinds of positive activities and decide what they like."[30]

Missing from the CDC's agenda for VERB, as the campaign is called, is a plan for telling kids to stop eating junk food, or encouraging them to turn off television. David Shea, one of the advertising executives recruited for the campaign, explained, "Tweens consider eating chips and watching TV to be fun, and the ads won't lecture them that couch-dwelling, high-fat living is bad for them."[31] Well, of course not. Many of the companies working with the CDC have a vested interest in keeping children in front of the tube munching junk. Mr. Shea, for instance, is the creative director of Frankel Chicago,[32] which also has McDonald's as one of its clients.[33] McDonald's spent $510.5 million on television advertising in 2002.[34] Where would they take their business if Frankel executives were encouraging kids to stop watching TV?

Saatchi and Saatchi, one of Frankel's sister companies, is handling the advertising. You met them in an earlier chapter—they're the ones who did the premier advertising industry study on children, using psychologists and anthropologists. They also handle marketing for General Mills products, including Fruit Roll-Ups.[35] General Mills ranked fifteenth in corporate spending on TV advertising in 2002, to the tune of $540 million.[36] As the makers of all sorts of snacks and cereals, General Mills might not be thrilled to have Saatchi and Saatchi lure children away from television, sugared cereal, or fattening snack food.

Let's look at the CDC's main media partners. There's Viacom, which owns Nickelodeon and MTV. *They* certainly don't want kids to stop watching TV. Also on board is Channel One,[37] the company discussed in chapter 5, known for piping commercially sponsored television news and ads for snacks and sodas such as Skittles, M&Ms,[38] Reeses Pieces,

Pepsi,[39] Snickers,[40] Twinkies, and Mountain Dew[41] into schools across the country.

So, instead of suggesting that children stop sitting in front of screens or stop eating junk food, the campaign has a web site that seduces children into—guess what!—more screen time. Web site visitors have been able to expend calories by going cyber-skateboarding and shooting cyber-hoops in an ad for the movie *Like Mike.* On one visit, clicking on a button for bowling tips led me straight into the cyber-arms of Channel One. The campaign also features a live touring show sponsored by Nickelodeon.

As in other kinds of marketing, food marketing follows the principle of selling at any cost. In recent years, marketing literature has focused on the need for food to be "fun." The food industry refers to the phenomenon as "eatertainment."[42] Food commercials aimed at children don't talk as much about "great taste" as they do about having fun—associating food with action, friends, excitement. None of these are good reasons for eating.

Fun has always been an element of food marketing aimed at children. Remember "Snap, Crackle, and Pop"? Campbell's Alphabet Soup? What has changed is the intensity of the marketing and the nature of the fun. It was fun to listen to the crispy rice grains crackling before you ate them. It was fun to try to find your name in a bowl of Campbell's soup. Once again the marketing industry has upped the ante. Now there are "fruit" snacks in the shape of checkers pieces, fruit snacks incised with shapes that kids are supposed to punch out to make Nickelodeon cartoon characters.

"It used to be [that] food marketers grabbed kids' attention with packaging graphics and good taste," said Lisa Piasecki, spokeswoman for the Quaker Oats Company. "Kids today are so media-savvy, they want everything in life to be interactive, including their food. It has to have great taste, but it also needs to deliver entertainment value."[43]

Wait a minute. Hasn't food has always been interactive? Eating is one of the ultimate participatory experiences, engaging most of our senses—sight, taste, smell, and touch. Since when does food need to deliver entertainment value other than that provided by eating it?

Central to many of these campaigns is a strategy designed to convince both parents and children that these foods are a necessity—that Fruit Roll-Ups, for instance, meet some basic need. For example, I found a series of interesting statements in a Canadian article on colored condiments. "How are parents supposed to cope with picky eaters?" its author asked:

The solution, marketing experts say, is technicolor condiments. "Kids are living
in a world that is more colourful than the black-and-white-TV world we grew
up with," says dietitian Althea Zanecosky. "They expect everything, including
food, to be more colourful. . . . We have to stop being such purists," she says.
"You have to do whatever you can to encourage kids to eat a variety of foods. If
you can find a nutritious food that has been coloured to make it more attractive,
I think that's OK."[44]

But a condiment like Funky Purple Ketchup is not a particularly good
source of nutrients; nor are Fruit Roll-Ups or many other popular snack
foods. The world that kids are living in today is not more colorful than the
world we lived in as children. Color television may be more colorful than
black-and-white, but children are not (or shouldn't be) living in television.

Another major advertising theme surfaced in an article in the trade
journal *Confectioner*, in which marketers are urged to position candy as a
means of "fulfilling children's unmet needs for control." Gene Del Vecchio, author of *Creating Ever-Cool: The Marketer's Guide to a Kid's Heart*,
is quoted extensively:

"Kids respond well to products that allow them to make their own choices and
give them a sense of control," says Del Vecchio. That is because kids have very
little control over their own lives—either at school where the teacher is in charge
or at home where parents set the ground rules.

Candy can help satisfy the child's unmet desire for control in a number of
different ways. For one thing, Del Vecchio notes, kids frequently get to choose
their own candy purchases. "Candy is at the top of the list of what kids spend
their own money on," he notes.

At a deeper, more profound level, candy can be positioned as a way of "empowering" kids. Del Vecchio cites the example of Jelly Belly jelly beans.
"They've got it," he says of the Jelly Belly Candy Co. "They've created a product where kids can mix and match their own great flavor sensations."[45]

Del Vecchio isn't the only marketing expert who suggests using candy
to make children feel powerful. Tim Coffey, chairman and CEO of the
WonderGroup, described the same tactic for a candy called Airheads. In a
CNN interview, Coffey said, "Airheads is one of those candies that most
adults don't know about, but every kid does. They're uniquely formulated

for kids' taste, and we portray that brand in a way that . . . speaks to their, again, this notion of power and freedom, that . . . eating an Airheads allows you to do things you might not be able to do all the time."[46]

The notion of using any kind of food to foster empowerment is troubling, and the use of candy, which is filled with completely empty calories, is especially so. Is it good for children to equate candy with empowerment? The people I know who struggle with food issues spend all too much time trying to disentangle themselves from their emotional associations with food, yet we have the marketing industry actively encouraging these kinds of connections. Not only that, kids with serious weight problems may be especially vulnerable to the emotional appeal of food commercials. A 1998 study in the *International Journal of Obesity and Related Metabolic Disorders* suggests that obese children are more susceptible to the message implicit in food commercials: that food will enhance their lives.[47]

The conception of food as empowerment may be the most damaging and dangerous of the ways the food industry exploits children's vulnerabilities, but there are others. It also takes advantage, for instance, of parents' desires to raise literate children. Cardboard books developed just for babies feature images and characters from snack-food advertising campaigns—such as an *M&M's Counting Book* and the *Froot Loops Count and Play Book*, whose covers are designed to replicate the products' colorful packaging.

Literacy experts encourage parents to read to babies and toddlers, citing gains in literacy and the promotion of positive parent-baby bonding. Babies and young children whose mothers or fathers read to them—especially when their parents take them on their laps or read to them at bedtime—associate warm, snuggly feelings with reading, and reading itself becomes a pleasurable experience for them early on. All to the good, but meanwhile, one assumes that if they are reading the *Hershey Kisses Counting Board Book* or the *Skittles Riddles Math Book*, they are gaining equally warm, snuggly feelings about certain kinds of food.

Even as kids are bombarded from infancy with messages to chow down foods that experts tell us are practically guaranteed to make them obese, they—girls especially—are being sold the notion that they are supposed to be impossibly thin.[48]

When my daughter was in the seventh grade, parents were notified by the school that several girls in her class were vomiting and using laxatives

to control their weight. At the same time, a friend's daughter was hospitalized because she had stopped eating. Meanwhile, a colleague was concerned about his eighth-grader, who was dieting and exercising to the
point of exhaustion. It's not surprising that anorexia and bulimia are growing problems: most of the models in ads—even those for junk food and especially female models—are all thinner than the national norm for healthy
people. It has even been suggested that bulimia is the only adaptive behavior for children, especially girls, who watch a lot of food commercials—
everyone on the tube is skinny, even as they are devouring fattening food in
huge quantities.[49] Concern about weight begins early: forty percent of
nine- and ten-year-old girls are on diets.[50] A mother confided to me recently that her five-year-old daughter was complaining that her thighs
were too fat.

Meanwhile, a joint study of adolescent girls at Brigham and Women's
Hospital and Harvard Medical School found that their discontent about
body image was directly correlated to how often they read fashion magazines, which are filled with ads featuring underweight models. American
icons such as Miss America have gotten thinner over the years to the point
of undernourishment.[51] It's hard to miss the irony that even as regular people increasingly struggle with obesity, the models we hold as ideals of female beauty are getting thinner.

In 1998, researchers obtained the Body Mass Index (an estimate of
body fat based on height and weight) for 500 women who were models
and found that almost half qualified as malnourished according to the
World Health Organization's standards.[52] Researchers in Italy and Scan-
dinavia show that girls with eating disorders are more susceptible to messages about body image and are more psychologically dependent on
television than girls with normal eating patterns.[53,54] Girls' tendencies to
compare themselves to models increases with age and is greater for those
with lower self-esteem.[55] One of the most telling studies of the impact of
depictions of women on television showed a significant increase in eating
disorders among adolescent girls on the island of Fiji after television was
introduced there in 1995.[56]

Nor are girls alone in their dissatisfaction with their bodies. Eating disorders among boys can also be linked to commercial culture.[57] The biceps
of bestselling action figures such as GI Joe have increased dramatically
over the past twenty years to well beyond that of any real-life soldier. When
GI Joe's measurements are extrapolated to real life, his physique is as un-

7

Peace-Keeping Battle Stations and Smackdown!: Selling Kids on Violence

LAST FALL I got a phone call from a father who worked for an advertising agency specializing in marketing to children. "My daughter's been e-raped," he said. E-raped? Someone had broken into his eleven-year-old daughter's instant messaging service and, in language both violent and sexually explicit, shared sexual fantasies about what he'd like to do to her. What shook this man up more than anything was his daughter's response. She didn't tell her parents about the message, but rather passed it on to a friend who did tell *her* parents. His daughter's stance was, "It's no big deal."

"This brought home to me," he said, "how much children have become commodities. Advertisers treat them like things. We inundate them with sexual and violent imagery and we expect that somehow it won't affect their behavior or values. And I work in this field!"

Among the toys marketed to kids in the 2002 holiday season at JC Penney and other stores were a rather Orwellian war toy for three-year-olds called a Peace-Keeping Battle Station and an Army Forward Command Post, consisting of a machine-gun-toting soldier in a bombed-out house. For more upscale shoppers, FAO Schwarz was carrying Lingerie Barbie, featuring the ubiquitous bombshell in a bustier, stiletto heels, and pink garters. The top selling video game was Grand Theft Auto: Vice City, in which a character kills a prostitute after having sex with her.[1] While this version of the larger Grand Theft Auto franchise is rated M, for mature audiences, it's a favorite among teens and preteens. I've seen it advertised on television during programs that the broadcasting industry has decided are suitable for kids as young as fourteen.

Meanwhile, in 2003, Toys "R" Us was selling an action figure derived from the offerings of the World Wrestling Entertainment corporation: According to the Toys "R" Us cyberstore catalogue at Amazon.com, the manufacturer of the figure, Jakks Pacific, recommended the toy for children age four and older. Toys "R" Us, however, recommended it for kids ten years old and up.[2] Action-figure Lita is wearing a cropped shirt sporting the logo "Girls Rule!" and low-riding cargo pants revealing a significant swath of her minuscule thong underwear. I applaud Toys "R" Us for disagreeing with Jakks Pacific about the toy's appropriateness for preschoolers, but it's hard to understand why they think it's appropriate for preteens.

The marketing of violence and sex to children are linked phenomena. As these examples demonstrate, that's often how they're sold to kids—through every sort of media outlet and through the toys and other licensed products connected with media programs. This chapter focuses on violence, but the principles of child development discussed here are also relevant to my discussion of marketing sex in the next chapter.

People concerned about the violent toys or media marketed to children are often accused of holding a sanitized view of childhood or of depriving children of natural and constructive outlets for aggression. Having spent a great deal of my career engaging children in play therapy, I am the last person to think that childhood is all sweetness and light. It is absolutely clear to me that children are capable of deep fear and great rage. The children I see for therapy have neither guns nor swords nor media-linked action figures when we play together. Nevertheless, they frequently and enthusiastically commit terrible acts of fantasy violence. My puppets are routinely eaten by monsters, poisoned, starved, and abandoned. These violent or cruel-seeming fantasies emerge, however, from the children themselves, from their own needs and experiences. Fantasy play is a natural and constructive way for children not only to express their feelings but also to gain a sense of control over an often confusing and frightening world.

Most psychologists and early-childhood educators recognize the need for many children to play out scary, violent themes like war, abandonment, or injury. This is especially true if they are exposed to disasters either in real life or on television news. Professors Diane Levin and Nancy Carlsson-Paige, child development specialists who have written extensively about children and violence, argue that the impetus for healthy, adaptive war play—or any kind of play with scary and/or violent themes—

should come from the children themselves and not from the toys we give them or the media to which they are exposed.[3]

In the 1950s, 1960s, and 1970s, parents used to worry primarily about toy guns: Should boys (it was mostly boys then) be given such things to play with? My mother used to say that if a child needed to play with a gun, he or she would make one—out of fingers, carrots, clay, or whatever was available. On the other hand, she also talked about my cousin Karl, who had desperately wanted a toy gun, which his parents refused to buy him. At the age of fourteen, he got a paper route and bought himself a BB gun with his own money. She was quick to point out that he did not grow up to be a mass murderer, or any kind of murderer, for that matter. Nor did my husband, who has fond memories of his Hop-a-Long Cassidy six-shooters. While I do believe that buying a child a toy gun, especially while advocating for nonviolence, sends a confusing message, I also recognize that one such purchase is not likely to set a normal, healthy kid on the road to committing mayhem.

By the 1980s, however, explicitly violent media programming, and the licensed toys and other spin-offs that followed in its wake, became much more prevalent in children's lives. In the year after the deregulation of children's programming, seven of the ten bestselling toys had violent themes, and all of those were media-based.[4] Now, in addition to that one potential toy gun or rifle, parents are coping with highly realistic, violent video games and a television culture reflecting a murder rate of one every twelve minutes, witnessed by an estimated thirteen million children each night.[5] (In a bizarre twist, during the 1990s, there seemed to be less violence in adult programming than in programs targeting children: according to one study published in 1995, 50 percent of characters in adult programs were either victims or perpetrators of violent crimes; in children's programming 79 percent of characters were victims or perpetrators.)[6]

In his influential book, *The Uses of Enchantment,* psychologist Bruno Bettelheim wrote about the cathartic value children can derive from the original versions of fairy tales, which (in contrast to later, expurgated versions) often feature rather gruesome tortures and deaths for their villains.[7] Those who use his argument to defend the proliferation of increasingly graphic scenarios in visual media are not taking into account the difference between words and visual images. Children listening to fairy tales are free to imagine, in however much detail they choose, the horror of a monster or a violent death. Visual images, on the other hand, are much, much more powerful. Besides, the bloody scenes washing over children in countless movies, videos, and television programs are not of their own making—they are someone else's vision and cannot be controlled.

When people worry about media violence, they mostly worry—and they're often right to do so, as we shall see—about children imitating violent behavior. Violent movies or television programs can also be harmful to children just because they're frightening. Do you have at least one vivid memory of a scene from television or the movies that truly terrified you when you were a child? I do. In fact, research suggests that most of us do.[8] Media-induced fears can cause reactions ranging from general anxiety to nightmares, and these can last for a long time. One of my earliest media-influenced memories is a close-up of the wicked queen transformed into a witch in Walt Disney's *Snow White*. I was terrified, and (I know this sounds funny now, but it wasn't at the time) the film triggered a spate of dreams about my mother being poisoned by apple juice.

It's sad, but it seems that children are frightened by TV and films more often than we, their parents, think they are.[9] This suggests that children may be reluctant to share their fears with us—and sometimes with good reason. Alvin Poussaint recalls being in a theater watching an extremely violent film. As someone was being decapitated on the screen, a very young child began screaming and crying, only to be slapped by his mother for disrupting the movie.[10] I ache for that child—who had no control over what was coming at him and then was punished for responding in a perfectly normal way. Yet young children frequently watch movies and television programming intended for adults. In 1986, one researcher found that almost half of the four- to ten-year-old children he interviewed had seen Steven Spielberg's shark epic, *Jaws,* and a significant number had seen the horror film *Friday the 13th.*[11] I suspect that the numbers are higher today, given the proliferation of channels on television and of TVs in the home. In fact, characters from R-rated horror movies, such as *Chucky*—about a serial killer trapped in the body of a doll—frequently figure into the play of more than one of the young children with whom I work.

It's not surprising that one of the consequences of exposing children to an abundance of media violence is that they become desensitized to it.[12] Desensitization is a common defense against fear. I'm sure that, by now, the little boy who was slapped by his mother can sit through all sorts of violence without batting an eye. Is desensitization a good thing? How does it affect our inclination to prevent wars and other violent and horrific tragedies televised nightly on TV news?

I found myself in what may seem like an esoteric quandary about desensitization when the movie *Titanic* came out. On the one hand, I was reluctant to let my ten-year-old daughter see the blockbuster hit because I couldn't bear the thought of her being haunted by visions of all those bodies floating in the ocean. On the other hand, I was reluctant because I couldn't bear the thought that she *wouldn't* be affected by visions of all those bodies floating in the sea. The sinking of the ocean liner *Titanic* really happened. People died, unnecessarily, for greed. Isn't horror an appropriate response to those deaths? I didn't want her to be devastated, nor did I want that tragedy to be trivialized. Mostly, what I wanted was for a trillion-dollar blockbuster infringing on my life as well as my daughter's to disappear. Guess what? It didn't. I managed to postpone her viewing those drowning bodies for about a year. By then I realized that *Titanic* was only a drop in a tidal wave of media marketing that was overwhelming our lives.

Another way to frame discussions about the marketing of media violence and sex to children is to think about the power of narrative in the transmission of cultural values. Stories, fables, morality plays, and even guerrilla theater have long been used as means of educating young people—inculcating societal expectations, fomenting change, or maintaining the status quo, and reinforcing current notions of good and evil. The power of stories (I'm using the term "stories" broadly to include ads and music videos which may be without a plot but nonetheless serve, through visual imagery, to encourage projection and identification) to affect real life lies in their capacity to draw us, even momentarily, into believing that a created world is real, and to present characters that remind us of ourselves as we are and/or as we wish to be. As we see ourselves in these characters, they become "like us." We may consciously or unconsciously adopt their behaviors, values, and attitudes as our own.

When I use my puppets for play therapy, I deliberately choose to imbue them with characteristics that are similar to the particular child I'm seeing at the time. They may be about the same age, have the same family constellation, or be struggling with a slightly altered version of the same issues. The more children see my puppets as similar to them—the more they identify with my puppets—the more they are likely to incorporate my puppet's behavior into theirs.

I was once working in a hospital with a little boy whose beleaguered and caring mother went home one night to get a decent night's sleep. The little boy was pretty upset at her departure—both angry and grief-stricken. While she was gone, we pretended that my puppet was in the hospital and that *her* mother went home overnight. My puppet kept saying, "I'm mad and I'm sad and I know my mom will be back again," and she eventually told her mother about her sad and angry feelings. When the little boy's mom returned, she was greeted with, "Hey Mom! Audrey Duck was mad and sad when her mother went home," opening up an opportunity for the two of them to talk honestly about his feelings.

Because children's attitudes and values are not as solidified as those of adults, they are more impressionable. The stories we create for them—about ourselves, our values, and our culture—have a profound impact on their development. Most of the educators, health professionals, and parents who use stories to influence children's behavior do so with their best interests in mind. However, most of the stories reaching children through commercial media—replete with special effects, amazing animation, or snazzy camera work—are designed primarily to turn a profit, not to educate or enlighten them. The sex and violence inundating children on various screens exist not because parents, teachers, or artists think such content is good for children, but because sex and violence have proven to be extremely profitable attention-grabbers. As noted earlier, children represent not only a source of profits in the present but also a vast reservoir of revenue in the future as well.

Because advertising and marketing work to create a continuous need for products, one of the most powerful techniques media marketers employ to hook children is to exploit their aspirations. Marketing companies conduct research with kids that is designed to elicit information about—among other things—who and what they'd like to be. These aspirations might involve a certain age or body type, and attitudes or qualities such as toughness, power, and invulnerability. Findings from such studies lead to the creation of media products and marketing campaigns. If characters populating these creations successfully manifest qualities or characteristics that children long to embody, kids will identify with them.

When marketing to teens or preteens, companies frequently focus their research on "alpha" kids, who have been identified as leaders or trendsetters.[13] Once those kids adopt a trait or product, it becomes "cool," and the whole phenomenon of peer pressure kicks in. Selling "cool" is so important to marketers working with teens and preteens that *KidScreen* magazine actually held an "Understanding Cool" conference in 1998.[14]

Just as adolescents search for an identity separate from their parents, they often want to fit in with their peers. Dave Seigel, marketing expert and co-author of the *The Great Tween Buying Machine,* comments on marketing to preteens: "Peers become increasingly important as children get older, so they want to know that a product will help them fit in and make them popular."[15] Kids who want to be "cool" look to their alpha peers for those cues. It's not unusual for companies to give kids they've identified as trendsetters products to use and to give away to their friends. Once what is being sold is popular, other companies wanting a piece of the market create similar products, or create products that are a more extreme version that will appeal to trendsetters.[16] In a cynical nod to social and political movements, this exploitation of young teens' and preteens' need to belong is referred to as "grassroots" marketing.[17]

The word "aspirational" turns up a lot in marketing literature these days, especially in the context of selling to children. For instance, teens are seen as aspirational twentysomethings and twelve-year-olds are described as aspirational seventeen-year-olds. When it comes to mass media, it's not just that kids are buying products—or persuading their parents to buy them. They are also buying into the behavior, values, and attitudes of characters designed to attract and hold their attention in order to sell video games, shampoo, CDs, and numerous other products.

There are media producers who acknowledge the power of television, movies, and video games to influence behavior. Nearly a decade ago, Brandon Tartikoff, the former head of NBC, said, "I definitely think that moving images influence behavior. . . . TV is funded by commercials, and most commercials work through imitative behavior. They show someone drinking a cup of hot coffee saying, 'mmmm,' and then they expect you to go out and buy Yuban!"[18]

Marketers routinely make use of children's desires to emulate those they admire by using famous actors and athletes to sell sneakers, for instance, or candy. As we all know from our own experience, kids, preteens, and teens pick up intonations, mannerisms, and behavior from the big and small screens. For a while it seemed as though every thirteen-year-old I encountered spoke in questions. Even answers to questions sounded like inquiries. For instance, "I'm fine?" rather than the declarative "I'm fine," was the usual response to "How are you?" They all seemed to sound alike, and they all sounded like the teenagers appearing on television shows.

Marketers and media producers also make use of the natural human fascination with conflict and violence to capture the attention of the audiences they want to reach. Since the 1970s, movies and television programs for adults have included greater amounts of violence and have grown more explicit in depicting it. Over the past two decades, as children have come to be seen as an important audience (read "market demographic"), much of the commercial programming designed for them has become increasingly violent as well. With video game and toy tie-ins, media violence extends its reach beyond commercial television and movies to become ever present in children's lives—with predictable results.

Ed Albino, a fellow employee at the Judge Baker Children's Center and the father of a four-year-old boy, complained to me recently that the movie *Power Rangers* was shown in his son's after-school program. When he picked his son up, all of the boys were racing around, kicking each other à la Power Rangers. When his son got home, all he wanted to do was play Power Rangers. Ever since the original *Power Rangers* TV series debuted in 1993, parents, teachers, and early-childhood experts have voiced serious concerns—even outrage—at its impact on children's play. In particular, they've been concerned about children imitating the kind of violent fighting depicted on the screen.[19] This year, the Power Rangers are back in the form of teenage *Power Ranger Ninja Storm.* According to the *New York Times,* the show's executive producers are aiming for an over-fourteen audience.[20] Then why is it a cartoon shown on Saturday mornings? Who's up on weekend mornings? Certainly not teenagers! Nor are teenagers likely to buy the accompanying action figures.

Most of the therapists and teachers I meet recount similar incidents. Their experience represents another disturbing trend: not only is much of children's programming more violent than ever before, but children are being exposed to material ostensibly intended for adults earlier and earlier in their lives. A school psychologist recently told me about her unsuccessful attempts to wean one of her students from watching professional wrestling:

> I was in a therapy session with a nine-year-old boy, who regularly watches wrestling on TV with his mom and brother. I have raised my concerns about the show with his mother as her son has real trouble with his anger and has become

physical in the past. He has also witnessed a great deal of domestic violence between his parents, who are now divorced. His mom repeatedly dismisses my
concerns, saying, "It's a time that we all get to be together, and the boys know it
isn't real fighting." During the session the student and I were working on anger-
management, one of the goals in his treatment plan. I asked him if he could tell
me of a time recently when he was angry at someone, so we could work on some
verbally appropriate ways to let someone know when he is angry. He said, "I'm
really mad at my brother right now!" When I asked about it he said that his ten-
year-old brother did a "jack-hammer on me last night and it really hurt." I asked
what a "jack-hammer" was, and he said, "It's a wrestling move where you pick
someone up and drop him on his head." They were having a disagreement and
his brother became physical with him.

The wrestling programs this family watches regularly, featuring live-
action violence by real people who look as though they are actually hurting
other people, are offerings of World Wrestling Entertainment, Inc., common known as the WWE. You might have seen the WWE when you were a
kid. It used to be called the World Wrestling Federation (WWF) until the
company lost the right to use those initials to the World Wildlife Fund a
few years ago. In its current incarnation, WWE programs exemplify some
of the most graphic examples not only of violence but also of the ways that
sex and violence get mixed together in media marketed to children.

Unless you grew up in the 1990s, the WWE has changed dramatically.
If you've never seen their current version of wrestling, I suggest you take a
look, preferably without your children. WWE programs are on both network and basic cable stations. They are broadcast Sunday, Monday,
Thursday, and Saturday nights.[21] Two syndicated programs are on at different times in different areas and, in addition, WWE produces pay-per-
view programs throughout the year.

If you don't have the time or inclination to watch, here's some information about the content. A study conducted at Indiana University analyzed fifty weeks of *RAW*, a cable program that, admittedly, may be the
most extreme version of televised wrestling, which is rated TV-14 (meaning that it's deemed appropriate for teens fourteen and older). Among
other things, it quantified lewd behaviors such as crotch grabbing (1,600
times), excessive violence such as the use of chairs, garbage cans, and other
objects as weapons in wrestling (609 times), kicks to the groin (273 times),
and poor sportsmanship in the form of attacking the referees (50 times).[22]

The study documents behaviors, but it does not fully reflect the anti-social messages embedded in WWE programs. WWE programs are a celebration of power and its abuse. Over and over again, at least four times a week, the WWE programs depict a world in which those who are physically or economically powerful have license to hurt, degrade, and humiliate those who are less powerful. It's a confusing world, where fantasy and reality mix. In addition to wrestling, the programs feature an ongoing soap opera about the wrestlers and their rivalries and relationships. The stories include a character named Vince McMahon, who is the owner of the fantasy WWE. The fantasy Vince McMahon is played by the actual Vince McMahon, the real owner of the real WWE. For younger viewers, this merging of reality and fantasy is particularly confusing since they will have trouble understanding, let alone holding on to the concept of two McMahons, one real and one fictional.

An extraordinary video from the Media Education Foundation, called *Wrestling with Manhood*,[23] addresses the disturbing behaviors and values the WWE promulgates, focusing on what its shows teach boys about manhood. One thing the WWE teaches them is that men are bullies. Day after day, large wrestlers pick on smaller ones, beat them, jump on them when they are unconscious, and taunt them for being weak. To cheers from fans in the audience, characters display an exaggerated relish at humiliating their opponents or their underlings both physically and psychologically.

Men on the WWE bully mostly, though not entirely, from a position of physical strength. They also bully from a position of power. On the programs, Vince McMahon routinely uses his power to hire and fire as a tool for humiliation and what looks a lot like torture. For instance, one wrestler, in order to save his job, is forced to fight three other wrestlers, all of whom apparently have a grudge against him. To the "sportscaster's" and the audience's delight, he is beaten in this grossly unfair fight, which culminates—at the urging of the audience—in a table being thrown and broken on his prone, practically unconscious body. In another scene, shown in *Wrestling with Manhood,* McMahon makes one of his workers literally kiss his naked rear end.

Bullying is an escalating problem among schoolchildren.[24] The National Institute of Child Health and Human Development reports that almost 30 percent of sixth to tenth graders report being bullied, bullying other people, or both.[25] Of course, by itself, the WWE (or any other media programming) doesn't directly cause children to be bullies, nor does it directly cause any of the other behaviors identified in the study. However, the WWE *does* present a world in which bullying—in the form of taunting, humiliating, and torturing the less powerful—is glorified by applause, laughter, and other forms of approval. In the world of WWE, conflicts are resolved by violence, people are rewarded for cruelty, and the arbitrary whims of one powerful person are law. Surely this is not a vision we want our children to buy into, and while the WWE has allegedly toned down some of its programs, such as *Smackdown,* cruelty and domination continue to be predominant themes.

The WWE presents an extremely graphic and violent form of bullying, but at present, prime-time television is rife with behaviors associated with bullying, including public humiliation, a derivation of enjoyment at someone else's expense, and a disregard for other people's feelings. On the current—extremely popular—spate of reality shows, such as *American Idol,* which features people competing on the basis of talent, this takes the form of hosts who make nasty remarks about aspiring performers. On shows like the *Fear Factor,* contestants put themselves in the position of eating raw entrails or live beetles. Many of these programs are on during what used to be called "the family hour," between 8:00 and 9:00 P.M. A decade ago this time slot was the venue for programs like *The Cosby Show* and *Family Ties,* which featured high-quality scripts, well-regarded actors like Bill Cosby and Michael J. Fox, and relationships built on respect.

Even preschool children are not exempt from WWE marketing, primarily through licensed products sold in toy stores. The WWE joins media makers of all kinds in one of the most common, effective, and least publicized means of marketing violence to children—especially young children. Over the past few years, WWE "toys" have included trading cards featuring a WWE hero laughing as he holds a decapitated woman's head and an action figure showing wrestler Matt Hardy dropping a female wrestler on her head. In recent years, WWE has labeled some action figures appropriate only for kids twelve and over, as have other R-rated enterprises such as the *Spawn* and *Matrix* franchises. But these ratings are in small print, tucked away on the back of the packaging; at Toys "R" Us, these figures are displayed with a variety of other action figures. The Federal Trade Commission's recommendation is that action figures or other licensed products associated with M- or R-rated media should not be marketed to young children *at all.* (According to the FTC, video games are especially prone to that practice.)[26] That recommendation seems to have fallen on deaf ears.[27]

Like many corporations, the WWE also markets to children by performing "good works." Through its community outreach program, the WWE sponsors a program for schools and libraries called "Get R.E.A.L." (an acronym for Respect, Education, Achievement, and Leadership).[28] I can't help but marvel at the hypocrisy of a company that turns a profit by routinely glorifying bullies and promoting the disrespect of women, fair play, and rules while simultaneously claiming to teach children respect.

The WWE is a past sponsor of the American Library Association's teen read week. They sponsored "Get R.E.A.L. Read," a tour in which WWE stars read aloud in public libraries around the country. The WWE's interest in reading certainly coincides with their commercial interests: they also have a deal with Simon and Schuster to publish, among other things, young adult books.[29] Current "Get R.E.A.L." programs include an essay contest for elementary school, junior high, and high school students. What's the prize? A WWE assembly at each winner's school.

By their own admission, 40 percent of WWE viewers are kids under the age of eighteen, and the company has pushed the envelope of what's acceptable entertainment for children and adolescents, whom they court assiduously.[30] A study from Wake Forest Medical School found that, at least for high school students, a correlation exists between watching the WWE and risky behaviors. For high school boys, watching wrestling regularly is associated with, among other behaviors, starting a fight with a date, being a date fight victim, carrying a gun and other weapons, fighting, using nonprescription Ritalin, and driving after drinking. For girls, the relationship between watching wrestling and similar health risk behaviors is even stronger.[31]

Once again, it's important to note that "associated with" does not mean "causes." It means that kids who watch wrestling are more likely to engage in these behaviors than other kids. It could be that they were prone to risky behavior anyway. But even if that's so, can it be good for them to be watching shows that glamorize violent resolutions to conflict? Is it good for any children? Most child development experts would say no, and they might cite, among others, a study done in 1994 in Israel, which documented what researchers describe as an epidemic of schoolyard injuries caused by kids imitating wrestling moves; an epidemic that followed the introduction of WWE programming in that country.[32]

Given that children spend more time engaged with media than they do engaged in any activity other than sleeping, it's hard to see how they could escape being affected by the content of media's advertising and programming. In addition to the study cited above, there is plenty of research to back this—especially about violence. I'm sure that it would be easier for everyone if media violence had no negative impact on children's attitudes and behavior. It does. And given that it does, it would be convenient if media violence were the sole cause for children's violent behavior. It isn't.

On July 26, 2000, the American Academy of Pediatrics, the American Psychological Association, the American Academy of Child and Adolescent Psychiatry, the American Medical Association, the American Association of Family Physicians, and the American Psychiatric Association issued a joint statement on media violence. After reviewing more than a thousand studies conducted over thirty years, they reported a consensus in the public health community that "viewing entertainment violence can lead to increases in aggressive attitudes, values and behavior, particularly in children."[33]

While acknowledging that the effects of entertainment violence on children are complicated and may vary from child to child, the statement identifies several measurable effects:

- Children who see a lot of violence are more likely to view violence as an effective way of settling conflicts. Children exposed to violence are more likely to assume that acts of violence are acceptable behavior.

- Viewing violence can lead to emotional desensitization toward violence in real life, and it can decrease the likelihood that one will take action on behalf of a victim when violence occurs.

- Entertainment violence feeds a perception that the world is a violent and mean place. Viewing violence increases fear of becoming a victim of violence and results in an increase in self-protective behaviors and a mistrust of others.

- Viewing violence may lead to real-life violence. Children exposed to violent programming at a young age have a higher tendency for violent and aggressive behavior later in life than children who are not so exposed.[34]

Several aspects of this document are noteworthy, not the least of which is the fact that these gargantuan organizations, representing thousands of health care professionals, were able to come to agreement. The report acknowledges the complexity of human behavior and the diversity of children's responses. It states quite clearly that, while media violence is not the sole cause of behavioral violence, it is a contributing factor.

Since the joint report was published, more evidence about the harmful effects of media violence on children has emerged. Recently, a longitudinal study by researchers from the University of Michigan reported that children who consumed a lot of television violence in early childhood are more at risk for antisocial and violent behavior as adults. This correlation remains even if we take into account class, race, and initial levels of aggression.[35] Another study documents the changes in neurological patterns—changes in the brain itself—occuring when kids play violent video games.[36] This study, as stand-alone evidence, is too small to be conclusive, but it certainly points to the need for further research.

A month after the public health community made its statement, the Federal Trade Commission published the results of their investigation of the marketing of violence to children by media companies. The report shows, unequivocally, that in violation of even their own—self-imposed—rating systems, the television, movie, and music industries do, in fact, market violent content to children. Follow-up reports show that some improvements have been made, but not many.[37]

For parents, educators, health care professionals, and activists concerned about media violence, the confluence of the two reports was encouraging. At least, we thought, these reports should be the cornerstones of reasonable public debate and problem solving. We were wrong.

A few months after the reports were released, twelve-year-old Lionel Tate went on trial for murdering a six-year-old girl named Tiffany Eunice. He fractured her skull, lacerated her liver, and broke her neck. The jury rejected his defense attorney's claims that he was practicing wrestling moves learned from watching World Wrestling Entertainment programs on television. Tate was found guilty and sentenced to life imprisonment.[38]

First and foremost, Tiffany Eunice's death from violence at the age of six is a heartbreaking tragedy. So is the fact that a twelve-year-old killed her. I'm of the opinion that it's also heartbreaking for Lionel Tate to be serving a life sentence for something he did as a child. Whether or not you agree with me, this case can be seen as a mirror reflecting all sorts of social ills, from poverty and flaws in our delivery of social services to problems in the criminal justice and juvenile justice systems. Predictably, the case also triggered a civil lawsuit and a minor media circus, both of which embody much of what's wrong with our national dialogue on the impact of marketing violence to children—simultaneously trivializing, sensationalizing, and politicizing the inquiry into the relationship between media violence and children's behavior.

In the trial's aftermath, an organization called the Parents Television Council, described variously as a "watchdog group," a "conservative watchdog group," and "an extremist group," was sued by the WWE for making a fundraising video that blamed WWE for Tiffany's murder. In its suit, the WWE claimed that the PTC was responsible for convincing several corporations to pull their sponsorship from WWE television programs. The boy's lawyer, Jim Lewis, was also named in the suit. Eventually, WWE won a judgment against the defense attorney and $3.5 million from the Parents Television Council. As part of the settlement, Brent Bozell, a politically conservative columnist and CEO of the Parents Television Council, wrote a retraction letter stating, "Neither 'wrestling' in general, nor WWE specifically, had anything to do with [Lionel Tate's actions]. Of that I am certain."

Unlike Mr. Bozell, Lionel Tate's lawyer refused to recant. According to an Associated Press report, Lewis wrote in his own court-ordered letter of apology to the WWE that he "still believe[s] that television violence influenced Lionel Tate to be insensitive to the physical harm and tragic death of his playmate, Tiffany Eunice." [39] Meanwhile, the WWE declared a victory for wrestling and for the First Amendment.

I don't know whether watching wrestling on television influenced Lionel Tate or not. Nor do I understand how Brent Bozell could be so certain at one point that it had "caused" Tiffany's murder and then be so certain that it didn't. But I do know this: The boys that I've seen for play therapy at the day-care center where I work, ranging in age from four to eight, bring World Wrestling Entertainment moves into our sessions. They all watch WWE programs—at least they used to. The problem of WWE-inspired play at the center was so severe that the director sent a letter home to parents asking that kids be kept from watching it. Last year, Haikim, a slight, friendly four-year-old, confided in me that he didn't like his older brother. "He always wants to play wrestling," he complained. "So we do. And then I start crying."

It's not easy to stop a media juggernaut. The Rock, one of the all-time most popular WWE characters (now pursuing a film career), spoke at the Republican Convention in 2000. Today, WWE productions continue to make "top ten" lists for media popularity. In 2002, the WWE's *RAW*, on TNN, was *the* top-rated basic cable program. WWE *Smackdown*'s "Shut Your Mouth" hit the best-seller lists for electronic game rentals. WWE soundtracks sold well enough to be awarded platinum album status by the American Recording Industry Association in 1999,[40] and gold status in 2001.[41]

Eventually, I suppose, the WWE will lose its popularity. As I write, their earnings are down.[42] But even if the WWE fades from view, something else equally or even more disturbing is likely to take its place.

Some people argue that violent media is harmless to children if the good guys win. In other words, it's fine for children to witness people being blown up, shot, or beaten if it's all for a good cause. Actually, there's strong evidence that the reverse is true—that being exposed to a mix of pro-social and violent behaviors in the same program can have even more of a negative impact on children than a program portraying violence.[43] This makes sense to me, in that positive outcome becomes a justification for violent behavior and reinforces a child's tendency to identify with, and want to behave like, the hero or good guy engaging in violence. It's important to remember that programming most of us might agree is perfectly appropriate for adults—programs we enjoy and even admire—may have unintended effects on children and their social behavior.

In my own experience as a therapist, a mother, and a children's entertainer, I am repeatedly reminded that even when we accept the idea that observation and imitation are important components of the way children learn about the world and how to behave in it, it's not always easy to see things from their point of view, or to assess ahead of time how they are going to respond to various kinds of stimulation. For example, one way that troubled children can learn how to change their behavior and cope more effectively with what scares or upsets them is by observing how adults or other children react positively and effectively to the same kinds of challenges they face.

This process is called modeling. When I engage children in therapeutic puppet play, I am always careful about what my puppets do and say. Although they are fantasy creatures, the children relate to them as if they are "real," and can learn new ways of being in the world from our interactions. Films, video and television programs can also help kids develop important pro-social behaviors such as cooperation and altruism and the ability to delay gratification.[44] Sometimes, however, even the most well-intentioned efforts produce unforeseen effects.

As a performer, I've found that it's sometimes hard to predict what behaviors children—especially young children—will choose to imitate. Early on in my performing career, I decided to include something about name-calling in one of my live performance pieces. I was going to have my puppet Audrey Duck call another puppet named Cat-a-lion "stupid," and then spend some time dealing with the ramifications—Cat-a-lion's hurt feelings and Audrey's sense of shame and guilt. The piece started out well enough. Audrey called Cat-a-lion "stupid," in her best taunting voice. She repeated it several times. The children were riveted. But then I heard a little voice from the audience calling out, "Stupid!" Then another voice joined the first one. "Stupid!" Suddenly I had a whole audience of kindergartners calling Cat-a-lion stupid. This was not the response I anticipated!

I should have known better. Young children have not yet developed the ability to process, or remember, a whole plot. Their perception of events tend to be somewhat fragmented, and they do not have the same capacity as older children or adults to synthesize all of the elements of dramatic presentations. Nor do they necessarily link consequences with the actions that precipitated them. They cannot grasp irony, and tend to be grabbed by and remember especially dramatic, funny, scary, or relevant parts of the action. When you add to the mix the fact that young children do not have great impulse control, it's not surprising that my audience that day burst out in a resounding chorus of "Stupid!" The lesson this incident taught me came in handy later, when I began to create video programs designed to help children cope with difficult issues. It kept me alert to messages in my scripts that I didn't intend, or want, to convey; a script designed to promote ethnic diversity, for example, could also inadvertently promote sexism if the male and female characters in it were presented only in stereotypic gender roles.

Even brilliantly written programs like *The Simpsons,* which airs during what used to be called the family hour, adds to a confusing cultural milieu for children around issues of violence and sexuality. *The Simpsons* is broadcast Sunday nights at eight, EST. On average, during the 2001–2002 season, over 1.4 million children between ages two and eleven tuned in to watch it each week.[45] In Boston, where I live, reruns are shown daily at 6:30 P.M. Presumably, millions more young children watch it then.

As a show for adults, *The Simpsons* often serves up good social commentary, but that doesn't mean it's a great program for kids. From a child development perspective, in fact, it's likely to be harmful. The problem? Humor on *The Simpsons* is rooted in irony and satire, neither of which is readily understood by children. In fact, young children seem to have more trouble comprehending irony than any other kind of humor.[46] Until the age of about six, children are unable to understand verbal irony even when it's delivered in a markedly sarcastic tone.[47] Irony and satire in *The Simpsons* is much more subtle than that.

Identifying the humor in irony and recognizing satire as a distorted commentary on reality requires sophisticated cognitive processes. These include being able to hold two disparate images in one's mind simultaneously and having a thorough understanding of the actual event, object, value, or person targeted by the distortion. Even eighth graders can have trouble recognizing the humor in satire or irony.[48]

I love satire and, as my friends and family know, get a kick out of irreverence. I even liked the extremely violent movie *Pulp Fiction,* which I thought was a funny and provocative commentary on, among other things, the mundanity of evil—but I wouldn't want a child to see it.

When children are exposed to satirical television programs or films before they are equipped to understand them, they are likely to be confused or even frightened by distortions in the narrative. Since kids tend to remember what is novel, these distortions are what they are most likely to remember, except they will understand them at face value, and not as the humorous take-offs intended. If you can imagine *The Simpsons* as understood by someone who doesn't grasp irony and who takes the values espoused in its stories literally, it becomes a show about people who are often disrespectful of or mean to each other, not a show making fun of people who are disrespectful or mean. It's an important distinction.

For example, in one episode Marge accidentally gets breast implants that increase her breast size to the point of being grotesque. Homer is thrilled. She's embarrassed and humiliated. While it ends with Marge getting a breast reduction, the bulk of the show consists of her being ogled and harassed by men. As adults, we can understand this show on several levels, including as a comment on male obsession with breast size. How does a young child, who takes things literally and tends to focus on the most startling or unusual part of what he or she sees and hears, understand that particular story line? What message is he or she getting about breasts and their size, or about what men value about women?

In another episode, a clown named Krusty runs for Congress primarily to help the Simpsons change the airline flight pattern over their house. The plot is a wonderful riff on nasty children's entertainers, corrupt politicians, and a political system that favors the rich and well-connected. It also includes scenes of Krusty the Clown smoking a cigarette and of Homer Simpson getting drunk and being beaten up on the floor of the U.S. Senate. Young children will miss the satire, but—because preschoolers tend to remember what is most scary, exciting, or emotion-laden—they will probably remember the smoking, drinking, and violence. Yet *The Simpsons* is currently being heavily marketed to young children, which was not true at the time of its inception.

On a recent visit to Toys "R" Us, I found a whole section devoted to Simpsons toys, marked as appropriate for children four and up. Because *The Simpsons* is animated and people incorrectly perceive animation as a children's medium and because of its time slot, parents and network censors (yes, they still exist) assume that it's fine for kids to watch. According to the president of the animation house that produces the program, "You can get away with stuff in animation you can't get away with in live action. The audience is more forgiving. When the words come out of animated characters' mouths, the censors are a little more generous and accepting. . . . When Bart Simpson insults his father, it's a joke, not something that offends the real parents watching."[49] Their preschool children, however, wouldn't inherently understand those insults as jokes. When they watch their parents laughing at a child insulting a parent, they may well get the message that brattiness, or disrespect, is on their parents' list of approved and/or amusing behaviors. Yet in many families, a child insulting an adult would be grounds for punishment. They might even be slapped or spanked. It's incredibly confusing for children. *The Simpsons* is only one

8

From Barbie and Ken to Britney, the Bratz, and Beyond: Sex As Commodity

"I'M NOT A PRUDE. Really I'm not," explains a journalist, the father of ten-year-old Jennifer. "But I'm concerned about the way sex and sexuality is used on television these days. It's not about sex for love or even affection—it's about using sex as a way of getting power. It works that way for both males and females. What a terrible message to send to our kids."

I had to laugh—not because I think he's wrong, but because I often hear myself beginning conversations about sex in the media and children with the same phrase: "I'm not a prude, but . . ."

The journalist and I feel the need for a disclaimer because, in public dialogue, complaints about the portrayal of sex in the media usually come from political conservatives—often from the religious right. I find that people who come down—as I do—on the side of sexual equality, for instance, and/or a woman's right to choose, sex education in schools, gay rights, birth control, and the right for school libraries to own *The Catcher in the Rye*, pride ourselves on being sexually enlightened.

We might believe in fidelity, but we do not necessarily think that sex without marriage is a sin. We acknowledge that children are curious about sex at an early age, and that they are sensual beings. We want to have open, honest, and factual discussions with our children about sex, and we try to frame our sexual ethics in terms of intimacy, love, integrity, and respect. We would prefer that they manage not to have sex in high school, although, as one mother sighed to me after she discovered her seventeen-year-old son in bed with his girlfriend, "Why would I think that my son would be in the 25 percent of seniors who aren't having sex?" We will do everything we can to help our kids prevent pregnancy and sexually transmitted diseases (STDs), and we have friends, family members, and colleagues who tend to associate criticism about sex in the media with a kind of evangelical, moral rigidity. Therefore, we have to assure ourselves and everyone else that "we're not prudes, but . . ."

How we think and feel about sex, how we were raised, and our own sexual experiences have an impact on our hopes and fears about children's sexuality and how we feel about the sexual messages and imagery they encounter in the media. As for me, I hope that the young people in my life experience sex uncoerced and in the context of love—or at least with tenderness, mutuality, and respect.

My hopes may not jibe with yours. You may ascribe to a stricter or more relaxed code of sexual ethics. Whatever values and aspirations you want to pass on to your children, I suggest that before, during, or after you read this chapter you take some time to remember your own adolescence. Think about when and where you learned about the mysteries of sex, and about what it means to be a man or a woman—and how men and women should look and how they should treat each other.

Did the popular magazines, movies, TV programs, and music in your teenage life have any impact on your ideals for beauty, virility, sex, or romance? Spend some time leafing through today's youth-oriented magazines like *Teen People*, *YM*, or *Seventeen*. Listen to radio stations that play top-forty hits and/or rap music. Watch MTV and the commercials that air during televised sporting events. Rent PG-13 movies. Explore the major venues for commercial children's television programming, such as Nickelodeon, Disney, and Fox Family. Surf the Web. Forget about pornography sites—instead, check out corporate sites that market to teens and preteens. As you peruse these outlets, think about how much time your child spends engaged with media (which, for the average child in the United States, is almost forty hours a week after school). I'm hoping you'll do this for your own education, for your children, and for my sake . . . so you won't think I'm a prude.

I mentioned in chapter 1 that the marketing world is abuzz with the idea that children are "getting older younger." For reasons physicians don't really understand, girls are beginning to develop the body changes associated with puberty at an earlier age. For white girls, the mean age for sprouting breasts and pubic hair is ten, and for African American girls, it's nine.[1] But breast buds do not a woman make. There is no evidence that girls' emotional development is keeping pace with physical changes. Given how confusing, embarrassing, and even frightening it must be for girls to experience hormonal shifts before they even reach double digits, it would make sense if adults in this country focused on how to help them cope. What's the best way to help girls navigate when hormonal changes occur before they may be ready emotionally or cognitively to make responsible decisions about sexuality, let alone sex? What's the best way to help boys, who lag behind girls in sexual development, cope even as their female friends and classmates are changing before their eyes?

While the percentage of teens having intercourse has dropped some-what in recent years, it has risen among girls under age fifteen.[2] According to the CDC, about one-third of ninth graders have had sex.[3] Thirty-three percent of ten- and eleven-year-old kids think that the pressure on them to have sex is a big problem.[4]

Even as kids are having intercourse at younger ages, many report that they are not getting adequate information about sex from their parents or in school.[5] While more than two-thirds of public schools require some kind of sex education, more than one-third of those schools require that abstinence be taught as the only option for unmarried people. These either prohibit teaching about birth control or teach about it only in the context of its failures.[6] Fifty-one percent allow contraceptives to be discussed as a means of preventing STDs, while 35 percent do not.[7] Even though most parents want sex education programs to teach about birth control,[8] at least for now it's likely that more schools will be joining the abstinence-only bandwagon. In 2003 the Bush administration, which holds the purse strings for funding sex education programs, is pushing heavily for abstinence-only programs.[9]

So where do kids go to learn about sex? They frequently turn to the media. More than half of teens report getting some or most of their information about sex from television (remember that "information" comes not just from facts, but from the way sex and sexuality are depicted).[10] When asked where they got information or advice about sex in the previous month, 64 percent of sexually active teens named the media rather than parents, friends, or teachers.[11]

Unfortunately, girls in the throes of early sexual maturity are especially vulnerable to media messages. Researchers at University of North Carolina have found that such girls are more likely to seek out programs containing sexual content on television and more likely to see R-rated movies. Most troubling is that, more than their nonpubescent friends and more than older teens, they interpret media messages as approving of teens having sex.[12] However, young teens are not finding media sex to be as wonderful as it looks on the screen. The younger a girl is when she first has intercourse, the more likely she is to report that it was unwanted,[13] and in a national survey of sexually active teens, 81 percent of 12- to 14-year-olds said that they wish they had waited.[14] In fact, almost 90 percent of all the teens surveyed said that they would advise their younger brothers and sisters to wait until they are at least out of high school.[15]

What troubles me is that even as we allow marketers to inundate children with highly charged sexual messages, we are not doing a good job of helping kids responsibly cope with their burgeoning sexuality. Author and educator Jean Kilbourne says, "Sex in advertising has far more to do with trivializing sex rather than promoting it, with narcissism than with promiscuity, with consuming rather than with connecting. The problem is not that it is sinful but that it is synthetic and cynical."[16] I would extend her assessment to include much of the sex portrayed in mass media, especially in media competing in the teen market. While there are always exceptions, the function of mass media sex is as likely to be the creation of profits as the creation of art.

Sex as commodity is not a new phenomenon. Sex or sexuality has been exploited since the beginning of advertising to sell everything from cars to candy bars. These days it's also used to sell the media offerings that attract the viewers marketers want to reach. Ads for TV programs, movies, and music highlight sexual content, just as they highlight violence.

Because the goal of most commercial television program producers is to gain and keep enough audience share to attract lucrative licensing or advertising deals, program content is designed to grab viewers' attention as they click through myriad program options. Content is also designed to lure viewers away from videos, DVDs, computer games, and other electronic media. As a result, the research showing that teens are particularly attracted to programming that features portrayals of prostitution, extramarital sex, and sexually active singles[17] is likely to spawn more programs about prostitutes and sexually active singles marketed to teens.

What I discovered in doing research on this topic is that children are barraged with sexual messages from media to a greater extent than most people, including myself, realize. While there is not as much research about the impact on children of sexuality in media as there is the impact of violence, our knowledge is growing. Among thirteen- and fourteen-year-olds, heavy exposure to sexually oriented television is correlated with increased acceptance of nonmarital sex.[18] This should not come as a surprise. Since most thirteen-year-olds can't even envision being married, they are more likely to identify with stories and images depicting teenagers or young singles than those that feature married couples, and most of the media messages about sex marketed to children celebrate it outside the context of marital bliss. We also know that viewing sexual violence on television can lead to a greater acceptance of real-life sexual violence.[19] Boys exposed to violent sex on television, including rape, are less likely to be sympathetic to female victims of sexual violence.[20]

When we think about sex and sexuality in media, we need to expand our thinking beyond hugging, kissing, intercourse, or other sexual acts. Equally potent are the messages kids get about what it takes to be attractive, how men and women treat each other, and what's valuable about being male or female. As with violence, when it comes to portraying sexuality in media popular with teens and preteens, the images produced by the WWE, including the series *RAW* (rated TV14), are particularly upsetting. While women wrestlers, called "divas," are presented as both sexy and physically strong, they are constantly vulnerable to domination as well as physical and psychological humiliation by men. They may have their clothes ripped off, be doused with vomit, or be forced into sexual acts even when unconscious. A stunning example of a particularly cruel form of sexual harassment on a WWE program is shown in the video *Wrestling with Manhood*, which I referred to in the previous chapter. A female wrestler is ordered by Vince McMahon, the owner of the WWE, to strip off her clothes down to a minuscule bra and panties, get down on her hands and knees, and bark like a dog—in front of a cheering, hooting crowd.[21]

The last time I watched *RAW*,[22] in preparation for writing this chapter, a man in the process of being fired by Vince McMahon offered him two "hot lesbians" as an appeasement. The "lesbians" were played by two sexy young women who held hands as they walked into the ring and paraded around as the crowd cheered. After a minute, the man bargaining for his job announced with great excitement that they were "bisexual" lesbians.

Once again, I need to issue a disclaimer. I think it's fine for fourteen-year-olds, or younger children, to learn about homosexuality and all kinds of lifestyle choices. This, however, was a depiction of women as owned by men who can offer them as gifts or bribes. This presentation of female lovers begins as a voyeuristic male fantasy and, with the news that the women are bisexual, morphs into a fantasy about women as sex slaves.

How does a fourteen-year-old viewer process this kind of stimulation, particularly if he or she is not receiving countering information at home or at school? For that matter, how do younger kids process that information? WWE programs are among the favorites of eight to eleven-year-olds.[23]

The WWE presents an extreme version of the treatment of women as objects, of sex and violence as linked, and of sex as a commodity, but kids of all ages are saturated on a daily basis with messages about sex that fit somewhere along a continuum that includes less extreme material.

As parents of middle school children know all too well, the group most vulnerable to sexual messages in media and marketing are preteens. Tweens are currently the hottest market demographic around. Marketing mavens describe them as easier targets than teenagers because they are more "benign and not as cynical" and are "very accessible and very open to new ideas."[24] These characteristics, plus the fact that they evidently "get their way more with parents than little kids"[25] mean that they are, as one cable television executive enthused, "a ripe audience to exploit."[26]

The creation of tweens as a marketing demographic reads like a testimony both to the marketing industry's willingness to exploit children's vulnerabilities and to advertisers' disregard for children's welfare.

Beginning in the 1970s, as the changing needs of families outstripped the services provided by public institutions, the phenomenon of "latchkey kids" came to the attention of people who cared about children. Millions of elementary school kids were home alone from the time they finished school until their parents returned from work. By the 1980s, the phenomenon sparked studies of their school performance, calls for after-school programs, hotlines for kids to call if they became frightened, and books written to help children survive on their own at home. Parents at work worried that their kids were going to be prey for all kinds of predators and instructed them to not answer the door and to tell people who called on the phone that their parents were busy in the next room.

These kids did not go unnoticed by Madison Avenue, and a new marketing demographic sprang from the vulnerability of children alone at home, unsupervised. As Alan Toman, president of The Marketing Department, explained in the *Chicago Tribune* in 1988, "Latchkey kids are a natural for a lot of consumer products. . . . We are just beginning to see companies approaching this particular kids' market, taking seriously how many purchases kids control and calculating how much potential they represent."[27]

That year, the Thomas J. Lipton company (now owned by Unilever) put out a magazine called *Kidsmart* aimed at latchkey kids and their parents. The magazine contained safety tips and fun projects as well as four pages of ads for Lipton packaged foods such as soup, fruit snacks, and fruit drinks.[28]

For children whose parents felt safer with them at home than roaming the streets, the major activity was watching television. In 1988, the *New York Times* reported that 80 percent of American kids were watching TV after school. According to the *Times,* "Marketers have been responding. The value of commercial time sold to national advertisers for syndicated children's programs primarily between 3 P.M. and 5 P.M. on weekdays grew from nothing in 1982 to $107 million last year."[29]

The eighties also saw marketers flocking to the newly created cable television stations. Ellen, a young woman now in her early twenties, recalls, "When I was twelve, my mom started working and I watched MTV every day after school until she came home." Campbell's, for instance, created a soup music video to sell Chunky Soup on MTV. In a prescient twist on the refrain of the day, a vice president of research at Nickelodeon announced, "The latest European research shows that product preferences develop at a much earlier age than anyone had ever thought. . . . As people begin to understand this, to see how brand loyalty transfers to adulthood, *there is almost nothing that won't be advertised as for children* [italics mine]."[30]

Of course, the phrase "latchkey kids," referring as it did to kids who were fending for themselves and taking on household responsibilities, is rather downbeat, so the advertising industry created "tweens." In the marketing world, kids who are in third grade are lumped together with kids in sixth grade who may or may not be entering puberty, and with even older kids who are probably in the midst of it. Since marketers exploit children's natural tendency to look forward to growing up, and to choose slightly older kids as role models, it's no accident that kids are acting out sexually at younger ages than did previous generations; they're targets for intense marketing campaigns, many if not most of which are designed to encourage them to dress and act like teenagers and young adults. According to marketing wisdom, teens are "twentysomething wannabes"[31] and twelve-year-olds want to be seventeen.[32]

Often a kind of feedback loop between advertising agencies and their clients comes into play, one that ups the ante even further, especially when it comes to fashion. As a 2001 Associated Press story explained, "Designer

Betsey Johnson recognizes the market power of tween girls—whether they're spending their own money or their parents'. 'Five-year-olds want to look like their twelve-year-old sisters,' says Johnson. 'Teens and young twentysomethings look great, and little girls want to do the same—and do it faster.' "[33] As a result, girls especially—even very young girls—are being targeted for clothing and accessories that are more appropriate for their older friends and relatives.

According to Sharon Pommer, a vice president of Alloy, a teen and tween mail-order company and "lifestyle" web site: "Tweens aspire to look like older teenagers, so our assortment for them encompasses the look of the average fifteen-year-old. . . ."[34] What might this mean? Before parents raised an extremely vocal outcry, retailer Abercrombie and Fitch was marketing thong underpants to ten-year-olds.[35] That Abercrombie was marketing sexy underpants to ten-year-olds is disconcerting; to make it even worse, these were decorated with sexually provocative phrases such as "Wink Wink" and "Eye Candy."[36] Meanwhile, Betsey Johnson's vice president of marketing describes the clothes they market to kids as "age-appropriate with an edge."[37]

That "edge" comment troubles me. The 2002 *American Heritage College Dictionary* defines "edge" as "a provocative or discomfiting quality, as from audacity." "Edgy" is defined as "daring, provocative, trendsetting." Various dictionaries associate "edge" with having a sharp or biting quality. There's also an element of hardness or danger associated with the word. In slang usage, it can be used to mean drunkenness, or as a euphemism for "knife." It's understandable that many teenagers, who are in a search for identity and for whom rebellion is an important part of that search, "edge" can be an attractive quality. But now we have marketing experts peddling that quality to younger and younger children. The results are not just little girls in highly sexualized clothing. The "edge" being marketed to kids also involves behaviors and values, particularly related to sex.

In 2002, according to *Woman's Wear Daily*, a market research firm called Teen Research Unlimited found that in their study of 2,000 teens and tweens, "Aspirational age is dipping down into the tween market."[38] Therefore, the article concludes, "The tween girl's emulation of pop stars, TV personalities, and older siblings means she wants to wear the same sassy looks as her idols." In this context, of course, "sassy" is a euphemism for "sexy"—tight, tight, belly-baring shirts, tiny halter tops, and "low rider" pants, very short shorts, or tiny little skirts.

It's no accident that tweens are emulating pop singers. The music industry has discovered tweens, too. Ten- to fourteen-year-olds account for
9 percent of all CD sales.[39] Whose music are they buying? For the past few
years, a large chunk of change has been going to Lolita-like girl singers
such as Britney Spears, Mandy Moore, or Christina Aguilera, who dress
like quintessential male fantasies of teenybopper hookers, sing songs about
sex written by middle-aged men, and are marketed to kids on formerly "kid
friendly" cable stations such as Nickelodeon.[40] Children's stations such as
Nickelodeon, Disney, and Fox Family now focus programming around
music to such an extent that *Billboard* calls them the "Pied Piper for this
demographic."[41] Another music venue for marketing to kids is Radio Disney, which broadcasts on fifty-two stations nationwide and is streamed
over the Internet.[42]

Billboard's choice of the Pied Piper as an analogy is both more apt and
more sinister than the publication probably intends. (As I noted in chapter
1, consider the fate of the children from Hamlin Town who were susceptible to his music.) In the same article, a record company executive inadvertently reinforces the image of kids being led to their doom by deceptive
marketing. According to Paul Orescan, vice president and marketing director at MCA, "Those outlets are like the Good Housekeeping seal. . . .
Parents are concerned about content, but they don't worry about the
artists they see on the television shows after school. So when the kids see
their albums at Wal-Mart and say, 'Hey, this is great,' they have no fears
about buying it."[43]

Maybe parents should be concerned. Nickelodeon, for example, does
have a reputation as a television station that is good for kids. In its early
years it was noncommercial, and it still produces some good, thoughtful
programming, but in the words of one Nickelodeon executive I talked to,
"Nickelodeon has changed. It's not as kid-friendly as it was when I
started." Today, it's an understatement to say that parents' blanket acceptance of Nickelodeon as being safe for kids is misguided. Owned by Viacom, Nickelodeon is a feeder station for MTV. When they feature, through
on-air concerts and the Kids Choice awards, pop singers like Jennifer
Lopez, Mandy Moore, Jessica Simpson, and Britney Spears, they are
promoting a whole dubious package—lyrics, clothing, and image—to
preschoolers and preteens.

A four-year-old named Darlene first introduced me to Britney, who
turned up repeatedly as a character in her play. The singer—whose popu-

lar song at that time contained the chorus "Hit me, baby, one more time," which can be interpreted as a glorification of physical abuse—was absorbed into this little girl's consciousness as a heroine and portrayed as such week after week. In *Billboard*, a Nickelodeon executive rationalized the media brand of sexuality being marketed to young children by saying, "Kids at each age hear and see what their developmental level is adjusted to. At 6, they're not translating the lyrics or the suggestions."[44] Well, yes . . . and no.

Getting a true handle on what early-elementary or preschool kids might understand is complicated. Yes, they probably don't understand lyrics that feature irony, innuendo, or metaphor because they take things so literally. That's exactly why the lyric "Give me a sign / Hit me, baby, one more time" is problematic for them. Whatever the symbolic intent of "Hit me, baby," it's likely to be lost on younger kids who will take it at face value— a female voice inviting someone to physically harm her. Fortunately, for the same reason, the sexual innuendo in Aaron Carter's hit song *Candy*, or many songs by the young rapper Lil' Romeo, probably sail right over their heads. However, the lyrics of songs marketed to teens and tweens contain more explicit sexual references than most adults probably realize.

A study by the Center for Media and the Family has looked at sexual content in lyrics. Researchers picked a radio station in Minneapolis favored by twelve- to seventeen-year-olds and rated the music using a system similar to the categories used in many studies of sex on television. The following are examples of how various lyrics were rated:

> *"Oh baby, baby / The reason I breathe is you / Boy you got me blinded / Oh pretty baby / There's nothing that I wouldn't do / It's not the way I planned it / Show me how you want it to be"* (Britney Spears, "Baby One More Time").
> This is coded as containing no sexual content.

> *"And get this, a Drew Carey love triangle. Three guys, one girl, hey, use your imagination. . . . So, if you're looking for a better way to spend time with your valentine, stay home for Valentine's the ABC way—a twosome, a threesome, and a free-for-all!"* (ABC, "Valentine Wednesday").
> This is coded as sexual innuendo, "not at all explicit."

> *" . . . It was so dumb / shoulda used a condom. . . . Let him do his thing / I'm the one he's loving / I'm here to show y'all / having the kid ain't meaning nothing /*

That ain't keeping him / Especially if he in love with another chick / Then you're stuck with the baby mother shit" (Foxy Brown, "My Life").
Coded as sexual innuendo, "pretty explicit," including discussion of responsibilities and consequences.

"It's been three weeks since you've been looking for your friend / The one you let hit it and never called you again. . . . You act like you ain't hear him then gave him a little trim. . . . Plus when you give it up so easy you ain't even fooling him / If you did it then, then you probably fuck again. . . . The quick to shoot the semen stop acting like boys and be men. . . ." (Lauryn Hill, "Doo Wop [That Thing]").
Coded as direct discussion of sexual intercourse, "very explicit," including discussion of planning, the benefits of sexual patience, and fidelity.

"Give me some room / Oh y'all just want to dig in my womb / You don't even know me / Want to fuck my friends? . . . Leave you numb / Make me come / Five more times, need five more bottles to get my shit wet / You ain't even sucked the tits yet! . . . Fuck you right" (Foxy Brown, "Tramp").
Coded as direct discussion of sexual intercourse, "very explicit," outside of a preexisting relationship.[45]

This particular study found that of the 159 songs of the top-ten-selling CDs, 42 percent contained sexual content. Twenty-three percent contained innuendo or seductive lyrics, and 19 percent contained direct description of sexual intercourse. Overall, 20 percent of the airtime on this radio station contained sexual content, including 45 percent of the music played and 9 percent of the commercials. For kids who watch music videos, the visual images attached to the lyrics probably ups the sexual charge by an unknowable amount.

"If it was just the music, it would be different," says Marlene, the mother of two girls who are ten and thirteen. "It's the visuals that are a problem. Now, once they hear the music, they want to see the videos and the videos are all about sex. My eighth grader comes home with her friends and watches MTV after school. I don't think it's great to get into culture battles with your kids, but every so often I find myself walking in and turning it off."

Like violence, visual images of sex and sexuality probably have more impact on a wider range of children than similar content conveyed in language or the written word. After talking to Marlene, I sat down to watch what was on MTV in the afternoons, remembering the book *Reviving Ophelia,* and author Mary Pipher's description of watching the station from a hotel room in the early 1990s:

> I was shocked by the sexual lyrics and scenes. In the first video, openmouthed and moaning women writhed around a male singer. In the second video, four women with vacant eyes gyrated in low-cut dresses and high black boots. Their breasts and bottoms were photographed more than their faces. . . . [46]

I have since discovered that breasts and bottoms are *so* 1990s. These days, the focus is all on crotch shots. MTV's content has gotten more extreme, even as its audience is getting younger.[47]

Meanwhile, speaking of crotch shots, I hate to think of young pre- or postpubescent girls watching the videos currently up on Britney Spears's web site.[48] Britney's most recent offering features her, alone, dressed in tight low-rider pants and a tiny top, writhing in what looks like the agony and ecstasy of sexual frenzy (honestly, I hate writing that because I sound like someone's old maiden aunt, but bear with me). The effect is enhanced and emphasized by the camera work. Think of the camera as the eye of the beholder, saying, "This is what's important about what I'm photographing. I want you to see what I see," to the viewer. The eye of this particular beholder sees close-ups of a girl's gyrating crotch, her blond hair flipping, and her face looking with heightened longing and desire into the (beholder's) eye. If you think of the video as a commercial selling Britney, it's not a huge step to see her as meat on the hoof being sold as parts for consumption. Buy her hips! Buy her crotch! Look at those juicy lips! The camera tells us what's important about Britney Spears. For young girls who identify with her, it's telling them what's important about themselves as well.

According to a study from the Center for Media and Public Affairs, music videos contain about ninety-three sexual situations per hour, or one and one-half per minute. Eleven of those scenes (or one every five or six minutes) was what the center labeled "hard core"—material depicting behaviors including intercourse and oral sex.[49]

Emory University researchers assessed the number of hours a group of African American girls from poor neighborhoods watched rap music videos per week. One year later they found that girls who watched more than fourteen hours of rap music videos a week were more likely to have multiple sex partners and to be diagnosed with an STD than girls who watched less.[50]

As the rap industry faces continued criticism for lyrics promoting violence and demeaning women, Lil' Romeo, a twelve-year-old rapper, is being touted as "great" for tweens because his lyrics contain no cuss words or violent images. However, his video for the song *True Love*[51] features a cute young guy positioned next to, or in front of—you guessed it—youngish (but older than he and his audience) women, dressed in skimpy clothes and dancing suggestively. What does this video tell us about Lil' Romeo? He may be young, but he's powerful enough to attract and dominate sexy older women. Marketing experts would probably give high marks to the Lil' Romeo video. Dominion (power, force, mastery, domination, control, and so on) is one of the qualities marketers encourage corporations to highlight in products marketed to tween boys. For tween girls, products should be associated with relationships and closeness.[52] The *True Love* video is a lesson to girls as well, teaching them what they have to do to get close to cool (or hot) guys—dress in skimpy clothes, wiggle your body alluringly, and give him the spotlight![53]

Lil' Romeo is following in the footsteps of another million-dollar rapper, Lil' Bow Wow, who at fifteen brags in his raps that he's, "a lil' man with big checks . . . big girls wanting to teach me about sex. . . ."[54] One thirteen-year-old girl I know, whose mother objected to the violence and the depiction of women in rap music, argued, "Would you rather I listened to rock? That's all about drugs!"

Performers who were thought controversial for teenagers a few years ago are now tween favorites. The homophobic, misogynist, and talented Marshall Mather, better known as the rap star Eminem, was one of the nominees for Nickelodeon's 2003 Kid's Choice awards. Never mind that his CDs are rated Parental Advisory and his movie, *8 Mile,* was rated R (children under 17 admitted only with an adult). Never mind that his lyrics present a demeaning picture of women. Kids under twelve flocked to see *8 Mile.* They begged their mothers and fathers to take them to see it—and lots of parents acquiesced.[55]

In spite of the fact that I find Eminem offensive, I thought *8 Mile* was pretty good, and not just because—as an ex-Detroiter—I got most of the in-jokes. It was a better-than-average movie, but I wouldn't take a young kid to see it. The combination of a well-done, steamy sex scene and some nasty interactions between the central character's mom and her boyfriend make it a film about teenagers for adults. Eminem's new status as a movie star, his recent Academy Award, and his appearance on the cover of teen magazines (which cater to tweens) lend a veneer of respectability to him and to the values his music espouses.

Eminem's transformation from "fringe" to "mainstream" has become a common phenomenon in the music business. Rap, once an ingenious grassroots expression of the plight of young, impoverished, urban African Americans is now brought to kids by Sprite and a variety of other products. When a phenomenon that was once considered to be extreme—like rap—sells out to corporate culture, it often becomes widely popular. When that happens, kids with rebellious, creative, or free-thinking tendencies have a problem. They want to be nonconformists, but the symbols of their nonconformity (from skateboard culture to hip hop) become popularized. The more adventurous—and often angrier—kids seek out increasingly outrageous expressions of their rebellion. In media, this often means more graphic violence, more outrageous behavior, and more explicit sex.[56]

It's not just the sexuality sold in music and music videos (or the sex used to sell them) that is barraging kids. In 1995, the American Academy of Pediatrics reported that the average teenager was likely to hear nearly 14,000 sexual references, innuendos, and jokes on television per year.[57] That figure is likely to be higher now. The Kaiser Family Foundation has been tracking the amount and kinds of sexual messages found in television programs since 1998. In 2003, 83 percent of the top twenty shows watched by teenagers had some sexual content—ranging from verbal references to depictions of intercourse. Forty-nine percent contained sexual behavior, and 20 percent included sexual intercourse. The top teen shows included an average of 6.7 sex scenes for each hour they were broadcast. Shows watched by teenagers were more likely to contain sexual content than programs favored by any other age group, including adults.[58]

What's hailed as good news is that the overall number of programs containing references to risk and responsibility surrounding sexual behavior has increased from 6 percent in 2000 to 15 percent today.[59] That is good news for teenagers, and may be a sign that media producers are becoming more responsible, but some parents find even some safe-sex media messages problematic for their preteens—who often like the same programs as teens.

Although she was talking about radio and not television, this mother's comment to me about condom ads is relevant here:

> I was driving in the car with my ten-year-old daughter, who has just gotten into rock music. We were listening to some local teen station when a condom commercial came on. I'm happy to have my daughter learn about condoms—but this was about the sensual pleasure afforded by this particular brand—complete with groans, squeals, and grunting. It wasn't about safety or responsibility. Yes, it was an ad for condoms—and that's a good thing, I guess. If my kids are going to be having sex, I want them at least to use condoms. But this ad was titillating. It may have been an ad for safe sex, but it was also an ad for any kind of sex!

No discussion about marketing sex to kids would be complete without a discussion of the Internet. Since the Net's inception, there has been a huge furor about on-line pornography, as well as repeated and failed attempts by Congress to censor it. My e-mail service provider—through an academic institution—does its best to filter out spam. This past year or so, however, I find that I'm encountering a bewildering array of sex-based messages in my in-box with subject lines such as "Bald Twats On-Line" and ads for various sex toys. Even with filters, parents worry about the spam sent to their kids and about predators entering chat rooms. Most kids are warned at an early age not to meet in person anyone they meet on-line and not to give out personal information. Parents, with varying degrees of success, use Internet filters for their younger children. Kids are told to stay away from pornography sites, and lots of parents use the "history" function on their web browsers to keep an eye on the sites their children visit—until their kids catch on. But assaults by pornographers and sexual predators aren't the only sources of sexually explicit material likely to be accessed by teens and tweens on-line. Most parents wouldn't blink if they found Alloy.com among the sites that their tween was visiting. Alloy has been a rising star among businesses targeting teens and tweens. It is a catalogue and "lifestyle" company, which means that in addition to clothes, they put out a girls' magazine/catalogue four times a year, and their web site is designed to be a place where young girls turn for fun. Alloy is even partnering with Penguin Books to publish a series of young-adult books on subjects such as dream analysis and beauty.[60]

Since I've ordered clothes for my daughter from Alloy, I was interested in the company. I visited its web site recently to look at what kind of clothes it was selling, but when I reached the home page I noticed a button that said "Real Life." I'm always interested in corporate versions of real life, so I clicked on it and came upon a button that said "Sex?s [*sic*]." One more click and a notice flashed on the screen: "Hey you! Read this. This page is intended for mature users ONLY." [61] One wonders if anyone at Alloy actually thinks that a message like that will be a deterrent to younger kids. Instead, it seems like an invitation to any self-respecting child to forge ahead. On the left side of the screen, I saw a column similar to advice columns found in most teen magazines these days: "All My Friends Are Doing It. Should I?" To the right was a bulletin board, inviting postings. It was headed, "What Do You Think?"

Alloy's justification for the bulletin board can also be found on the site. The portion that interested me is the following:

> We also provide a forum for teens to talk about issues they might be too embarrassed to bring up in real life, and a place where they can learn how to deal with these issues.
>
> We feel that teens come to Alloy to learn something, to lend a hand, or to voice a particular point of view. The vast majority of users respect the community here. Still, we've taken steps to monitor the site 24/7, and we use state-of-the-art filtering software to discourage harmful language. Our editors also participate in conversations to help keep teens on track and to discourage irresponsible behavior. . . ." [62]

As I read through the postings, I struggled to understand how this column discouraged irresponsible behavior, or how it was helpful to the girls (and some boys) participating. Not only that, since all of the names are pseudonyms, we really don't know who's writing in. It seems like a great site for someone who gets off overstimulating young girls. For instance, some of the postings contained detailed sexual fantasies such as the two from someone whose screen name is "Hot Gurl":

> *I see u standing there ur so hot. i reach out and grab ur boobs. we start humoing each other harder and harder then i grab u and throw u on the bed where i take off ur clothes*
> *we're both lying there with our bras and thongs I slowly take of ur thong with my teeth and lick ur pussi* [sic][63]

Some of the postings revolved around technical questions:

> *hey umm every one, how do u do a b.l.o.w job? do u just suck on it or do u really actually blow? thanks*—blonde_baby56[64]

> *hey blonde_baby no you don't blow you suck and lick it*[65]

One contributor who identified herself as fourteen years old wrote that *"I kno what sex is but I dont kno how to 'do it.' . . ."*[66]

Some of the questions, like this one from "Sweet n Sour," just made me sad:

> *How do u give a good hand job? and also can u guyz give me some ideas on what to say 2 my mom when i get my period?*—sweet n sour[67]

It's the juxtaposition of these two questions that worries me. First of all, this girl isn't asking what a hand job is. She's asking how to do a good job at giving a hand job, which indicates to me that she's at a point in her sexual activity where that's either happening or going to be happening and she's only worried about her capacity to perform. At the same time, she's too uncomfortable with her body and/or her mother to even know how to tell her mom that she's menstruating.

Sweet n sour got a couple of answers to her question about hand jobs. Here's one from Jen:

> *when u give him a handjob use spit and go fast then slow ans* [sic] *squeeze my boyfriend likes that. . . .* [68]

Certainly, there are chat rooms galore on the Internet filled with this kind of dialogue. Other than mandating the use of filters on computers in public libraries, the government has failed to find ways to regulate pornography in cyberspace. My sense is that probably there's not much we can do about it. We can use filters at home—an imperfect solution because they tend to block too much or too little.

What sets Alloy.com apart is that Alloy is a legitimate corporate entity with a great reputation in the teen/tween fashion world. It's described as a "leading teen catalogue and lifestyle web site."[69] Alloy's PR material claims that its demographic of choice is boys and girls in the United States between the ages of ten and twenty-four, although I've seen the company described as targeting ages eight to seventeen.[70] It claims to reach 24 million kids and provides a "host of marketing and advertising services to marketers seeking to reach the Generation Y audience."[71] Merchandise sales from its catalogues and web site targeting teens and tweens rose 35 percent, to $167.6 million in 2002.[72] The company's executives are quoted in the mainstream press as experts on tweens.[73] The web site attracts advertising from all sorts of companies catering to tweens. On the days I looked through the Alloy bulletin board described earlier, the ads popping up on the screen were for Herbal Essences and Disney's tween hit *Lizzie McGuire*, which (ironically) is supposed to be a good "clean" media fare for tweens.

Because Alloy and the companies that advertise with Alloy are legitimate, mainstream corporations, the material on Alloy.com has a certain legitimacy with kids that the pornography popping up on their screen independently—or even the porn they go looking for—does not. It's confusing to see, for instance, messages like those from "hot gurl" brought to them by Herbal Essences.

In the course of writing this chapter I had a conversation with Jane Brown, a professor of communications at the University of North Carolina who has written extensively about the impact of media on children's behavior. I commented that, given the amount of sexual stimulation that kids were exposed to and given the state of their hormones, it was surprising to me that they weren't in a constant state of sexual arousal. She talked about the concept of "jolts per minute" as a means for media producers and advertisers to keep us interested in their products. The goal *is* to keep us in state of arousal, and both violence and sex are effective ways of doing that.[74] She reminded me that studies of media violence show that we can become habituated to it and that it takes increasingly graphic and extreme images to give us the rush of adrenalin we might have initially experienced viewing milder scenes. Finally, she theorized that the same was likely to be true of sexual images. As kids get exposed to more and more sex in the media, they become desensitized to it, seeking out increasingly explicit and extreme sexual images to get the same rush they used to get from more moderate images. I can see her point. After I read the postings on the Alloy site, looking at the sexually evocative but not pornographic ads in *Seventeen* seemed pretty tame.

What's also possible is that advertisers will use sex to market to increasingly younger audiences. In a sense that's already happening, even in the world of toys. As the rest of us worry about what the business world's conceptualization of eight-year-olds as miniteenagers does to our children, toy manufacturers worry about what it does to profits. Sometime during the past few years, Mattel discovered that the age for playing with Barbie dolls was slipping. Once the favorite of older girls, Barbie was now being relegated to the preschool market. What's a toy company to do?

Enter the Bratz. The Bratz hit the market as the brand that was going to bring tweens back to doll play. They are hip and sexy—much sexier than Barbie, who, in spite of her conical breasts and tiny waist, always seems fairly asexual, even in a bathing suit. Not the Bratz. The Bratz radiate a cartoonlike, street-smart, in-your-face combination of sex and toughness. On the official Bratz web site, they are posed to show off their lush butts and melon-sized breasts.[75] The Bratz have that "edge" we talked about before. They radiate a sense of humor (a characteristic I never associate with Barbie), but are they good for kids?

MGA entertainment created the Bratz for the tween market (described in relation to these dolls as beginning at age seven). In a smart marketing twist, they have been positioned to lure back to dolls girls who have gotten older younger. Ads for the Bratz appear on Nickelodeon's *Sunday Night Tee-NICK.*

Mattel couldn't take a threat to Barbie's throne lying down, so they've retaliated with a new, bigger-lipped, bigger-hipped, belly-button-baring "My Scene" Barbie. Wearing a ton of makeup, Barbie is transformed into a Bratz wannabe, and is even being advertised on MTV. Barbie temporarily zoomed past the Bratz in audaciousness when Lingerie Barbie (called "pornographic Barbie" by some of my more radically feminist friends) appeared in FAO Schwarz in 2002. By shelling out $40.00, eager buyers could get Barbie in black lingerie, garters, and a bustier. After a consumer protest, the dolls were taken off the shelves at FAO Schwarz while Mattel claimed publicly that this particular Barbie was intended for collectors and was being marketed only to people over fourteen.[76] I know that adult men and women collect Barbies, but, really, do girls over fourteen play with dolls? Not if kids are getting older younger.

Actually, what seems to be happening with these so-called "tween" dolls is that younger girls are buying them. The Bratz made it to the 2002 "Hot Toy Picks" list put out by Toys "R" Us—but not for tweens.[77] No, the sexy little Bratz are bestsellers for five- to seven-year-olds, who are now going to be getting even older even younger. I expect they'll soon be turning to MTV in droves.

Many parents still find it hard to make a connection between their children's behavior and what kids absorb through their media experiences. A psychologist colleague of mine was in a quandary because one of the first graders she works with was bragging about her boyfriend to her classmates—explaining in graphic and colloquial detail about how she "did sex" with him. There is absolutely no evidence that this child has been sexually abused. Her mother reports that she does have a TV (with cable) in her bedroom. She does watch R- or PG-13-rated movies. Her mom is worried about her daughter's precocious interest in sex, but absolutely refuses to have "the talk" with her. For children who by nature are more impulsive, more curious, or even more sensual than other children, or for children whose parents can't or won't educate them about sex, the barrage of media messages can be devastating.

9

Marketing, Media,
and the First Amendment:
What's Best for Children?

W HEN CONFRONTED with the complex issues and passions evoked by
marketing sex and violence to children, I was initially reluctant to leap into
the fray. Every attempt to formulate my thoughts led inevitably to natural
disaster metaphors ranging from "quagmire" and "sinkhole" to "tsunami"
and "avalanche." I knew I was heading for trouble.

The problem is that in this country it's virtually impossible to talk
about curbing children's exposure to media sex and violence without addressing controversial and passion-engendering questions of morality,
artistic freedom, the role of government in media regulation, and the free-
speech guarantees of the First Amendment to our Constitution. Unlike advertisements and product placements created to sell junk food to kids—or
even advertising strategies that are designed to bypass regulations and sell
them alcohol and tobacco—the marketing of sex and violence involves the
content of expressive media productions themselves, including movies,
television programs, videos, video games, and music. Most of the motivation for drama—that which holds our interest in a narrative—stems from
conflict and the expression of basic human drives. In contrast, despite
product placement, hamburgers are rarely a plot point, nor do we hear
much about artistic freedom when it comes to selling sugar cereals.

We are a pluralistic nation, and our attitudes about sex and violence
are often rooted in moral and religious beliefs. The Torah, the Koran, and
the New Testament all weigh in on violent and sexual behaviors. What
their teachings mean, of course, is open to interpretation—giving rise to
lots of modern-day confusion about sin. Most of us agree in general that it's
wrong to physically hurt another person, yet, as a society, we seem to tolerate and even applaud spanking, war, and self-defense. We disagree more

about sex, except insofar as most of us think (at a minimum) that it should
be consensual and that our own children are too young to be having it.

There are voices of reason in the debate, but they are often drowned
out. The loudest condemnations (especially about sex) and many of the
calls for regulation that reach the public ear seem to come from extreme
conservatives and the religious right, whose arguments invoke God, a universal morality, and a stunning disregard for large portions of the Bill of
Rights.

While arguing vociferously against government intervention in areas
that are known to have an impact on youth violence and teen pregnancy
(poverty, mental health, gun ownership, or sex education), they lobby with
equal fervor for government control of media content. Meanwhile, their
opposite numbers—who seem to consist mainly of media makers and
rather doctrinaire left-wingers—support government interventions in the
form of gun control, federal poverty programs, and sex education in public
schools, yet oppose any regulation of how media is marketed. They tend to
equate any media content rating systems with censorship, and wave the
flag of the First Amendment while remaining in complete denial of the idea
that the media have any influence at all on children's behaviors or values.

For people like me—concerned about children's exposure to media
violence and about precocious, irresponsible sexuality even as I support
the First Amendment (to say nothing of separation of church and state)—
this dichotomy is a problem. I sometimes find myself in agreement on this
particular issue with people with whom I disagree about almost everything
else. It's a mess, made messier because public dialogue is increasingly influenced (some would say "controlled") by sound bites and headlines that
can never do justice to complex issues.

Tussles about media content go at least as far back as the development
of media for the masses. By the end of the nineteenth century, parents and
clergy worried about the effect on morality of "Penny Dreadfuls," cheap
novels sporting rather lurid covers designed to appeal to, among others,
children. In the mid-twentieth century, or "back in the day," as my daughter would say, they worried about comic books and their possible negative
impact on youth. Concerns about mass media content intensified with the
advent of television.[1]

In the early 1950s, in response to these concerns, and to avoid federal
regulation, the National Broadcasters Association created a standards and
practices code, which included a section stating that broadcasters were ac-

countable to the American public for, among other things, "respect for the special needs of children . . . for decency and decorum in programming and for propriety in advertising." [2]

The same decade, often referred to as the Golden Age of Television, also saw the beginnings of a whole range of creative, prosocial children's programming. From the perspective of the twenty-first century, it's pretty obvious that the 1950s were a golden age of broadcasting only if you were Caucasian, were willing to sign a loyalty oath, and expressed no radical political opinions. The children's programming created then was not even remotely commercial-free.

In fact, through what is called "host selling," commercials were incorporated right into the body of various shows. I recently spent some time at the Museum of Television and Radio visiting programs I loved as a child. I watched Buffalo Bob, host of the extremely popular *Howdy Doody Show,* hawking Wonder Bread ("It builds strong bodies twelve different ways!"). On my still all-time favorite program, *Kukla, Fran and Ollie,* characters were speaking warmly about their "good friends" at Whirlpool or RCA and reading aloud from *Life* magazine.

As a result of activism in the 1970s, the FCC banned host selling in 1974. The ban still exists, having survived the deregulation of children's television in 1984. However, given the increase in cross promotions and product licensing, de facto host selling is a component of almost all children's television programs in existence today.

Still, among the broadcasting community there was some acknowledgment that children deserved special consideration in programming; indeed, the promotional hook of television as a benefit for kids was used as a selling point to American families. By the beginning of the next decade, once televisions were established in most American homes, broadcasters began to cut back on children's programming and concentrate on prime-time viewing, which grew increasingly violent over the years.

In 1968, to avoid regulation, the Motion Picture Association of America (MPAA) came out with a rating system: G (fine for all ages), PG (parental guidance), R (children under 17 admitted with a parent), and X (so-called "adult" movies). In 1984, they added PG-13 (not recommended for children under 13). NC-17 (no child under seventeen admitted) replaced the X rating in 1990 after pressure from film makers who felt that the X rating was being applied to serious movies which were being lumped in with pornography. [3]

In the 1980s, Tipper Gore successfully led a movement to get the
music industry to provide similar rating labels for music recordings.
(When I talk with parents today who used to be critical of Tipper Gore's
work, they inevitably refer back to her advocacy and are so much more
supportive now that they have children.) Television executives managed to
avoid instituting a rating system until 1996, when the Telecommunications Act mandated that every television set contain a "V-chip" that would
allow parents to block out violent or otherwise objectionable programs.

Under threat of government intervention, and as a necessary part of
the V-chip technology, the television industry created ratings for shows—
to be broadcast along with them—so that parents could program the
V-chip to block out shows that contained content they felt was inappropri-
ate for their children. The V-chip has not been a howling success. Only
one-third of parents with V-chip televisions use it.[4] There are lots of reasons for this. It's been under-advertised (some would argue that it has
barely been advertised at all). It's hard to set up. The ratings themselves are
complicated and inadequate.

Meanwhile, parents, health professionals, educators, and advocacy
groups have been fighting unsuccessfully to get the industry to create a
more useful descriptive code, one that communicates content rather than
age-appropriateness. As mentioned earlier, research combined with anec-
dotal evidence suggests that children will be more attracted to programs
aimed at older kids than they will be to those labeled for their own age
group. For instance, the mother of an eleven-year-old boy complained to
me recently that her son's initial response—sight unseen—to any movies
rated G or PG is that they are babyish. R ratings, or M (for "mature") ratings for video games, are often a draw rather than a deterrent for young
teens and preteens. Just the fact that the video game and television industries have chosen "Mature" or "Mature Audience" as a label shows a certain dishonesty about their intent. To be seen as mature, or see themselves
that way, is an important component of what adolescents and preadolescents are striving for. "But Mom, I can handle it!" is a common rejoinder to
parents' attempts to limit media access. One mother complains that her
son's friends refuse to come over because he doesn't own any violent video
games with "Mature," thus "cool," ratings.

As a parent, I have found film and television ratings useful in an arbitrary kind of way. However, I do think that associating ratings with age
lends a peculiar message to children about violence. Such ratings suggest

that being able to tolerate or enjoy watching people get hurt is a sign of maturity, something children should look forward to as a reward for growing
up. Some television programs voluntarily identify the reason for their rating, whether it's violence, language, or sexuality, but they aren't required to
do so. More than one father has told me that seeing scary or violent movies
is a point of honor for his preteen sons and their friends. "That wasn't
scary," is a common refrain.

Violence is marketed to children so intensively that parents find themselves making all sorts of devil's bargains with what kinds of violence they
will and won't allow. One mother of a thirteen-year-old finally decided that
her child could buy video games that involved killing fantasy creatures but
not games that involved violence against humans. At the same time, she
recognized that she could not control which video games he played at
other kids' houses.

As the United States was gearing up for the 2003 war in Iraq and
Americans were supposed to be defending themselves against terrorism, I
attended a panel discussion evaluating the V-chip. Representative Edward
Markey, a veteran of many of the children's media wars, commented, "The
parents of the United States know more right now in two weeks about how
to duct tape the saferoom in their house and how much water they should
have than they know about this V-chip in their TV set." Educating parents
about how to use the V-chip is not a priority for anyone in the media industry. In fact, it is in their best financial interest for parents to remain ig-
norant about the device. Every child viewer lost to a program is one fewer
consumer for the products they sell.

However daunting the task, I knew when I began this book that I
would have to leap into the First-Amendment-children's-media-and-
marketing morass. It's the only time I ever yearned to be a lawyer. I at-
tacked the problem in the following way—months of fretting, followed by
months of reading,[5] interspersed with endless conversations with a wide
range of people, all of whom have passionate and sometimes widely different perspectives on the meaning of free speech. I spoke to lawyers who informed me in no uncertain terms that all I had to say was "A corporation is
not a person," and I spoke with lawyers who told me with equal authority
that, in law, a corporation absolutely had to be treated like a person so that
it could be regulated.

The people I spoke to included, but are not limited to, Marjorie Heins,
director of the Free Expression Policy Project; Gary Ruskin, from Com-

mercial Alert; Angela Campbell, from the Georgetown University Law
Center; and journalists, child development experts, my husband, my colleagues in Stop Commercial Exploitation of Children, and a random seat-
mate on a flight to Texas who turned out to be Noam Chomsky ("Gee, Dr.
Chomsky, you're going to be awfully sorry that I'm sitting next to you, but
I'm writing a book about marketing to children. . . ."), with whom I had
subsequent helpful discussions.

Ultimately it's up to policy makers and legal scholars to give shape to
how this country deals or doesn't deal with children, marketing, media,
and the First Amendment. I think their work should take place in the context of widespread public debate *in the context of what's best for children.*
Since free speech as it relates either to corporations in general or to advertising in particular is based on interpretations of the First Amendment
rather than what it actually says, this conversation should take place un-
constrained by how the Supreme Court is currently interpreting the Constitution.

After struggling to sort through the issues, I decided that what I can
offer are some points for framing that discussion. If we get the dialogue
right, we have a better chance of getting the results right as well. With that
in mind, these are some points we need to consider:

THE WORDS "ADVERTISING" OR "MARKETING" ARE NOT
INCLUDED IN THE TEXT OF THE FIRST AMENDMENT.

The actual text of the First Amendment[6] addresses political and religious
expression, free speech, freedom of the press, the right to assemble, and
the right of petition. As recently as 1942, the Supreme Court voted unani-
mously that advertising was not protected under the rubric of free speech.
In recent years, the Court has been changing its mind and granting increased protections for commercial speech or advertising.

Artists, corporations, and any other entities have the right to produce
the media or products they choose, but the government (of the people, by
the people, and for the people) should have the right to regulate how those
products are marketed—especially to children.

ADVERTISING TO CHILDREN IS NOT ANYONE'S INALIENABLE RIGHT.

I find that discussions about marketing to children often devolve into arguments about advertising as an inalienable right. Usually, this refers to the rights of the marketers, but I have to admit to being startled when a reporter asked me, "Don't children have the right to be marketed to?" Well, no. That's like saying sheep have a right to be wolf bait. Children do have certain rights protected by law in this country—the right to be educated, for instance—but being targeted in the marketplace is not among them.

THE GOVERNMENT IS NOT THE ONLY THREAT TO FREEDOM OF EXPRESSION, ESPECIALLY WHEN IT COMES TO THE MASS MEDIA.

I'm puzzled that people concerned about freedom of speech don't seem to be worrying about corporate control of media content[7] as much as they worry about government regulation.[8] For instance, in the year 2000, free speech advocates railed against the government's involvement in inserting antidrug messages in television programs, while at the same time there was little mention of the influence of corporate interests on media content, which represents an equally destructive, and more pervasive, threat to free speech.

Certainly it was a violation of the First Amendment when the White House Office of National Drug Control Policy actually reviewed the messages incorporated in television scripts. However, the current trend toward deregulation of media ownership (which began while Jimmy Carter was president, intensified during Ronald Reagan's tenure, and is continuing through the present) has led to a consolidation of media ownership to such an extent that only a few companies control most of the media—and therefore most of the media content available to Americans.

Under the guise of the Family Friendly Programming Forum, big advertisers, including McDonald's, Coca-Cola, Kellogg, and General Mills, give money toward the development of "family friendly" programs. The Forum appears to focus its efforts on affecting the creation of prime-time shows that are free of violent and sexual content. One of their creations, *The Gilmore Girls*, received some critical acclaim and was held up as a program that could be popular without containing sex or violence. Kellogg's, a member of the forum, was one of the main sponsors of *The*

Gilmore Girls. Guess what the Gilmore Girls ate for breakfast? Kellogg's
Pop Tarts.[9] Given the childhood obesity epidemic, just how family
friendly are the advertising practices of food companies like Kellogg's,
General Mills, Coca-Cola, and McDonald's? Is any corporation in the
business of marketing directly to children truly family friendly?

In addition to providing networks seed money to develop programs,
the Forum offers scriptwriting scholarships to film schools at New York
University and the University of Southern California. It has provided seed
money to some networks to create programming.[10] We would be naive to
assume that the course of creative flow will be uninfluenced by either of
these gifts. The Forum's vested interests are likely to be directly protected
simply because it holds the purse strings. Would a beneficiary of the
Forum's benevolence be likely to create programs critical of the advertising
industry, for instance? How much influence will a Forum scholarship have
on the creativity of cash-strapped film students? Will they really want to
begin their film careers by alienating an entire consortium of potential fun-
ders by using their beneficence to create scripts critical of corporate practices?

When corporate sponsors of media programming take part in its creation, their power extends beyond being able to decline sponsorship.
They are able to shape programming at its inception. What it means for the
rest of the population is that, for all the glitzy bells and whistles made possible by new technology, media programming in the twenty-first century is
going to function a lot like radio and television once did in the 1940s and
1950s, the "good old days," when the sponsors of programs like *GE Theater* and *Kraft Playhouse* exercised inordinate control over program content, even picking contestants for quiz shows and vetting scripts for the
merest suggestion of a competitor's name. It seems to me that anyone concerned about free speech has to take on corporate control of media content
as well as government control.

TELEVISION NETWORKS WERE GIVEN THE RIGHT TO BROADCAST
—FOR FREE—OVER THE PUBLIC AIRWAYS IN EXCHANGE FOR AN
OBLIGATION TO SUPPORT THE PUBLIC INTEREST.

In the 1920s, the government formally leased the public's radio airways to
commercial interests and began to regulate broadcasting through the Federal Radio Commission. In the 1930s, with the invention of television, the

FRC was dismantled and the Federal Communications Commission (FCC) took over its mission. From the start, broadcasters' adherence to public interest has been one criteria for license renewal. Initially, there were limits on commercials, and requirements that broadcasters air news and public affairs programming. However, the definition of "public interest" has changed over the years.[11] These days, supporting public interest seems to mean simply adhering to FCC regulations, which have been diminishing significantly in number and domain over the years.[12] Is it in the public interest for children to be exposed to violent and confusing sexual images during the hours they're most likely to be watching TV? Is it in the public interest for children to be targets for marketing products through ads that manipulate their vulnerabilities? If not, don't we, the public, have a right to hold broadcasters responsible for airing those ads?

As part of the 1996 Telecommunications Act, Congress gave existing commercial broadcasters rights to broadcast through the expanded digital spectrum for free—at an estimated loss to the public of over $70 billion.[13] While each broadcaster now has multiple channels for broadcasting, there has been no channel set aside for commercial-free programming. It has been pointed out that if broadcasters were to be charged a fee for their use of the digital spectrum, the government could earn $2 to $5 billion annually that could then be spent on a truly public, truly non-commercial broadcasting system.[14] Since government expenditures for public broadcasting are currently in the $250 million range,[15] imagine the commercial-free programming that a few billion more dollars could create—including programming for children.

WE, AS A SOCIETY, HAVE TRADITIONALLY RECOGNIZED THAT CHILDREN ARE NOT ADULTS—SINCE THEIR LACK OF COGNITIVE, SOCIAL, EMOTIONAL, AND PHYSICAL DEVELOPMENT, AS WELL AS THEIR LACK OF EXPERIENCE, MAKES THEM PARTICULARLY VULNERABLE TO EXPLOITATION. THEY ARE ENTITLED TO AND HAVE BEEN ALLOWED MANY SPECIAL PROTECTIONS IN OTHER ARENAS UNDER THE LAW.

We have child labor laws, laws that children must stay in school, laws prohibiting sale of alcohol and tobacco to children, and laws that attempt to protect them from pornography. Even if the Supreme Court decides, through rulings on test cases, that marketing "speech" should be completely protected under the First Amendment, there are still precedents suggesting that marketing to children—including marketing sexual and violent media content through ads as well as promotions with toys, food companies, and fast-food restaurants—should be excluded from such protections.[16]

At this point, the law does suggest that children have a right to be protected from speech that is harmful to them[17]—from, for instance, pornography or what gets classified as adult entertainment. One problem is that, other than outright pornography, we can't seem to come to an agreement on the definition of "harm." If it could be proven that viewing violent media is a "sole or primary cause" of harm or harming behavior, excluding the media violence marketed to children from First Amendment protections would be legally justifiable.

Many factors, both environmental and biological, determine attitudes toward violence and violent behavior. There's enough evidence (see the one thousand studies over thirty years cited in the public health community's Joint Statement on the Impact of Entertainment Violence)[18] that media violence is one of those factors, although there's no evidence that it's ever the sole factor.

As one media researcher pointed out to me, the study that could prove that violent media was a sole factor in violent attitudes or behavior would be unethical, and therefore will never be done. Such a study might look like this: Two groups of children matched in age, gender, socioeconomic status, and risk for violence would have to be divided accordingly and locked in two separate rooms for an extended period of time. One would be fed a steady diet of media violence while the other would be fed some other kind of media. Perhaps a third group, equally matched, could be allowed to play. Then their behavior would have to be observed for another extended period of time, perhaps years. Because there are (thank goodness) restrictions on how human subjects can be used in academic research, no public institution could conduct this research. It is interesting to note, however, that since market research is subject to no government restrictions on the use of human subjects, including children, it is theoretically possible for some corporation to do it.

Aside from such an unethical study, some people think that the best way to prove harm would be research using brain-imaging techniques to show how the brain processes violent media. One such study, conducted at Kansas State University in 2003, showed intriguing results using a sample too small to be conclusive. It suggested that children's brains respond to media violence as though it were a significant life event, storing information the same the way they would store a post-traumatic stress memory.[19] Another study shows that the brains of children with a history of violent behavior respond differently to media violence than those with no such history.[20] More such research will be conducted over the next few years.

TOOLS THAT ENABLE PARENTS TO CONTROL WHAT THEIR
CHILDREN SEE ON TELEVISION ARE NOT A VIOLATION OF THE
FIRST AMENDMENT.

The V-chip to allow parents to screen certain programs based on their ratings is now embedded by law in all television sets, and its use has not yet been challenged in the courts. However, Replay TV, a device enabling people to skip over commercials, is currently the subject of a lawsuit brought by various media companies against its maker, Sonic Blue.

I'm ambivalent about both of these devices because they allow us to dodge the underlying issue of public and corporate responsibility to children. Kids from families whose parents can't or won't use the V-chip are not going to benefit from it. The fact that viewers can skip commercials is now a major rationale for the escalation of advertising embedded in television programming instead of just surrounding it. On the other hand, changing the political and social landscape that frames policies relating to media and advertising to children is likely to take a long time. In the meantime, these devices do provide some relief to some families.

One problem with both the V-chip and Replay TV is that their value to parents is undermined by ignorance and greed. Thus far, the V-chip is used only minimally.[21] Many salespeople selling televisions don't know how to program the V-chip, nor has it been promoted with any major public service campaign. It is not in media corporations' immediate best interest to limit access to programming for any segment of its audience. Replay TV, which is being positioned as an anticommercialism device, has partnered with Coca-Cola to run commercials while a program is on pause.[22]

With the advent of digital media resulting in technology that combines the Internet and television, issues relating to media content, marketing, and the First Amendment as they apply to children are going to become even more complex. Without government intervention, or the real threat of government regulation, there is no evidence that we can count on media

10

Joe Camel Is Dead, but Whassup with Those Budweiser Frogs?: Hooking Kids on Alcohol and Tobacco

A MOTHER WHO HAPPENS to be a child psychologist writes to me: "I was driving my eight-year-old daughter to a school concert. She was all dressed up and feeling great about herself. 'You know,' she said seriously, 'when I'm dressed like this, I feel like when I'm in high school, I'm going to smoke.' 'What?!' I shrieked, slamming on my brakes in my best therapeutic style. 'Are you nuts? Where did you get that idea?' My daughter stroked her skirt complacently. 'All the pretty girls in high school smoke.' "

Another mother complains via e-mail, "My husband and I are baseball nuts. My nine-year-old son, Matt, is rapidly acquiring our passion. We often watch games on television, but I don't know what to do about the endless run of beer commercials during the games. I know we can talk to him about drinking, and we do, but he's constantly exposed to all of this glamour, fun and excitement centered around beer—to say nothing about all those pseudo-sexy women! We've tried muting the sound. We've tried everything short of depriving ourselves of watching the games. It's not fair."

Children are important to the alcohol and the tobacco industries. According to the National Institute of Alcohol Abuse, people who start drinking before the age of fifteen are four times more likely to develop a dependency on alcohol than those who start drinking when they're twenty-one.[1] Lifetime alcohol abuse and dependence is greatest for those who begin drinking between the ages of eleven and fourteen (or younger),[2] and the alcohol industry depends on alcoholics for a significant portion of their profits.[3] In combination, adults who drink excessively and underage drinkers account for almost half of all alcohol sales in the United States.[4] Tobacco companies need to keep creating smokers to replace the 440,000 who die each year,[5] so it's essential for business that they get children to start smoking. The younger children are when they begin to smoke, the more likely it is that they will be become regular smokers and the less likely that they will ever successfully quit.[6,7,8] If a person can reach the age of twenty without beginning to smoke, he or she has almost no likelihood of starting.[9] Ninety percent of smokers began before they turned eighteen.[10]

It's illegal to sell alcohol to anyone under twenty-one. It's illegal to sell cigarettes to children under eighteen. When it comes to marketing to children, the alcohol industry periodically comes under government scrutiny and, in 1998, the tobacco industry became subject to some government regulations. Yet children and teenagers continue to be targets for marketing by both industries.

There is significant public health concern about children's consumption of alcohol and tobacco—enough so that consumption of each is tracked through more than one ongoing government survey of risky behaviors among youth. For all the similarities between the two, there are differences as well. Tobacco is inherently addictive and harmful to adults as well as children, even when used as intended. While alcohol can be addictive, it is certainly possible for many people to drink in what alcohol abuse counselors call "low-risk ways" without harming themselves. On the other hand, of the approximately 9.7 million drinkers between twelve and twenty, close to 20 percent engage in binge drinking and 6 percent are heavy drinkers.[11] By about seventh grade, 20 percent of students have tried alcohol. By eighth grade, that figure rises to 50 percent.[12]

Alcohol is implicated in four of the leading causes of adolescent deaths, including automobile accidents, suicide, homicide, and unintentional injuries.[13] Researchers estimate that alcohol is involved in one-third to two-thirds of adolescent "date rapes" and sexual assaults.[14] Almost 30 percent of fifteen- to seventeen-year-olds say that alcohol or drugs influenced their decision to engage in sexual activity. About one quarter of that same group said that drugs or alcohol caused them to do more sexually than they intended or were comfortable with.[15]

When it does not employ animated amphibians, today's alcohol advertising grabs the attention of teens and preteens by exploiting the same vulnerabilities as ads for clothing or accessories. Populated by ever-so-slightly-older beautiful people, these ads offer the promise of an ever-so-fun-filled life brimming with sex, lack of bothersome inhibition, and raucous parties, all centered around alcohol—mostly beer, although hard liquor is marketed to young people as well. All your loneliness, insecurities, or awkwardness will disappear, these ads promise, with a Bud, or a Coors Light, or a Heineken. Kids are getting the message. Most of them drink not because they like the taste, but to relax, to feel more mature, be more uninhibited, or because it's supposed to be fun.[16]

Alcohol companies swear that they are targeting twenty-one- to thirty-four-year-olds, but the themes and media techniques that characterize beer advertising, for instance, have undeniable appeal for teens as well. For example, the industry has a self-imposed rule that models in commercials need to be at least twenty-five,[17] but as we know from the way marketers characterize teens and tweens as "aspirational," models who look old enough to be in their twenties have great appeal to teenagers. Besides, many of the models in beer commercials I've seen look young enough to be under twenty-one. The themes or stories portrayed in some alcohol commercials seem more relevant to underage drinkers than anyone else.

As I noted earlier, underage drinking in this country is monitored by various annual and biannual government surveys. The statistics they report can be confusing because some surveys track by age and some by grade. However, in the first few weeks of my research for this chapter, when all of the numbers were starting to blur, I came across one that stopped me cold.

According to Mr. Jeff Becker, president of the Beer Institute (call me provincial, or alcoholically challenged, but I didn't know there *was* a Beer Institute), 83 percent of adolescents don't drink.[18] To give weight to his statement, he attributed that fact to the Department of Health and Human Services. Based on your experience of today's teenagers, does that figure surprise you? My eyebrows certainly went up. It runs counter to the observations of most of the students, teachers, health care professionals, and parents I know, as well to the data from all those government surveys, all of which suggest that the figure is significantly lower.

In fact, alcohol is the drug of choice for middle and high school students, and beer is the alcoholic drink they prefer.[19,20] Teens and preteens are drinking more than they did a generation ago and are beginning at an earlier age.[21] On average, kids begin experimenting with alcohol when they are about thirteen.[22] According to the latest available data from the Centers for Disease Control, about one-fifth of eighth graders have had a drink in the past month, and one-sixth admit to having been drunk in the past year.[23]

Underage drinkers are essential to the economy of the alcohol industry. They drink almost one-fifth of the alcohol consumed in the United
States. In 1999 teens (and preteens) spent about $22 billion of the $116
billion Americans spent that year on beer, wine, and liquor.[24] Most of that
money—about $17.2 billion—was spent on beer.

I asked the Beer Institute, which, it turns out, is the malt beverage industry's trade association, where they found the data to support their
claim. They e-mailed me a graph from a 2001 Department of Health and
Human Services survey showing that 16.4 percent of twelve- to seventeen-
year-olds reported having had a drink in the previous thirty days. According to the same survey, almost 34 percent of twelve- to seventeen-year-olds
reported drinking in the previous year. More than 10 percent reported
binge drinking—defined as having more than five drinks in one day—at
least once in the previous month.

Of the national surveys I've seen on alcohol abuse, that particular
Health and Human Services survey (from the Office of Applied Studies,
National Household Survey on Drug Abuse [NHSDA], 2000–2001), reports the most positive statistics on adolescent drinking. The NHSDA
consistently reports rates below surveys by the Centers for Disease Control, which also document incidents of risky behavior.[25] One probable ex-
planation for this discrepancy is that the former is conducted at home with
a parent in the house, although not necessarily in the room, while the latter
takes place in school, with no parent present. Even so, I could find no evidence that even remotely suggests that 83 percent of adolescents don't
drink.

I called the Beer Institute back and explained that their reading of the
data was confusing to me. Mr. Becker, who returned my call, said that he
stood by his statement and referred me to an epidemiologist who would
explain the numbers to me. The epidemiologist, who also consults to the
tobacco industry, evinced surprise at Mr. Becker's interpretation of the
data and said that she would get back to him. "He's a very nice man," she
said. I'm sure he is, although I'm still not clear what that had to do with the
discussion at hand. (A few hours after my conversation with the epidemiologist, I received an e-mail from her saying that she already communicated to Jeff Becker the proper figures. The e-mail thanked me for bringing
the issue to their attention and assured me that "the industry's intention is
to be diligent, comprehensive, and accurate when it comes to reporting national statistics that address underage drinking.")

I'm reporting this interchange because it reflects my experience throughout writing this book. The public health community is taxed with conducting intensive, scrupulous, and often expensive research to document the effects of advertising on children, while industries devoted to advertising and promotion—or the industries that profit through marketing to children—merely issue statements saying that the research is false or inadequate. Meanwhile, children continue to be barraged with advertising—including advertising for products such as alcohol or tobacco, which are known to be harmful to them.

Thanks to major grants from large foundations such as the Robert Wood Johnson Foundation and the Pew Charitable Trusts, we are beginning to accumulate more data about adolescent exposure to alcohol advertising. Kids—particularly those who watch sports on television—are inundated with alcohol ads. Alcohol companies reach teens (and preteens and—as we shall see—even young children) through commercials on television and radio and in magazines. They also reach children through media promotions, product placement in movies and television programs, and through sponsoring sports events and rock concerts.[26]

Teens (including twelve-year-olds) see more commercials for alcohol on television than they do for skin-care products, jeans, and snacks like potato chips.[27] In 2001, alcohol companies spent over $31 million on ads during thirteen of the fifteen most popular shows among kids twelve to seventeen, including *Friends, That '70s Show,* and *Survivor Africa.*[28] Many of these shows are also watched by younger kids. According to A.C. Neilsen data, on average more than 2.1 million kids between two and eleven watched *Survivor Africa* each week. Over 1.3 million were watching weekly episodes of *Friends.*[29]

In 2001, the alcohol industry reached 89 percent of teens who watch television. The average teen viewer saw 245 alcohol commercials on the tube that year. Teens who are heavy viewers saw more than three times that amount. They are also more likely to drink. A study from Stanford Medical School showed that the more television kids watched in ninth grade, the more likely they were to have begun drinking eighteen months later. The likelihood increased 9 percent for each hour of television watched.[30]

Of course, television commercials represent only a fraction of the total amount of advertising to which kids are exposed. The industry spent about $218 million on radio advertising last year, up from $176 million in 2000, with 81 percent of those millions coming from the beer industry.

The Center for Alcohol Marketing and Youth at Georgetown University found that almost 40 percent of radio ads monitored in 2002 were aired on stations favored by teens. Commercials for certain brands of beer such as Budweiser and Coors Light were more likely to be heard by twelve- to twenty-year-olds than by adults aged twenty-one to thirty-four.[31]

The alcohol industry also advertises in magazines popular with teens.[32] In 2001, ten magazines that have a significant youth readership, *Vibe, Spin, Rolling Stone, Allure, Car and Driver, Maxim, Glamour, Motor Trend, In Style,* and *Sports Ilustrated,* accounted for almost one-third of alcoholic beverage advertising in magazines. Topping this list in spending on alcohol ads is *Sports Illustrated,* which took in $31 million in alcohol advertising that year and was reported to have a youth readership of 6,127,000 in 2001.[33]

Among the alcohol brands advertising in these magazines are "alcopops," or "malternatives," such as Doc Otis' Hard Lemon Malt Beverage and Smirnoff Ice Premium Malt Beverage. Malternatives are marketed as "low-alcohol refreshers," but actually they contain more alcohol than beer. Teenagers see 60 percent more print ads for malternatives than do adults over the age of twenty-one.

The ads themselves are particularly attractive to teens. For instance, a Sam Adams beer commercial shows a young guy in the midst of a large party lying to a cop who is responding to a complaint about noise. The camera lovingly follows this guy's hand as he hides his beer bottle behind his back. "Uh, you must have the wrong address," he says. This ad brilliantly plays into adolescent identity issues—feeding into a defy-authority, us-against-them mentality. The viewer is definitely rooting for the kids and not the cop.

As author Jean Kilbourne eloquently points out, beer ads are not kind to women, either.[34] One Miller Lite commercial even features a young man putting an electronic dog collar on a girl. A Coors commercial features rapid-fire MTV-type camera work, a pounding beat, and two blonde, extremely voluptuous, gyrating twins. The lyrics featured in this commercial (to a beat so compelling I have not been able to get it out of my head for days!) are:

> I love playing two-hand touch,
> Eating way too much,
> Watching my team win.

> . . . With the Twins.
> I love quarterbacks eatin' dirt,
> Pom poms and short skirts,
> . . . And those Twins.

That the association of Coors Light and sexy women would appeal to teenage boys goes without saying. This particular commercial would probably qualify as "edgy" since it implies that the protagonist is "loving" not just one woman, but two. As an anticlimax (as it were), what's also interesting about this ad is its focus on sports. I don't know if beer advertisers read the same studies I do, but if they do they would have come across one in 1995 showing that white adolescent boys prefer beer ads with sports images to ones without.[35] Drinking is more prevalent among boys than girls (although the girls are catching up). White male teenagers are an important market for beer advertisers—they drink more than, for instance, their African American counterparts.[36]

Coors has gone public with their intent to market to a younger crowd—but according to them, it's the twenty-one to twenty-nine demographic they're after.[37] Other Coors commercials feature the same kind of glorification of rowdy overindulgence, as well as music by rap stars Dr. Dre and Kid Rock. It's all in sync with the kind of extreme, outrageous behavior that saturates MTV and that is spilling over to reality TV.

Coors's new advertising campaign has elicited criticism even from the beverage industry itself. Tom Pirko, president of Bevmark LLC, a consulting firm, called at least one of the new Coors offerings ". . . sophomoric and stupid. These are obviously not mature adults in their twenties."

Mr. Pirko seems to understand why Coors—which is the number-three beer company in the United States—has upped the advertising ante. "There's blood in the water," he said in an interview. "They are in a wonderful position right now. There's no better time to do what they are doing to win market share. It's time to invest and spend." Miller, which is the number-two beer company, had better watch out. The Miller executive interviewed in the same story was quite admiring of Coors's endeavors. I expect that we are going to see even more outrageous beer-selling behavior over the next few years.

The industry claims that advertising affects only brand choice, not the decision to drink. That seems to be true for adults, but for children it seems to affect both. Beer companies spending the most on advertising

make the brands most favored by teenagers.[38] Kids also report that advertising has more impact on their desire to drink than on the brand they consume.[39]

Even as alcohol executives consistently dismiss the relationship between advertising and underage drinking, the amount of money they
spend on advertising increases each year.[40] Alcohol companies spent at
least $4 billion to market their products to Americans in 2001.[41] Spending
for radio, television, and print ads alone has outstripped inflation by 20
percent since 1975, and that's not even where the bulk of money is being
spent. A larger chunk of advertising budgets is going for what is called "un-
measured" advertising, such as sports promotions or product placement,
which heightens the capacity of companies to insinuate their brands into
adolescent culture.[42]

Mr. Becker from the Beer Institute has this to say about current beer
industry advertising: "We know that we have critics, but our consumers
love our ads and that for us is very, very important."[43] I can't help but wonder to which consumers he's referring. Children as young as seven have
considerable awareness of beer brands and are as adept as twelve-year-olds
at matching logos to particular brands of beer.[44] Those animated,
adorable, and croaking shills, the Budweiser frogs, are beloved by children. While Budweiser states in no uncertain terms that the ads do not target children, they could have been created from a how-to manual for
marketing to kids. Gurus in the world of marketing to children routinely
suggest that ads targeting children include cartoon characters and/or animals in their ads because children immediately recognize cartoon messages as intended for them.[45] Dan Acuff, in *What Kids Buy and Why*, talks
about the "strong affinity very young children have to animals and animal
characters."[46]

For older children, humor and music are appealing. So it's no surprise
that more nine- and ten-year-olds recognize the frogs than recognize the
Mighty Morphin Power Rangers, Smokey Bear, and Tony the Tiger. Only
Bugs Bunny fared slightly better.[47] In a 1998 survey conducted with kids
between ages six and seventeen, a market research firm found that the Bud
frogs topped the list of their ten favorite commercials. Nor is it a surprise
that, according to the study, the ad campaign's appeal to children is attributed to humor, animals, animation, and music.[48]

I have not been able to find information on the amount of alcohol advertising that reaches children under twelve, but given how familiar they

are with beer brands and beer ads, it's clear that they are not exempt from the bombardment. Of course, exposure is only part of the equation for advertising's effectiveness. The Prevention Research Center in Berkeley, California, has been documenting alcohol advertising's effects on children by studying their awareness of alcohol advertising and its effects on their beliefs about drinking as well as on their intent to drink. A study of fifth and sixth graders found that those more aware of beer advertising had more positive attitudes toward drinking and showed more intent to drink as adults.[49] About a third of children in grades four through six report that they have received a lot of pressure from their classmates to drink beer.[50]

What's particularly troubling about marketing alcohol to young kids— and about the way that it's marketed—is that it sets up what researchers call "expectancies" or positive attitudes about the effects and benefits of drinking. Having positive expectations about what drinking alcohol is like is a better predictor of future drinking habits than socioeconomic class. Expectancies can be traced to the impact of advertising because they are often exactly the messages that beer commercials teach—that good parties require beer, for instance.[51] Children as young as eight have been found to have "expectancies" about beer,[52] which makes me think that the baseball-loving mother I mentioned earlier has reason for concern—and anger. Shouldn't families be able to watch baseball together without having to worry about encouraging their children to drink beer?

The American Medical Association, concerned about the potential negative effects of alcohol consumption on adolescent brain development and the effectiveness of televised alcohol commercials, recently asked network and cable stations to restrict, on a voluntary basis, alcohol advertising to programs running after 10 P.M. It would certainly improve the chances of diminishing young children's exposure to alcohol advertising. It would also improve families' experience of watching sports on TV. Not surprisingly, the TV stations have not yet complied, and the alcohol industry is expressing outrage.[53]

Like food companies, alcohol companies have recently been marketing through a spate of paid product placements and promotions in movies, films, and video games, many of which are targeted at underage drinkers. Heineken paid for product placement in the *Austin Powers* films, which were a big hit among both teens and tweens.[54] Anheuser-Busch, something of a pioneer in product placement, paid millions for CBS to incorporate Bud Lite into *Survivor*.[55]

Leslie Moonves, the president of CBS, expressed enthusiasm about the effectiveness of embedding products—including beer—into the show. "We've had many repeat sponsors on *Survivor* because they really feel like they got their money's worth. . . . When somebody is jumping up and down because they have a beer as a reward and they make it seem like it's the greatest liquid they've ever drunk in their lives, that probably is more effective than having some model saying, 'Hey, drink Budweiser.' "[56]

Coors, which, as I mentioned earlier, is going after younger drinkers,[57] has a deal with Miramax, which is owned by Disney, to incorporate Coors beer into fifteen movies, the first two are *A View from the Top* (rated PG-13), starring Gwyneth Paltrow and Mike Myers of *Austin Powers* fame, and *Duplex*, starring Drew Barrymore and Ben Stiller. Myers, Barrymore, and Stiller all have particular appeal to teens.

I'm focusing mostly on beer in this chapter, but it's worth mentioning that the hard-liquor, or spirits, industry has focused on music promotions to raise sales. Courvoisier brandy spent $5 million to target young African Americans—presumably in the hopes of helping them achieve alcohol parity with white males—by joining all those corporations who have co-opted hip-hop culture through event sponsorships, billboards, and print advertising.[58] They hit the jackpot when rap stars Busta Rhymes and Sean Combs ("P. Diddy") released the single "Pass the Courvoisier." "Pass the Courvoisier" doesn't qualify for product placement since Rhymes and Combs were not paid for their plug, but their record's success in selling Courvoisier was a significant factor in the decision of executives at Island Def Jam records, a leading rap label, to purchase and market Amadale vodka.[59]

Alcohol manufacturers use the Internet to reach kids as well, with web sites filled with games, music, contests, and giveaways. In 1998, the Center for Media Education found that 82 percent of beer-related web sites featured content that was attractive to teens.[60] Not much has changed since then.

I was virtually "carded" at all of the alcohol sites I visited. I had to type in a birth date, and each site proclaims that it is only for people over twenty-one. It's laughable to think that kids are going to be deterred from a site they want to visit; all they have to do is type in a fake birth date. The fact that many sites refer to what they are doing as "carding" is also attractive to teens—it replicates the feeling of sneaking into a bar or club. On many, music starts even before the screen focuses.

The alcopop sites I looked at seemed particularly teen-friendly. For instance, the site for Jack Daniels Whiskey is fairly staid—not much on the
site moves and the colors are pretty dull. When I clicked into the Jack
Daniels Original Hard Cola site, however, all of a sudden the screen looked
three dimensional—like a hologram. A click on "hard facts" there got me to
some very sexy women playing pool (and drinking JDOHC, of course)
and the following message: "Learn all about Jack Daniels Original Hard
Cola, the exciting new drink that's been proven to cure an extreme case of
boredom." Of course, that's exactly the message we want kids to have—if
you're bored, drink! Jack Daniels Original Hard Cola, the message continues, is "a great tasting cola tasting malt beverage . . . that goes great with a
burger, in an ice cream float, or poured generously over cereal flakes."[61] In
other words, it goes great with a teenage diet.

Anheuser-Busch's site for Doc Otis' Hard Lemon, another alcopop,
starts out touting what a low-carbohydrate, low-calorie beverage it is—a
perfect come-on for girls.[62] At the Coors Light site, I entered a birth date
indicating that I was under-twenty one and was barred from the site after
being told "Sorry, but that's under twenty-one."[63] I hit the "back" button,
typed in a different age, and I was in.

At the federal level, regulation of alcohol advertising falls under three
separate government agencies: the Bureau of Alcohol, Tobacco, Firearms
and Explosives; the U.S. Food and Drug Administration; and the Federal
Trade Commission. However, none of these agencies focus on marketing
to children. At the state level, less than half of the states have any laws that
address marketing to underage drinkers, and they tend to look to the federal government to regulate advertising and alcohol industry practices.[64]

Therefore, when it comes to marketing to kids, the alcohol industry is
largely self-regulated. In 1999, an investigation by the Office of the Health
and Human Services Inspector General found that the alcohol industry's
regulations were too vague to be enforceable, or too narrowly cast to do
any good. The industry is not rigorously enforcing its own rules either. For
instance, regulations in the beer industry don't allow beer advertising to
suggest that any alcohol laws are being broken. It seems to me that the Sam
Adams commercial I described earlier could only be a party with at least
some underage drinkers. Why else would the young man hide his can of
beer from the police? There's no law against having beer at a party filled
with legal drinkers!

Until 1996, the regulatory code offered by the Distilled Spirits Coun-

cil of the United States (DISCUS) held that spirits could not be marketed
on television. Unfortunately, that's no longer the case, and ads are appearing on TV based on the discretion of each station.

As with the food industry, or with the producers of media violence, executives in the alcohol industry claim that there has been no demonstrated
causal relationship shown between advertising and underage drinking.
They point out that teens identify parents and peers as having much more
influence on their drinking habits. Even so, more than half of students in
grades five through twelve say that alcohol advertising encourages them to
drink. In the endearing but crazy-making way that adolescence is characterized by a deluded sense of invulnerability combined with genuine insight into societal ills, many teens will report that advertising influences
other kids but deny that it influences them.[65]

In any case, it's difficult to disentangle peer influence and media influence. Even if certain teens are susceptible to peer pressure but not to advertising pressure, the friends influencing them to drink could be
susceptible to marketing.

Given the nature of beer and alcopop ads, and the importance of children to the industry, it's hard for me to believe alcohol executives like
Frank Coleman, senior vice president of the Washington, D.C.-based
DISCUS, when he says that the industry is against underage drinking. To
bolster his argument, he told the Associated Press in 2002 that the industry spends $10 million a year on responsibility programs to fight underage
drinking.[66] That's all fine, but it's only a quarter of 1 percent of the over $4
billion they spend on advertising. As the Madison Avenue adage goes,
"You don't drink the beer, you drink the advertising."[67]

In case you think that the mom who loves baseball is exaggerating
about the beer ads, she isn't. During a May 30, 2003, Red Sox–Yankee
game, shown at 7 P.M., I counted ten beer commercials between the top of
the fifth inning and the bottom of the ninth. These do not include the two
"brought to you by" messages, or the two times announcers mentioned
Miller and Sam Adams beer in the course of their commentary. Nor does it
include a commercial for *The Matrix Reloaded*—a big hit with teens—
which might as well have been a commercial for Heineken since it looked
just like the one shown a few innings earlier advertising both Heineken and
The Matrix Reloaded.

As I said earlier, tobacco differs from most other legal products, including alcohol, because it is harmful even when used as intended. It has

the dubious honor of being the subject of the very first public health treaty ever issued by the World Health Organization, designed to limit the spread of smoking. One way WHO intends to do that is to restrict advertising.[68] How they will enforce the treaty remains to be seen. Aside from greed or adherence to extreme libertarian beliefs, it's hard to understand why to-bacco continues to be marketed to anyone anywhere, let alone to children. But it does. And tobacco marketing is effective, especially with kids. Eighty-six percent of teen smokers smoke Camels, Newports, or Marl-boros—the most heavily advertised brands.[69]

In 1998, after years of public health research, advocacy, and lawsuits, the American tobacco industry and forty states signed a Master Settlement Agreement in which, among other things, the industry agreed to stop in-tentionally marketing to kids. Within two years, the amount of money spent on advertising tobacco increased by 42 percent.[70] A year later my friend Zoe called me in my office, outraged that her thirteen-year-old daughter had just received a catalogue in the mail from a company selling all sorts of cigarette paraphernalia such as hats, backpacks, and T-shirts. Last week I walked into a convenience store across the street from my daughter's old elementary school. It's a store where kids stop in to buy candy and soda. Among the cigarette advertisements were those for a vari-ety of flavored brands from Camel—mirroring the same flavors as candy, or chapstick.

The cigarette companies may have changed the ways they do it, but they are still marketing to children. A look at some of the internal docu-ments generated by the tobacco industry from before the settlement ex-plains why, in the words of tobacco executives. A memo from Philip Morris (now Altria) says, "Today's teenager is tomorrow's potential regular cus-tomer . . . the smoking patterns of teenagers are particularly important to Philip Morris."[71] According to an executive from R.J. Reynolds, "Evi-dence is now available to indicate that the 14–18-year-old group is an in-creasing segment of the smoking population. RJR-T must soon establish a successful new brand in this market if our position in the industry is to be maintained in the long term."[72] Perhaps it's the executive from Lorillard who summed it up best: "[T]he base of our business is the high school stu-dent."[73] In other words, if tobacco companies stop marketing to kids, the industry goes up in smoke.

I'm not disparaging the Master Settlement. Although it by no means represents the end of the battle, it represents a huge victory for public health advocates. The steps taken by antitobacco activists and educators in the fight against tobacco companies can serve as a model for others advocating against major odds for children's health and well-being. For example, it limited venues for marketing. As a result, tobacco advertising has been curtailed on buses.

The settlement also served as the death knell for cartoon characters used as cigarette logos. However, the most famous one of all, Joe Camel, met his demise the year before, when pressure from consumer groups caused R.J. Reynolds to end that particular campaign. I, for one, am not sorry to see the old dromedary go. I remember taking my daughter to a shopping mall in suburban Detroit when she was less than two where we encountered a huge carboard cut-out of Joe. Her face lit up with joy and she went toddling over to him in delight. Like the Budweiser frogs, the camel was adored by children. At the height of Joe Camel's popularity, more than 90 percent of six-year-olds could identify his image as being associated with cigarettes—making him as recognizable a logo as Mickey Mouse.[74] He was quite popular with teens as well. During his first three years of life, Camels went from being a brand smoked by less than 1 percent of the under-eighteen market to a brand smoked by almost one-third of smokers under eighteen, which represented an annual increase of $470 million in sales for R.J. Reynolds.[75]

As a toddler, my daughter wouldn't have been susceptible to the ads that replaced him, but for teens, or preteens aspiring to be older, the new ones were equally pernicious and breathtakingly cynical. Take for example a Camels ad that I cut out of *Sports Illustrated* a few years ago. It shows a guy running toward a fallout shelter with a whole slew of cartons of Camels. A meteorite is falling from the sky about to destroy what is clearly middle-class suburban America—a clapboard house and a backyard with a barbecue. The Surgeon General's warning—a legal necessity for all tobacco advertising—is in the lower left-hand corner. In the lower right-hand corner is another larger, official-looking "warning":

Viewer discretion advised.
This ad contains:
FR: Falling rocks
CH: Cigarette hoarding
UM: Undercooked meat.

By aping the Surgeon General's warning label *and* the content ratings for movies and video games, the ad preys brilliantly upon adolescents' natural tendency to buck authority and to mistrust authoritative statements. Teens, who are often in struggles with parents about R-rated media, are set up to think that content warnings are stupid. The fake warning label is so ridiculously silly that it's easy to minimize the very real hazards of smoking—cancer, emphysema, and heart disease—on the real warning label.

Just as cigarette companies successfully exploit teen vulnerabilities in general, in recent years they have been especially good at exploiting young girls' concerns about their weight and appearance.[76] Teenage girls have been leading the way for new smokers for the past few decades; by 1995, they had virtually caught up with boys. One of the major reasons girls start to smoke is to lose weight or to keep themselves from gaining it. When Joseph Califano, former secretary of Health, Education and Welfare, was asked if he wished that he had done anything different during his time in office, he said that he wished that he had paid attention to the relationship between smoking and weight.[77] One of the claims tobacco companies make is that smoking kills the desire to eat. After Virginia Slims and other so-called "women's brands" were introduced in the 1960s, there was an unprecedented rise in the number of young girls who began to smoke.[78]

There have been no commercials for cigarettes on television since 1970 when Congress banned ads on TV and radio.[79] Instead, tobacco companies reach kids through magazines, billboards, advertising, displays—often in little convenience stores—sports and concert promotions, direct mail, and sales of branded clothing and accessories. Even teen magazines can't be considered free of tobacco advertising when they accept antismoking ads sponsored by cigarette companies or incorporate stories about tobacco companies' good works. Tobacco companies keep their names in front of kids by sponsoring antismoking ads on television. The notion that tobacco is just another product is fostered when textbook covers include tobacco company names among other advertisers' logos and ads for sneakers, pizza, or jeans.

Tobacco companies are forbidden to engage in product placement contracts with film and television producers, but even when they do not take money from tobacco companies, the media play a part in marketing smoking (and drinking) to children. Of eighty-one G-rated animated children's movies, more than half contained at least one sequence showing a character either smoking or drinking.[80] When smoking is incorporated regularly into children's entertainment—to which parents often accompany children—then tobacco use becomes normalized for kids, even for those who do not have smokers in their families. Unless parents take the time to comment on smoking as undesirable, children absorb the behavior as part of our cultural zeitgeist.

When I was taking my daughter to G-rated movies, much of my work at that time was focused on racial prejudice and diversity. Therefore, I understood the need to talk with her about the racism and sexism she encountered on the screen. It never once occurred to me to comment on the cartoon characters who were smoking or drinking.

Children absorb racial stereotypes and prejudices from the culture they encounter, and if no one talks with them about these issues or works to disavow the messages, they can become lifetime attitudes. It appears that the same might be true for children's attitudes toward tobacco. Studies show that kids who watch movies in which there is a lot of smoking are more likely to think that smoking is normal and that more people smoke than actually do.[81]

In 1998, the *Journal of the American Medical Association* reported that the cigarette brands teenagers are most likely to smoke are the brands most heavily advertised in magazines with high youth readership. As a result of the recent court battles, tobacco companies claim that they do not advertise in magazines that reach a high percentage of young people. The tobacco industry relies solely on circulation data—i.e., the age of the actual subscriber—to assess the number of young people who read a particular magazine, but recent research shows that circulation data is not an accurate method for estimating the size of the teenage audience; therefore, it is likely that tobacco marketers routinely reach a higher percentage of teenagers aged twelve to seventeen when placing advertisements in popular consumer magazines than circulation data shows.

Immediately after the settlement, the tobacco industry escalated the amount of money they spend on advertising in magazines that appeal to teens.[82] Four years later, California fined R.J. Reynolds $20 million for violating the settlement by advertising in magazines such as *Spin, Hot Rod,* and *In Style*.[83] According to Dr. Elizabeth Wheelam, who has been tracking tobacco ads since the settlement, after the recent downturn of the economy *Time* and *Newsweek* significantly increased the number of ads for tobacco.[84] These popular news magazines are frequently assigned as required reading in high school contemporary affairs classes.

The brands most popular with black adolescents are still heavily advertised in magazines favored by African American youth.[85] Actually, the brands that teenagers smoke are the brands that spend the most on advertising in any venue.[86] Cigarette advertising is extremely effective, and its effectiveness is so well documented that when the National Cancer Institute reviewed the research, they came to the conclusion that there is a causal relationship between advertising and first use of cigarettes.[87]

Teenagers are three times more susceptible to cigarette advertising than adults.[88] In fact, tobacco advertising appears to have even more influence on kids' decisions to smoke than exposure to family members or friends who are smokers.[89] It is even effective in influencing kids who are neither smokers nor susceptible to smoking to experiment with tobacco.[90]

What's really alarming—although not surprising—is that cigarette marketing can even trump good parenting. In a refrain commonly sung by advertising executives, the tobacco industry has long claimed that good parents can prevail over the industry's zillion-dollar efforts to ensnare children and keep their kids from smoking. In fact, the tobacco industry has paid for public service announcements on television implying that being actively involved with your children's lives is an antidote to smoking.

For some kids that seems to be right. For a significant number of others, that is not true. A new longitudinal study shows that what's called "authoritative" parenting—defined in this instance as active involvement in your child's life and maintaining a good balance between support and firmness—can cut your child's chances of smoking in half, but for the kids who start smoking despite their parents' best efforts, advertising is the major reason they begin.[91]

This study has ramifications well beyond tobacco advertising. At the time of the baseline research, Joe Camel was still around and was quite popular with teens and preteens. Researchers refer to tobacco industry documents revealing that the goal of that campaign was to associate Camels with themes of independence, coolness, imagination, sex, reality-based success (such as a date or good party), excitement (living to the limit, or at least imagining so), taking risks, and living on the edge.[92]

Of course, these traits, yearnings, and interests (or some combination of them) that are so tied up with normal adolescent interests and predilec-

tions are also what beer, clothing, music, and even food advertisers use to
market their wares to teens and preteens. It seems to me—and given the industry memos, it appears that this view is shared by marketing experts—
that kids vulnerable to those messages would also be more likely to use
products associated with the traits or characteristics they communicate.

Since my colleagues who conduct research are wary of generalizing
from tobacco to food or alcohol, it would be of great public service to replicate this study using marketing campaigns from other industries that employ the same tactics to hawk their wares to children. For that to happen,
the government, or major private foundations such as the ones currently
funding alcohol and tobacco research, will have to commit to broadening
their research about advertising to children beyond tobacco and alcohol.

Oh, and guess who the industry rag *Media Week* named Advertiser of
the Year in 2001? Budweiser. Why? Because, "If there was one campaign
this year that cut through the increasingly dense media clutter and became
a fixture in *playgrounds*, offices and bars around the country, it was the
Budweiser series of ads." [93] (The italics are mine.)

The alcohol and tobacco industries' pursuit of children threatens
more than their health. It encourages them to break, or at least circumvent,
the law. In that sense, it is obviously antisocial and differs from the practice
of marketing other products to kids. Yet it's a mistake to set them completely apart. Once we divorce advertising from the products being sold,
we find much of it embedded with antisocial messages—subtle and not so
subtle. All advertising—regardless of product—transmits lessons about
values. When it targets children, these values are often antithetical to the
lessons we want them to learn.

11

If Values Are Right, What's Left?:
Life Lessons from Marketing

I SPOKE to a scientist the other day who recently received a grant to study the effects of media violence on the brain. "I don't want to get all bogged down in the whole values thing," he said about his contribution to public debate about the issue. "I want this to be about science."

I sympathize with his desire to shy away from a debate about values. After all, they tend to be murky and unquantifiable. In the sociopolitical arena, values—especially so-called "family values"—have been ceded to political conservatives, in particular the Christian Right wing of the Republican Party. To the detriment of children, mentioning the word "values" to people of certain political persuasions (which I admit includes many of my friends, family, and colleagues) is at best a conversation-stopper and at worst grounds for ostracism. When it comes to talking about the impact of commercial media and advertising on children, however, we *have* to talk about values. Along with products, that's what corporations market.

We can't escape values—our own or those belonging to other people. Whether we're aware of it or not, whatever we voluntarily choose to do, say, or create communicates our values. The converse is true as well. Inaction, silence, and acts of destruction also reflect and express our values.

By the same token, all media content reflects and communicates the values of those in control of that particular medium. Because we usually experience media creations in the absence of the people responsible for them, it's easy to avoid conscious recognition of the values they communicate—unless the expression of those values has particular meaning to us. However, every image or word we and our children encounter in media is selected by someone who, perhaps in consort with lots of other people, discarded a whole lot of other words, images, and ideas along the way.

What we do and do not encounter in media is a conscious or unconscious reflection of some person's values—including the decision to compromise values in order to stay employed, gain power, make money, have a viable creative outlet, or even to avoid compromising other values.

The power of media to influence values and, by extension, the power given to the people who own media is one reason why advocacy groups ranging from the Center for Digital Democracy to the National Rifle Association are so alarmed by the consolidation of media company ownership. Even if we can choose among a hundred television stations, how much diversity of viewpoint do we have if each of the channels is owned by one of five corporations? We have even less if newspapers, book publishers, Internet service providers, television, and radio stations are all owned by the same companies as well. Everything from news to children's programming reflects the values of whoever is in charge of those corporations.

At this juncture, three corporations control most of the television programming that targets children. These are Viacom (which owns Nickelodeon and MTV), Disney (which owns ABC and all of the Disney channels), and Time Warner (which owns the Cartoon Network). The Fox News Corporation (which owns Fox Family and FX) also commands a significant child audience.

Many of the values we hold dear as adults begin to be formed in childhood, including those rooted in political, social, and religious beliefs. Babies are born value-free (but not free of value). They begin to absorb cultural, social, religious, and political values early in life. Our children learn values and absorb attitudes from us—their parents and families—but not from us alone.

We are not always conscious of the values we impart to our children (hence the old adage "Do as I say, not as I do," which even the most conscientious of us have probably uttered to our—usually teenage—kids at some point in our lives). They absorb values at school, from friends, in the community, and in churches, mosques, and synagogues. They also absorb values from the media. Teaching values to children is one of the things the media do best.

An article in the *New York Times* recently described a video game created for Hezbollah, a militant Middle East group that is on the U.S. list of terrorist organizations, the purpose of which is to shoot down representations of Israeli buildings and targets. According to a member of the game's design team, "Special Force" is designed to disseminate Hezbollah's "values, concepts and ideas."[1] When the white-power group, the National Alliance, released a game called "Ethnic Cleansing," a spokesman for the organization said, "We want to reach young people, and this is the medium that will do that. . . . We have an obligation to use [video games] to spread our message."[2] I condemn the hatred and violence fomented by these groups and their games, but I give them credit for being honest about their use of media to influence children's values and attitudes.

The U.S. Army has created a wildly popular computer game designed as a recruitment tool for young teenagers. It was presented to the public as career education, but I've seen no official recognition that it also promotes values. Aside from glamorizing violence, the game propagates the characterization of Arabs as Enemy with a capital "E." The cyber-terrorists pursued by young gamers are mostly dark-skinned and Semitic-looking. Their camps are situated in the desert, and described as located in a high desert with rolling sand dunes and wadis.[3]

Currently, the army issues a simulated game to teach urban warfare to its troops. It has been released in a commercial version called "Full Spectrum Warrior." The urban landscape in which the fighting takes place is designed to look like an Arab city.[4] One of the game's creators explained that they shifted the locale from a Bosnian-looking setting to one that looked more like an Arab city as the game developed because "We can't ignore the fact that we are in Afghanistan. We are in Iraq."[5]

If the villains children encounter in the media look like Arabs, aren't we sending them the message that Arabs are villains? This is the complaint that African Americans and Latinos have had for years about how they are portrayed on television. Video game makers, like film and television producers, actively deny that their products teach values or influence behaviors. Their stance is disingenuous. If the creators believed that they were not transmitting values and attitudes in their games, then why would they have taken care that "the U.S. soldiers act[ed] with discipline and professionalism."[6] It's absurd to think that children would notice the comportment of the soldiers but not notice the race or ethnicity of the enemy.

At least one game developer quoted in the *Christian Science Monitor* agrees. "[Game developers are] talking from both sides of their mouths. . . . When they talk publicly, or they testify before Congress, they'll talk about how games don't have any kind of profound impact. But when they talk to a major corporation, then go and have their [game's] protagonist walk around with a soft drink of Brand X, they're telling that company that games can influence people's behavior." [7]

Most of the parents I encounter, including me, care a lot about the values of the people to whom we entrust our children. Those who need (and can afford) child care carefully interview baby-sitters before hiring them. We visit day-care centers or nursery schools to ensure that we find one that is safe and that will reinforce the values and behaviors we try to promote at home. We may send our children to parochial schools to reinforce our religious values. If we're so inclined, we may choose a day-care center because its population is diverse, because it nurtures creative play, or promotes social skills such as cooperation and responsible conflict resolution.

Although there are always sad exceptions, we have some sense that the doctors, nurses, teachers, and day-care providers we choose have the well-being of our children at heart. In any case, they can usually be held accountable for their behavior by us, our community, professional organizations, and the government. We see their faces. They (usually) return our phone calls. I've been lucky, but in my experience the professionals who have had an impact on my daughter's life have held as a primary value the health and well-being of children.

With the proliferation of electronic media, however, our children's lives are shaped profoundly by people who do not know our children, and are accountable only to their co-workers, bosses, and clients. Because we don't encounter the people responsible for marketing campaigns directed at our children, it's unlikely that we spend much time thinking about their values. Clearly, the values that motivate their personal lives—how they treat their families, colleagues, and friends—are none of our business, but because marketing executives have so much influence over our children, I think that the values informing their work *are* our business.

I'm not suggesting that you and I have the same values. Nor am I suggesting that all people who market to children have the same values. What I am suggesting is that knowing how marketers characterize their beliefs about children and advertising is important information for parents and other people who care for, and about, children. This isn't easy to do. The best way to gain this knowledge is to attend marketing conferences. However, as I mentioned earlier, these are mostly prohibitively expensive, especially for the average parent. The next best way is to read marketing journals, books, magazines, and newsletters. Having spent the past several years immersed in learning about marketing to children from the point of view of the people who do it. I find that, in the course of talking or writing about how to market food, toys, and media to children, marketing experts also inadvertently or purposefully share their values.

For instance, one marketing executive commenting on the difference between selling food to children or selling food to adults said, "With kids you have to sell that it will taste good, that it will make them popular in school."[8] Wait a minute. Is it good for children to think that consuming a particular food, or any food, will make them popular? Is eating their way to popularity a behavior we want to inculcate in the younger generation?

From the perspective of values, the executive's statement is equally problematic. It assumes that children—especially teens and preteens—are universally vulnerable to, and motivated by, wanting to be popular. Assuming this is true, and it probably isn't for some kids, we can also assume that since the executive quoted was speaking in the context of a marketing campaign he created, this person is willing to exploit that vulnerability in order to sell a product.

An executive at Burger King explained the philosophy of their campaign to market what they call "Big Kids Meals" as follows: "We said you're a big kid whenever you're ready to be a big kid. . . . We're marketing to kids' attitudes about their age, how grown up they feel and how they like to be treated."[9]

This statement implies that children are the best judge of whether they are "big kids" or "little kids." Are kids "big kids" whenever they feel ready? Let's go back to the baby-sitter question. Would you hire a baby-sitter who, when faced with your six-year-old who wants the same rights and privileges as your eleven-year-old, gives in across the board because that's what your younger child wants?

Marketing the notion to children that they are, and should be, capable of free choice in the marketplace is an extension of a strategy that has been used in advertising targeted to adults for years. "Dispositionism" describes the belief that our choices manifest solely from who we are and are not influenced by either the environment or situations in which we find ourselves.[10] It's an appealing notion, especially because it provides us with a sense of complete control over our own destinies. It persists even though social psychologists have proven repeatedly that even as we cling to the belief that we have complete control over our choices, our decisions are heavily swayed by forces we often don't even notice. The most famous studies were conducted in the 1960s by Stanley Milgram at Yale, who asked participants, by pressing a button, to administer electric shocks to a student who was sitting in a kind of electric chair in another room. (It's important to note that the participants were not really administering shocks and the man playing the part of the "student" was not being hurt.)

Participants were asked by someone identified as a doctor to administer "shocks" of increasingly high voltage. They saw the man strapped in a chair and the electrodes placed on his head and then were taken to another room where they could no longer see him. The man in the chair was asked a question. When he got the answer wrong, the participants were told to administer a shock. At each wrong answer, the voltage increased. Eventually they could hear the man moaning in pain. He cried out that he had a heart condition. Eventually the man stopped screaming and became silent. The doctor said that the silence was interpreted as a wrong answer and the participants were told that the experiment must continue and they had to press the button. Finally, they were told to press one that appeared to administer 450 volts of electricity marked "extreme danger." Sixty-nine percent of the participants pressed that button when told to do so.

I remember reading Milgram's study in an undergraduate course on psychology and being horrified about what it suggested to me about human nature or, to quote that line from the old radio program *The Shadow*, "Who knows what evil lurks in the hearts of men." However, in the course of repeating his experiment with countless variations, Milgram found that participants' willingness to administer potentially lethal shocks varied depending on the situation and their perception of the situation, including factors such as location, who was giving the order, whether they were receiving counter-orders, and so on. Milgram's work, and the work of the social scientists who have conducted all sorts of variations on that work, say a lot about human nature. While our choices are often strongly influenced by our environment, we are often not conscious of these influences.

Marketers, however, are well aware that manipulating environmental factors has an impact on choice. Influencing choice while creating the illusion that our choices are not being influenced is the whole purpose of advertising. In the United States, freedom is one of our primary shared values. We do not like to be manipulated—at least we do not like to *think* we are being manipulated. Therefore, it is extremely important for marketers to perpetuate the illusion that all of our choices are "free." Burger King, for instance, clearly benefits from an advertising campaign based on the philosophy that kids should have control of their "bigness." Consumers spend more for Big Kid Meals. Do children benefit?

According to my local Burger King, a regular Kid's Meal consists of either a hamburger, a cheeseburger, or five chicken nuggets, a twelve-ounce. drink, and, as we say in the vernacular, a small fries. A Big Kids meal consists of a double hamburger, a double cheeseburger, or eight chicken nuggets, a fifteen-oz. drink, and a small fries. A child who decides to be a Big Kid and order the Big Kid's hamburger meal for instance, does get nine more grams of protein, but she also gets 180 more calories, nine more grams of fat, ten more grams of sugar and forty more milligrams of sodium.[11]

Burger King, and other corporations who market to children, also benefit from introducing children early on to the idea that they are and should be free to have control over their choices in the marketplace.

Rowan Williams, the current Archbishop of Canterbury, disagrees. In the context of describing his concerns about rampant commercialism, the Archbishop argues for supporting children's need to safely experiment with new identities and behaviors. One major difference between how children and adults are usually treated in Western society is that adults are expected to be competent and mature while children are expected to make mistakes and be rather irresponsible. Essential to a child growing into a well-functioning adult is the opportunity to experiment safely and, in the process, make mistakes and even behave irresponsibly.

According to the Archbishop, one major problem for children in an environment dominated by commercialism is that an unfettered marketplace is not a safe space for children to experiment. Their actions can result in real-life consequences that they may not be able to foresee and that may not be good for them. Williams focuses mainly on the commodification of children as sexual beings, but his concerns are applicable here as well. Little children need to experiment with being big kids, but given the rise of childhood obesity and the health risks associated with it, it seems pretty clear that Burger King, or any other fast-food restaurant, is not necessarily a safe place to start.

Next time you watch television—particularly at times when children are likely to be watching, between 4:30 and 9:00 P.M. on weeknights, for instance—ignore the programs and look at the commercials. Pay attention not just to the products being sold but to the values and behaviors each commercial promotes. I've found that a good way do this is to dredge up skills you probably learned in school for analyzing literature. Approach each commercial as you would a play or a short story. Identify the plot and the themes or ideas communicated by the plot. It's sometimes useful to identify the protagonist, the antagonist, and their motivations as well.

The McDonald's commercial shown in the child development presentation at the marketing conference I describe in chapter 1 is a good place to start. It's actually one of a series of commercials with similar plots, all revolving around children who are bored or sad until Ronald McDonald appears out of nowhere and transports them to McDonald's. As I remember, what the kids are bored with changes with each commercial. Sometimes it's classical music; sometimes it's what looks like a class trip to a museum or library.

Retold, the story could go something like this: Once upon a time there was a group of children who were bored being at a museum. Suddenly (borrowing a technique from ancient Greek playwrights, who occasionally wrote their heroes into dreadful situations for which there is no earthly solution, called *deus ex machina* or "god by machine"), Ronald McDonald appears and transports them to McDonald's, where, after the children are transformed from a state of boredom and unhappiness to one of bliss and wild enthusiasm, they presumably live happily ever after.

As for themes, the primary idea communicated is "McDonald's makes us happy." There are other ideas communicated as well. These include: "Passivity pays off," "Classical music is boring," "Museums are boring," and for the one in which an elderly librarian or museum docent shushes the kids sternly, "Old people are mean."

A commercial for milk shows a substitute teacher dressed as a milk carton who keeps getting everything wrong until the kids correct him. The plot is, "A substitute teacher shows up at school and is stupid and incompetent." The themes are: "Children are smarter than adults" and "Substitute teachers should be objects of derision."

Are these the ideas or values you want your children to learn? Would you send your child to a school that taught these values? How about a church, synagogue, mosque, or civic organization? Would you hire a babysitter with these values? As a society, we seem to believe that teaching values is the province of the family. However, children spend almost forty hours a week engaged with media, most of which is commercially based and not value-neutral. The values they are being taught by the people who target them for marketing are often diametrically opposed to those we try to teach at home.

· According to a poll by *USA Today*, 76 percent of adults in this country feel that too much emphasis on materialism is a serious problem in raising children.[12] Yet, by definition, the primary value communicated in just about any commercial is materialism—that buying the product advertised will make us happy (or "cool" or "fulfilled" or "sexy" or "popular" or "attractive" or whatever qualities our hearts desire). At the same time, these messages communicate implicitly and—in some instances—explicitly that not obtaining a product will render us miserable, unfulfilled, dorky, unpopular, or unattractive. A child who sees just a few such messages will probably experience them as specific to a particular product. When kids are bombarded with marketing, as they are today, the message they get is that *things,* not just a particular thing, will make them happy. For corporations, inculcating children with this belief is profitable because it promotes spending. For everyone else, as evidenced in the extreme by reports of kids killing each other for a pair of sneakers, and by the more mundane yet worrisome escalation of teen credit card debt, it can be a disaster.

As adults, with our experience, mature cognitive abilities and solidified values, one can assume that it's our responsibility to defend ourselves against messages intended to exploit or influence our value system. Children can't do that. What developmental psychologists have taught us is now graphically demonstrated through neural imaging. Children's capacities—to reason, to see beyond their own needs, and to manage their emotions—develop over time. Their values and behavior are influenced by their experience. Preschoolers are more susceptible to influence than older children and adults.[13] Teenagers can reason more effectively than eight-year-olds, but in addition to being buffeted by storms of hormonal changes, the frontal cortex, which governs higher cognitive functioning, including judgment, is not fully developed until their late teens or early twenties.

James McNeal, a psychologist and marketing professor, puts it this way: "Kids are the most unsophisticated of all consumers; they have the least and therefore want the most. Consequently, they are in a perfect position to be taken."[14] I would put it another way. Their brains are the least developed, they have the least experience and therefore they are in a perfect position to be taken. .

It turns out that things do not make us happy. In studies conducted across the globe, researchers find that relationships and job satisfaction are what bring us the most happiness. Not only that, people with predominantly materialistic values—those who believe happiness rests in the next car, CD, toy, or pair of shoes—are actually less happy than their neighbors.[15] People who live in countries where disasters—natural or otherwise—have left them bereft of food, medical care and adequate shelter, are significantly less happy than those who live in countries with a comfortable standard of living; but researchers have found no difference in the (collective) happiness of people in wealthy countries and of people in less wealthy countries whose basic needs are being met.[16]

In the film *The Gods Must Be Crazy,* an empty Coke bottle falls from the sky over Africa and is found by a man from a tribe of Kalahari Bushmen. Far from "civilization," they have never seen such an object and, because it falls from the skies, they assume that it is a gift from the gods, initially treating it with wonder and great respect. They discover myriad uses for the coke bottle, from rolling pin to musical instrument. It becomes indispensable. Soon there are problems. The Coke bottle cannot be divided. For the first time in this communal culture, disagreements emerge over ownership. Borne of envy, these small squabbles escalate first to arguments, then to violence. In alarm, the family elders decide that the gods have made a mistake in sending this object. They appoint the man who found it to journey to the end of the earth to cast the Coke bottle away. Most of the film is an often-hilarious account of his encounters with what we think of as the civilized world.

Now, I know that the cynics among you might argue that *The Gods Must Be Crazy* is mere fiction, and romantic fiction at that, but it does a great job of casting materialism—and the phenomenon of created need—in the harsh sunlight of the Kalahari Desert.

Materialistic values are harmful not just to individual health and happiness but to the well-being of our planet. For one thing, people with primarily materialistic values don't care that much about ecology and the natural world. For another, all too often things and the packaging they come in use up precious natural resources, are produced in factories that pollute the environment, and end up as litter and garbage that won't biodegrade.[17]

Let me acknowledge right here and now that all of this talk about materialistic values makes me anxious. Especially since I've been immersed in thinking about the impact of marketing on children, I'm doing my best to be conscious of how my life as I live it reflects my priorities and values. I have to admit, however, that I'm a sucker for certain products and the commercial messages that sell them. I've always wanted a Vegematic. My niece actually fulfilled my wish for a Miracle Mop. I started buying makeup when I turned thirty.

The commercials that most influence me change as I grow and develop. Currently I'm haunted most by those that prey on my fears about my daughter's future, like the one featuring two guys talking about college—one who clearly has the money to pay his kid's tuition and one who doesn't because he didn't use an investment broker who asked the right questions. The last thing we see is the guy who screwed up by not choosing that investment firm. He is a picture of guilt, remorse, and anxiety. Whether we actually have investment brokers, or whether they are or are not asking the "right" questions, many of us identify with those feelings, especially given the skyrocketing costs of college.

In other words, I make no claims to being unseduced by the material world. However, I know that a culture immersing children in consumerism is not doing a great job of teaching them to value the spiritual, humanistic, or ineffable splendors of life.

One of the best definitions of commercialism I've seen is offered by James Twitchell, who has written extensively about advertising and commercial culture—not, I may add, from a particularly critical point of view. According to Twitchell, commercialism consists of commodification and marketing. The former is characterized by "stripping an object of all other values except its value for sale to someone else." The latter involves "inserting that object into a network of exchanges, only some of which involve money." [18]

In the context of marketing to children, the "object" in commercialism certainly refers to the things that are advertised to children. However, it's important to remember that in the world of marketing, children themselves are commodities. In their role as audience for television programs, for instance, they are sold to corporations who buy advertising based on the number of viewers an ad can reach. (Of course adults are sold as audience as well, but since I am writing about marketing to children I am going to refer only to them.) Advertising agencies are paid for their capacity to deliver children for "ownership" by a particular brand, hopefully for life. As Mike Searles, then president of Kids "R" Us, put it in the late 1980s, ". . . if

you own this child at an early age, you can own this child for years to come.
. . . Companies are saying, 'Hey, I want to own the kid younger and
younger and younger.' "[19] Psychologists are paid by advertising agencies
and corporate marketing departments because they possess the tools to
deliver the minds of children for ownership. "Share of mind"[20] is the
phrase used in the industry to describe what corporations want from children.

When children are unprotected in the marketplace, they become commodities to be bought, sold or traded to facilitate profit. Unfettered commercialism strips children of their value and their values. In that sense it is
as much a threat to religion and democracy as Soviet-style communism
ever was.

I've been pleased to find that more august persons than I in various religious communities have expressed concerns about commercialism and
its impact on values. In recent years, Pope John Paul II and the Pontifical
Council have addressed commercialism's negative impact on the teachings of Catholicism. The council particularly addressed the problems associated with advertising to children. As I mentioned earlier, the
Archbishop of Canterbury writes about the harms done by treating children as commodities. When modern Jewish scholars like Rabbi Michael
Lerner address Jewish Renewal, they also write about rampant commercialism as counter to the teachings of Judaism. While—through no fault of
their own—Gandhi and Martin Luther King Jr. became posthumous shills
for Apple Computer, they both took strong stands against commercialism
in their lifetimes. The last time I heard a talk by the late Fred Rogers, who
in addition to his television work was a Presbyterian minister, he spoke explicitly and eloquently about greed as a threat to children's well-being.

I doubt that any of the above—living or dead—ever spent a lot of time
perusing marketing literature, but I wish I could hear what they had to say
about an article I came across recently in the British publication *Brand
Strategy*. Headlined "Brands: The New Religion," it begins solemnly,
"Identity and belonging are key issues for humanity today." The next para-
graph observes that ". . . What used to be trusted, reliable and consistent
sources of support and direction (education, government, religion, and
royalty), are now objects of a great degree of cynicism and rejection. So
what's left to hold on to? In each human being there is a basic capital of
trust, respect and love which needs to be invested into something or some-

body. The trouble is that it's becoming increasingly hard to find eligible objects for this investment."

So far, so good. But then comes the following: "Could," the author wonders, "brands take over the role that religions and philosophical movements used to own?" I certainly hope not.

The article likens a variety of brand strategies to the basic tenets of the world's major religions. Take Judaism and Islam. "From their core belief they invite worshipers to study, learn and evolve through an ongoing exploration of the original texts. Their philosophy could be expressed in one single notion: 'Think.' " I'm neither a scholar of Islam nor Judaism, but my friends who are might take exception to the idea that either religion could be summed up in a single notion—other than that of God.

Daniel Dumoulin, author of the article I'm discussing, cites a UK campaign for the Czech car, Skoda, as a "resonant" example of a Judeo-Islamic marketing strategy. "The brand's message invites its potential customers to consider the primary truth about cars. We are forced to realize that other car manufacturers surround or manipulate their truth with obvious, cynical tools: glamour, sexiness, ego-inflating codes and symbols. Skoda . . . invites us to face a different truth about the category they are promoting and the way we relate to it."

Meanwhile, Apple's marketing strategy is Buddhist, Procter & Gamble's campaign for a laundry detergent is likened to Catholicism, while Disney and Chanel are compared to religious totems that "convey a single-minded and universal meaning to people whoever, whatever, and wherever they are." The article concludes that religion and brands are converging. The former need to demonstrate their relevance to contemporary values and the future of the latter relies on "their ability to go deeper into the emotional/spiritual needs of their customers." [21]

It's the last sentence that has me worried. This article is not so different from one published not too long ago in a scholarly journal called *Psychology and Marketing,* titled "Children's Relationship to Brands: 'True Love' or 'One Night Stand'? " [22] This article describes the trend of characterizing brands as serving not only a functional/mechanical role as aids to living, but rather as fulfilling deeper needs for meaning and relationships. I take these articles, which could seem like jokes, very seriously. Over the years, I've watched children become inundated with products and their commercials—such as marketing the concept of food as plaything—developed from articles such as these. I can't imagine what form they'll take, but I expect that in the near future our kids are going to be seeing commercials that tap into their needs for meaningful relationships and spiritual life.

The importance of tapping into emotions in order to market products successfully has already been covered in a book called *Emotional Branding*.[23] McDonald's has been extremely successful in doing just that with children. As I mentioned in chapter 1, eight-year-olds in Australia would prefer to be taken out for a treat by Ronald McDonald than by their fathers, teachers, or grandfathers.[24]

Meaningful family relationships are certainly not among primary values communicated to children through advertising. Marketing messages aimed at children undermine family values in several ways. In the guise of empowering kids, they undermine adult authority. Referring to his experience working on the ad campaign that re-energized sales of Kool-Aid, an advertising copywriter said, "[O]ne really successful way to advertise to kids is to give them a sense of power, give them a place where they call the shots, instead of everyone telling them what to eat and when to go to bed and clean up their room."[25] As a result of this strategy, Kool-Aid ads began to feature "adults doing these slapstick reactions, falling on banana peels, wigs falling off. If we made adults look silly because they saw Kool-Aid Man and were shocked and frightened—the kids loved it because they were in control. . . . They called the Kool-Aid Man and he created chaos in the adult world."[26]

As an advertising strategy, undermining adults and creating chaos in the adult world may be a winner. Apparently for Kool-Aid it was. It's a strategy that seems to shape most of the advertising, and many of the commercial programs, aimed at children today. As a cultural milieu that envelops growing children, it's a problem. Children who watch a lot of television or movies are immersed in a world in which the adults—with the notable exception of Ronald McDonald and Cap'n Crunch—are largely absent, ineffectual, and stupid.

In 2003, more than a few of the commercials I watched added a new dimension to creating chaos in the adult world. These days, it's children who are doing it. A series of commercials for Nickelodeon magazine features tongue-in-cheek scenarios in which children scare and otherwise harass their parents into getting them a subscription. As these shenanigans progress, a voice says, "There are lots of ways to let people know that you want Nickelodeon magazine. How? You'll think of something." Others present children as ever so much smarter than adults. Cinnamon Toast Crunch gives us a fortune-teller who knows less than the children whose fortunes she is telling. A commercial for Wendy's shows a food service worker at a summer camp overwhelmed and confused by pandemonium in the "mess hall." And so on. In the name of empowering children, advertisers place them in a world pretty much devoid of adult wisdom. In the land of commercials, children have no need for adults. Except, perhaps, to buy them something.

Many of the commercial films and TV programs marketed to kids also choose to "empower" children by dismissing or diminishing adults. The father of a four-year-old told me about taking his son to see a G-rated animated film his son had seen hyped on television. "You know," he said, "some of it was clever but I found myself feeling uncomfortable. I couldn't help but notice that the 'coolest' kid in the movie was the one encouraging the hero to disobey his parents."

Because advertising agencies and corporations who market to children routinely hire child psychologists to help them shape their messages, the thinking behind their campaigns is rooted in psychological theory, but it's psychological theory run amok. Mastery, or a sense of control, is important to children. Fairy tales, or popular children's books from *Harry Potter* to Roald Dahl's *Matilda* often present child characters who triumph over mean adults. Children do get pleasure from imagining themselves as superheroes, or from identifying with kids who are oppressed and triumph over evil. Yet, as the Archbishop of Canterbury points out, the assumption is that children reading those books return to a world where they encounter some competent, caring adults who balance the fantasy.[27] Besides, the heroes in most popular children's books have adults in their lives who often serve as lifelines and positive role models. Harry Potter has Dumbledore and Ron Weasley's parents. Roald Dahl's Matilda has Miss Honey.

If children were seeing just one or two commercials or movies in which parents, teachers, and other adults are portrayed as incompetent, despicable, or stupid, it would be no big deal. With some exceptions, such as PBS programming or a few commercial programs such as *Blues Clues* or *Little Bill*, it's hard to find a film, television program, or commercial targeted for children in which parents—or any adults—are shown to be competent or even present. These days, the most loving, effective and competent adult children encounter in media—which takes up so much of their lives—is Ronald McDonald!

While the lessons children learn from commercial messages undermine religious teachings and family values, they are a disaster for democracy. A government "of the people, by the people, and for the people" requires a population characterized by certain attributes, including the capacity for critical thinking, cooperation, generosity, and nonviolent conflict resolution. Democracy depends on a populace that grasps the importance of checks and balances, and the delicate balance between individual rights and the greater good. They must see the value of diversity and eschew violence as a means of solving problems.

We are a population so saturated in consumerism that, after the terrorist attacks of September 11, we were exhorted by our government to go shopping as an expression of patriotism. Evoking patriotism as a justification for buying something certainly beats the normal reasons kids might give when they nag: "But Mom, everyone will think we're unpatriotic if you don't take me to the mall." In September 2002, when President Bush's chief of staff was asked by a *New York Times* reporter why the administration waited until the fall to launch its campaign for a war with Iraq, his answer was, "From a marketing point of view, you don't introduce new products in August."[28] However you felt, or feel, about that particular war, do you want your children to equate war with a new brand of sneakers? Do you consider war a product?

Being a good citizen is not the same thing as being a good customer. Citizenship in a democracy requires absorbing and adhering to a set of attributes and behaviors that can be learned beginning in early childhood. Cooperation, activism, critical thinking, peaceful resolution of conflict, and altruism are just a few of those qualities and behaviors essential in a democratic populace. Children may learn these at home, at school, or on the playground. They do not learn them in the marketplace. On the contrary, the attributes and behaviors corporate marketers want to instill in children are mostly antithetical to democracy.

Take brand loyalty, which has been described as the "Holy Grail" for marketers.[29] According to James McNeal, "We have living proof of the long-lasting quality of early brand loyalties in the cradle-to-grave marketing at McDonald's, and how well it works. . . . We start taking children in for their first and second birthdays, and on and on, and eventually they have a great deal of preference for that brand. Children can carry that with them through a lifetime."[30]

As brand loyalty increases, customers are less sensitive to changes in how much that brand costs. They are also less likely to notice or be susceptible to competitive promotions sponsored by other companies.[31] This allows companies to raise prices without a lot of complaint, and drives down the amount that companies have to spend on marketing. Brand loyalty means that a person might keep buying a brand even if their original reasons for purchasing it—such as cost—may no longer be valid, and even if it is actually in their best interest to buy the same kind of product from a different company. Brand loyalty is beneficial to a company, but not necessarily good for a customer.

By the same token, unthinking loyalty to a politician or a political party is extremely beneficial to elected officials and established political parties because it dulls a voter's inclination to make comparisons with other candidates and to examine voting records.

The habit of impulse buying, or making purchases based on the emotional appeal of a commercial without thinking through a decision, is another customer behavior that benefits companies and not consumers. If we look at most commercials these days, especially children's commercials (and especially children's commercials about food), they don't contain much useful information about the product. McDonald's commercials, such as the ones based on Ronald McDonald, don't even bother mentioning food. A healthy democracy depends on citizens who look beyond a candidate's surface promises and packaging to what they actually do and say. The slogan "Just do it," which has served Nike well for many years, implies that it's better not to think too much. Don't think about buying these sneakers. Just do it. Don't think about voting for this candidate or the issues he or she represents. Just do it.

Even going beyond brand loyalty and impulse buying, the messages in commercials undermine democracy. Commercials that show kids relying on a product or a magical being to solve their problems promote passivity, which is adaptive in a dictatorship but terrible for democracy. When passivity is combined with the kind of "me first" messages found especially in commercials aimed at teenagers, the overlying message is that there's no point in doing anything unless I benefit directly. Doesn't democracy rely on activism, cooperation, at least a modicum of altruism and citizens who understand the need for a balance between individual and majority rights?

I do know young people who are passionate about activism, but isn't there a connection between the onslaught of marketing messages and the fact that eighteen- to twenty-four-year-olds who grew up during the intensification of marketing are notoriously apathetic about voting? A healthy democracy relies on a population with a capacity for peaceful conflict resolution. Yet themes of violence and some kind of deceptive behavior are often found in children's commercials. In 1994, a study of 92 food commercials showed that 62 percent featured a violent theme.[32]

In the course of my research and writing this book, I found myself thinking a lot about Aldous Huxley's terrifying book *Brave New World*. Along the way, I discovered that Neil Postman, in the introduction to his book *Amusing Ourselves to Death*, captured the relevance of *Brave New World* to current commercial culture much better than I ever could. Writing in 1985, Postman begins:

> We were keeping our eye on 1984. When the year came and the prophecy didn't, thoughtful Americans sang softly in praise of themselves. The roots of liberal democracy had held. Wherever else the terror had happened, we, at least, had not been visited by Orwellian nightmares.
>
>   But we had forgotten that alongside Orwell's dark vision, there was another—slightly older, slightly less well known, equally chilling: Aldous Huxley's *Brave New World*. Contrary to common belief among the educated, Huxley and Orwell did not prophesy the same thing. Orwell warns that we will be overcome by an externally imposed oppression. But in Huxley's vision, no Big Brother is required to deprive people of their autonomy, maturity and history. As he saw it, people will come to love their oppression, to adore the technologies that undo their capacities to think.

Quoting Huxley himself, Postman goes on to write, "In *1984* . . . people are controlled by inflicting pain. In *Brave New World,* they are controlled by inflicting pleasure." Continuing in his own voice, Postman says, "Orwell feared that what we hate will ruin us. Huxley feared that what we love will ruin us."[33]

Twenty years later, there is certainly an argument that we should be worrying about Orwell's vision as well. But, when it comes to marketing to children, Huxley hit it right on the nose.

Speaking of noses, I've also been thinking a lot about *Pinocchio*— never my favorite children's story. You might remember, either from reading the book or watching the Disney version, that at one point Pinocchio is seduced into abandoning school and journeying with a lot of other boys to a country free of grownups and filled with pleasure. In the book it's called "Playland," a magical place devoid of adults where children play and cavort to their hearts content—until they are transformed into donkeys.

When I read the book recently I discovered that it didn't match my memory of what Playland was like, so I watched the way it was portrayed in the 1940 Disney movie. The first thing I noticed is that Walt Disney renamed Playland and called it Pleasure Island, a self-protective choice if he already had in mind the "land" that he was to develop a generation or so later. More important, Pleasure Island as created by Disney is an astonishingly evocative metaphor for the ways children are seduced by marketers today. In a magical setting, surrounded by exciting and alluring rides and fun houses, they are promised a life of total indulgence that is completely free—free of payment, free of rules, and free of consequence.

It's hard not to see the irony when, arriving at Pleasure Island, the boys stream eagerly into an amusement park where they immediately encounter a clown urging them to eat junk food. "Get your cake, pie, dill pickles, and ice cream," the clown chants. "Eat all you can. Be a glutton. It's all free! It's all free!" Chomping on sweets, to the accompaniment of carnival music, they are lured by another barker to "The Rough House! The Rough House!" "Come in and pick a fight, boys!" "Tobacco Row, Tobacco Row" still another barker chants, "Get your cigars, cigarettes, and chewing tobacca. Come right in boys and smoke your heads off. There's nobody here to stop ya." It's a party. They are even plied with free beer.

Huxley wrote *Brave New World* in 1932 as a cautionary tale for adults. Carlo Collodi wrote *Pinocchio* in the 1800s as a kind of morality tale for children. It was Disneyfied in 1940. Both stories warn that pleasure can be used as a weapon to subjugate people and rob them of personhood. Postman brilliantly lays out the connections between the culture created by modern commercialism and the world Huxley envisioned. As for why I keep thinking about *Pinocchio,* it's not hard to see his seduction by the adult proprietors of Playland/Pleasure Island as a pretty good metaphor for a frightening endpoint if advertisers' attempts to seduce children are allowed to go unchecked. Is that what we want for our kids?

12

Ending the Marketing Maelstrom: You're Not Alone

LAST WEEK I attended a meeting in San Francisco convened by a foundation interested in addressing the escalation of childhood obesity and its relationship to food marketing. I stayed in a little hotel with literary pretensions where various walls bear quotes from San Francisco literary luminaries. Each time I stepped off the elevator I encountered a line from the poet Kenneth Rexroth: "Against the ruin of the world there is only one defense: The creative act." Given the task ahead, it seemed particularly relevant.

When it comes to mitigating the harms to children caused by advertising, the easiest solution is to blame parents. It's certainly what the industry loves to do. Yet how can one family, alone, protect their children from an industry spending $15 billion annually to manipulate them? It's a struggle made more difficult because one of the primary techniques marketers use to manipulate children is to denigrate adults and undermine parental authority.

Advertising to children is out of control. It is unchecked, and escalating, as are the harms associated with it. That children are relentlessly targeted as consumers is both a social and a public health problem whose roots and solution lie primarily in public policy. Parents cannot solve this problem alone. Therefore, with a nod to the poet, even as we choose to act creatively, we need to act collaboratively as well.

Before we begin to argue about what's feasible or not in terms of policy, let's talk about what's best for kids. From that perspective, the answer is simple. *Let's stop marketing to children.* There is no evidence that it's beneficial. There's not even evidence that it's neutral. There's a growing and compelling body of evidence that it's harmful to their physical, mental, social, and emotional health. Let's stop marketing to children. It's not good for them.

I'm alone in my office as I write this, but I can almost hear a chorus of responses to that suggestion ranging in tone from despair to outrage and condescension. I've heard many of them in actuality: It's hopeless! Marketing is a fact of life! It's anticapitalist! It's anti-American! What about the First Amendment? Let the industry regulate itself! You want to put a billion-dollar industry out of business? It can never happen in this political climate! Are you nuts?

It's not hopeless. My colleagues and I have no illusions that attaining our goal of ending marketing to children is going to be either quick or easy, but it's not hopeless. And as we work together toward that end, we can certainly make significant changes along the way.

Psychologist Allen Kanner describes the sense of hopelessness that many of us feel when we think about challenging the power of corporations as a kind of "internalized corporate culture."[1] Such despair is often accompanied and exacerbated by the idea that believing anything else is unrealistic in the extreme and is likely to be characterized as "utopian." It's "utopian," I've been told, even to point out that if soda pop had not been so heavily marketed to children, perhaps we would not have to be in a position of having to market milk so heavily to them as well.

Just because marketing to children is a fact of life at this moment in time does not mean that it always has to be that way. At various points in our country's history, societal ills from slavery to child labor were all a fact of life. They are no longer.

As to the cry that it's anticapitalist? Many outspoken critics of marketing to children support capitalism. What they do not support is greed, or a kind of unregulated capitalism that gives corporations free reign to exploit whomever they choose in the interests of profit. They certainly do not support the kind of capitalism that allows for the manipulation of children to the detriment of their health and well-being.

Nor is wanting to stop marketing to children anti-American. As I pointed out in an earlier chapter, many of the values promoted by marketing messages aimed at children undermine the tenets of democracy. I also discussed the First Amendment in an earlier chapter. You may believe, as I do, that corporate advertising should not be given the protections of free speech, or you may believe that it should. In any case, children have often been given special consideration under the law and could be in this instance as well.

As evidenced by the explosion of child-targeted marketing, self-regulation is not working. The advertising industry does have a self-regulatory board called the Children's Advertising Review Unit (CARU). Its guidelines can be found at www.caru.org. The word "guideline" is critical here; CARU has no power to enforce compliance.

In 1993, a study of 10,000 commercials found that 98 percent were in compliance with specific CARU standards. However, the researchers also point out that many of the guidelines are so vague they did not lend themselves to empirical study.

The stated principles underlying CARU's guidelines look great on paper. For instance, advertisers are exhorted to take special responsibility to protect children from their own susceptibilities. Yet that suggestion, among others, runs exactly counter to what advertisers themselves say that they are doing. I've included several examples thus far showing how advertisers exploit children's developmental vulnerabilities. Here are a few more.

In an advice column published on his company's web site for advertisers who target children, Dave Siegel, president of the marketing agency WonderGroup, describes four- to seven-year-olds as "still operating on a relatively simple level," and notes that they "have yet to learn the memory aids of their older counterparts and tend to remember events in story form." He suggests that "use of repetition and likeable, recognizable characters will help the brand be remembered when kids hit the stores with their parents. Messages to this age group do not have to be rational as long as they contain a story strongly linked to the product so it is remembered." Siegel suggests that, since eleven- and twelve-year-olds are reaching puberty, marketers should "emphasize the social benefits of the product, particularly the ability to help the user interact with the opposite sex."[2] In a different marketing newsletter, Rachel Geller from the Geppetto Group points out that "teens use products and brands as tools to lower their anxiety, especially around the prom." She asks, "How can your brand help?"[3]

Another CARU principle suggests that while "many influences affect a child's personal and social development, it remains the prime responsibility of the parents to provide guidance for children. Advertisers should contribute to this parent-child relationship in a constructive manner." At least two chapters in this book point to the ways that advertisers deliberately undermine parent/child relationships both by encouraging children to nag and by portraying parents and adults as either absent or incompetent.

Advertisers are told not to exploit unfairly the imaginative quality of children. Yet isn't using a clown, or a talking bird, or any cartoon character to promote unhealthy food doing exactly that?

Aside from these specifics, there are some major problems with relying on industry self-regulation to market responsibly to children. The first is that once it goes beyond providing factual information about a product (what it is and where it can be purchased), advertising is inherently exploitive. Andrew Tuck, co-founder of Applied Research and Consulting, a consulting firm specializing in psychologically based market research with children and adults whose clients have included Channel One and the WWE, explains his work this way: "We try to understand what drives people's anxieties and aspirations—that's what influences their buying habits."[4]

As history has shown repeatedly, it's been government regulation, not self-regulation, that causes industries to curb exploitive practices such as child labor, sweat shops, and the dumping of toxic waste.

Finally, marketing to children is a huge industry. It's true that some people could lose their jobs if marketing to children is made illegal. I believe that we should worry about their potential unemployment in the same way that we should worry about the unemployment of people who have been "downsized" or lost jobs to the advent of automation and new technologies or because of the economy. We need to make more effort toward providing job retraining and support for people who lose their jobs as a result of forces beyond their control.

Marketing to children is a societal problem that cannot be fixed by one individual, or even one individual advocacy group, working alone. Its solution lies in collaborative efforts to influence public policy, similar to efforts that led to movements to gain rights for racial and ethnic minorities, women, laborers, and to protect the environment. It's not just that we need such a movement to protect children from commercial exploitation; such a movement already exists. It is a movement in its infancy, but it's growing.

Of course, no two movements are exactly alike, and this one differs from the others in several respects. Children, unlike the people who formed the core of the movements listed earlier, cannot advocate for themselves. Unlike the civil rights movement in the 1960s, which was able to use television to its advantage, commercial media companies have financial interests that could render them less sympathetic to concerns about marketing to children. Last but not least, all those other movements had better songs.

This movement has the potential to attract people with a wide range of interests and concerns who might not otherwise work together. Ralph Nader, Arianna Huffington, Hillary Clinton, and Phyllis Schlafly—who as a group probably don't agree on much—have all publicly taken stands against at least some aspect of marketing to children.

The word "movement" might be off-putting for some people, so let me explain what I mean. In this country, changes in policy that benefit people who have no political power (like children) generally occur when people start getting angry enough to take action. When enough people get angry they begin to find each other. They form an alliance (usually after a lot of power struggles, and endless disagreement about strategy and tactics), and begin working together for change. They raise public awareness. They look to academic disciplines such as sociology and psychology to build their case with data. They exercise their constitutional rights to assemble and to petition. They begin working through the courts.

My understanding is that that people in movements do not always speak in one voice. It's hard to reach consensus about which basket everyone involved should put their eggs in. There are loud voices asserting that there is one and only one way to approach the problem. We should only pressure corporations directly. We should litigate. We need to energize the grass roots. We should only be working on the Hill (Capitol Hill). We can't talk about a ban because we will alienate people in power. We should concentrate on schools. We should concentrate on food. We should concentrate on violence. We shouldn't bother talking about play because it's so hard to explain why it's important.

At the same time, once the powers-that-be—in this instance, corporations—recognize that a movement is beginning to form, they begin a reactive kind of dance. Initially, they may attempt to ignore the commotion. They may try to discredit or otherwise harm people challenging the status quo. They use their considerable financial resources to influence people in the government or to establish barriers and distractions. As a movement gains momentum, they may try to co-opt those who are co-optable through grants, sponsorships, and other financial incentives. They may try to mitigate their growing public relations problems, and avoid regulation, by setting up systems for self-monitoring.

Movements have phases. The civil rights movement, for instance, did not begin with *Brown* versus *the Board of Education* or the Montgomery bus boycott. Those successes were made possible by lessons learned from scores of other wins and losses years before.

The movement to stop the commercial exploitation of childhood is in its infancy. It stands on the shoulders of work done by individuals and individual organizations for years. The few regulations this country has in place to protect children from marketing are the result of work done in the 1960s, 1970s, 1980s, and the early part of the 1990s by a loose coalition of researchers, policy makers, and advocacy groups, such as Action for Children's Television, and in later years, the Center for Media Education. In those days, the National PTA—largely through the efforts Arnold Fege, who was its director of governmental relations at the time—worked closely with advocacy groups to regulate marketing to children. After leaving the organization, Fege has continued to speak out, especially on issues related to commercialism in schools. In an unfortunate sign of the times, however, the PTA began accepting corporate sponsorships from companies like Office Depot[5] and, most recently, Coca-Cola. In the last fifteen years of the twentieth century, as advertising to children began to escalate in earnest, individual outrage began to escalate as well. By the 1990s, the public health community began making an organized effort to do something about marketing violence to children. Professional organizations such as the American Academy of Pediatrics began to issue policy statements about advertising directed at children. In California, the Center for Commercial-Free Public Education was helping people all over the country work to stop commercialism in the schools. In 1990, the Children's Television Act was passed. The Center for Media Education, looking forward to the impact of new media on children, began focusing its attention on marketing to children over the Internet and spearheaded the Children's Online Privacy Protection Act. Commercial Alert began to use the Internet effectively as a tool for advocacy on behalf of children and families affected by commercialism. Dads and Daughters began mobilizing fathers to stop corporations from exploiting their daughters.

At the same time, Enola Aird formed The Motherhood Project to organize mothers to protect children from manipulation by commercial interests. In Alabama, Jim Metrock formed Obligation, Inc., and began fighting Channel One. The Alliance for Childhood was formed to counter environmental factors, including marketing, that affect children's healthy growth and development. Other groups such as the National Center of Media and the Family, Teachers Resisting Unhealthy Children's Entertainment (TRUCE), the Media Center at Judge Baker Children's Center, and the Center for the New American Dream began raising awareness about how commercialism was disrupting the lives of children and families.

Meanwhile, books, monographs, and articles were being published that began to raise public awareness. *Abandoned in the Wasteland, Selling Out America's Kids, Remote Control Childhood?, Deadly Persuasion,* and *Giving Kids the Business* are just some of the publications written in the 1990s that illustrate the various ways marketing has a negative impact on children and families. There was a lot of important activity on behalf of children in the marketplace, but it wasn't yet a movement.

That changed in the fall of 1999. The previous spring, Drs. Velma La-Point and Priscilla Hambrick-Dixon, at Howard University and Hunter College respectively, discovered that they were both interested in different aspects of the same issue—the impact of corporations on children's lives. With a $5,000 faculty grant from Howard, they decided to hold a small, interdisciplinary study group, including researchers and activists, to look at the problem. What was different about their approach is the way that they were framing the problem. It was not just about violence, or food, or toys, or clothes. They wanted to look at the whole of children's lives as they are affected by corporations.

In the course of finding participants, they contacted Gary Ruskin, the director of Commercial Alert, who immediately put a notice up on Commercial Alert's web site and sent out e-mail notices the organization's growing constituency. Suddenly, they were flooded with calls from all over the country from people who wanted to attend. The study group expanded into a full-fledged conference, bringing together academics, researchers, practitioners, parents, and activists representing a wide spectrum of interests, religions, and political affiliations. Conference speakers included Green Party member Ralph Nader; the senior senator from Kansas, Republican Sam Brownback; and Dr. Donald Vereen, from the Clinton administration's White House Office of National Drug Control Policy.

For me, and I suspect for others attending, the conference was a turning point. It was a great relief to discover that my growing concern about children and commercialism was shared by so many people. After listening to speakers whose expertise ranged from the impact of marketing in schools to the impact of marketing clothes on children, I began to understand that the problem was so much worse than I even knew.

Before the conference, Alvin Poussaint and I had already been writing about *Teletubbies* and other issues related to media and children. Upon my return, I continued to write other articles about marketing to children. It was in the course of researching those pieces that I happened upon the Golden Marble Awards. "The what?" you might ask. The Golden Marble Awards were, until this year, the advertising industry's celebration of marketing to children.

It was hard for me to believe that people were getting awards for doing a good job of manipulating children for profit. When I mentioned the awards to a variety of colleagues and friends, most of them responded with the same gasp of horrified disbelief. Even people who believed that efforts to stop marketing to children were useless experienced a sense of outrage that the phenomenon was actually being celebrated.

After hearing enough shocked responses, I began to think that the awards might be a good focus for raising public awareness about marketing to children. The Golden Marble Awards were given each year at a marketing conference called Advertising and Promoting to Kids—the same one I described in chapter 1—being held that year at the Grand Hyatt Hotel right in the middle of New York City. Diane Levin, Alvin Poussaint, and I decided that the three of us would hold a kind of mini-protest. We'd stand in front of the Grand Hyatt with signs. We figured we'd contact a few colleagues, send out a press release, and in some small way express our outrage and call public attention to what marketers were doing to children. We also sent a letter to all of the people who attended the conference at Howard asking if they wanted to join us. It turned out that several of them did. One of the first to call was Jim Metrock, the Alabama businessman who was (and still is) devoting himself to eradicating Channel One from the schools. In a wonderful Southern drawl, he said, "Dr. Linn, ah'm thinkin' of joinin' your demonstration." "That's fabulous," I replied sincerely, "Call me Susan." There was a brief pause. "Ah've never been in a demonstration before," he confided. There was a longer pause and then he continued, "Are we gonna get arrested?"

Calls began to pour in. Someone suggested that we get in touch with a young activist named Carrie McLaren who puts out a magazine called *Stay Free!*. Two years before, she had staged her own Golden Marble protest. With her help, and help from others, we were able to gather an impressive group of professionals, parents, and activists, all of whom had been working in their own ways to do something about marketing to children. Meeting briefly at Hunter College after the protest, we decided to form a coalition and expand our efforts the following year to use the Golden Marble Awards as a platform for raising public awareness about the harms of marketing to children. We decided to call our coalition Stop Commercial Exploitation of Children.

In 2001, building on contacts made the year before, we began working with other professionals as well as advocacy groups around the country. We rented a room in the Grand Hyatt, just like APK, and decided to hold a counter-conference. While marketers were in one section of the hotel educating attendees about advertising techniques designed to sell all sorts of things to kids, a coalition of health care professionals, parents, students, educators, and activists were down the hall describing the harms those techniques cause children.

With guidance from the activist groups represented on our steering committee (Dads and Daughters and the Center for Commercial-Free Public Education), SCEC initiated a grassroots effort to persuade Scholastic, Inc., the premiere youth publishing company, to withdraw sponsorship from APK and the Golden Marble Awards. A few weeks after the campaign began, Scholastic withdrew its support from the awards.

In 2002, when the Golden Marble Awards and the APK conference moved to a private venue (the Yale Club of New York), SCEC's counter-conference moved there as well. A week later, the British medical journal *Lancet*'s lead editorial, titled "Selling—and Selling Out—Children," had this to say: "Last week a couple of strange bedfellows met under the same roof in New York City. *KidScreen's* fifth annual conference on Advertising and Promoting to Kids took place on one floor of the Yale Club, while on another floor . . . Stop Commercial Exploitation of Children (SCEC) called attention to the effects of marketing and advertising on children's health."

Drawing from the presentations at the SCEC conference, the editorial asked, "What can be done about this truly toxic state of affairs? Some solutions are obvious: nutrition professionals need to divorce themselves from the food industry, or at least declare with whom they are working. Parents need to wake up and smell the chip[6] fat: fast-food chains are not educational institutions, no matter how many math and reading flash cards they hand out. More radical solutions should be considered: taxing soft drinks and fast foods; subsidizing nutritious foods, like fruits and vegetables; labeling the content of fast food; and prohibiting marketing and advertising to children. An advertising ban similar to that on tobacco advertising has

been recommended to the European Union. In the United States, litigation inspired by the success of the tobacco lawsuits is underway; parallels
between the tactics of the tobacco and food industries are striking."[7] Stories in international venues including the *International Herald Tribune*
and *Vatican Radio* followed.

In 2003, after three years of protests, Brunico decided not to hold the
Advertising and Promoting to Kids conference and did not present the
Golden Marble Awards.[8] SCEC declared victory.

I'm writing about SCEC because it's the aspect of this effort I know the
best, but our coalition is by no means the only evidence that a movement is
growing. Media literacy activists are organizing as well.

There is a lot of debate about the definition of media literacy. For our
purposes, it is the recognition that being able to think critically about the
images and information presented by media requires a set of learned skills.
Such skills are essential to functioning in the modern world. Media literacy
is relevant to any discussion about marketing to children because it is often
argued that teaching children media literacy skills is the solution to protecting them from marketplace manipulation. That argument, which
places the onus for protecting children on parents, teachers, and children
themselves, is one beloved by marketing experts for obvious reasons. It lets
them off the hook.

It's important to provide children with whatever tools they are developmentally capable of using to defend against marketing. In doing so, we have
to recognize that there are limitations. If, for instance, children under the age
of about eight do not have the cognitive structures in place to grasp persuasive intent, it is hard to see how we can educate them to resist it. Media literacy can lead older kids to skepticism about advertising, but it's not clear that
skepticism necessarily leads to changes in purchasing behavior.

On a radio program recently, an intelligent, honest and self-aware
thirteen-year-old girl talked about how she knows that advertising is manipulative. She described how deodorant companies, in order to sell deodorant, try to convince people that they smell in order to buy deodorant.
Then she laughed a little. "Of course, I'm wearing deodorant," she said.
When asked about logos on clothes, she said that she didn't buy clothing
with logos. She laughed again, "Of course, my hat has a logo." She went on
to explain that it was from a skateboard company called "Zoo York" that
was definitely "not cool" in any traditional sense. Her companion on the

program, an equally intelligent and self-aware thirteen-year-old boy, agreed and elaborated, explaining that they don't even advertise on television.

Two years ago, in *Sports Illustrated for Women*, the owner of a skateboard company commented "[Skateboarding] is pretty huge these days. I'd say probably 4 out of 5 young people are somehow affiliated with skateboarding—wearing the gear or riding."[9] According to the co-founder of Zoo York, "Style is a huge part of skateboarding, both in performance and in the way a kid is dressed."[10] Zoo York, which sponsors several top skateboarders, got into apparel a few years ago.[11] Described as a "cult brand" in the publication *Marketing*, Zoo York puts out a denim jacket with a do-it-yourself stencil created by a New York City graffiti artist. It's positioning itself as a brand appealing to creative kids who think of themselves as out of the mainstream—just like the girl wearing their logo on that radio program.

Those two kids are about as media literate as they come. They were doing a great job of resisting advertising, except where they were vulnerable. In this instance their vulnerability was around positive impulses to challenge conformity. How can we expect a thirteen-year-old girl—at the developmentally appropriate height of self-consciousness about her body—to resist deodorant commercials telling her that she smells bad? Isn't it too much to expect thirteen-year-olds, in the midst of an equally developmentally appropriate search for identity, to resist marketing that's carefully designed to convince them that buying a particular brand is a nonconformist act?

In October 2002, the founding meeting of Action Coalition for Media Education took place in New Mexico. ACME grew out of concerns from scholars, educators, and activists about corporate sponsorship of the Alliance for a Media Literate America. Over the years, AMLA's sponsors have included Time Warner, Sesame Workshop, and Discovery Communications Inc. Both Channel One and Turner Broadcasting have sponsored national media literacy conferences. With big money coming from big media corporations, it's easy to imagine that it would be tempting to limit the definition of media literacy to what can be done to help people decode media images.

Believing that the consolidation of corporate ownership of media is a profound threat to democracy, and concerned that corporate sponsorship of AMLA was a threat to free exchange of ideas, the founders of ACME left

AMLA to form a coalition designed not just to educate but to facilitate advocacy and activism around media issues, including the threats to freedom of expression posed by deregulation.

At the same time, the obesity epidemic is prompting public health lawyers, including those who were instrumental in the lawsuits against big tobacco companies, to turn their attention to the food industry's contribution to the problem. At the first annual meeting of a conference called Legal Approaches to the Obesity Epidemic, the consensus was that the food industry is most vulnerable around marketing to children. The same major foundations that have funded research about the impact of tobacco and alcohol advertising on children are beginning to turn their attention to food marketing.

Coalitions are being formed to deal with marketing-related concerns besides obesity, such as eating disorders and violence. The American Psychological Association and the American Academy of Pediatrics have each appointed a task force to address concerns about marketing to children. Media interest is certainly growing. In the past year major news programs such as *60 Minutes, 20/20, World News Tonight* and *Now with Bill Moyers,* just to name a few, have all done stories about children and marketing. High school students have protested the escalating corporate presence in their schools. Some refuse to wear logos. Others are creating art and theater pieces based on themes of anticommercialism.[12] Things are happening—or rather, people working together are making things happen.

As for concrete suggestions about what we as individuals can do about it, I'm going to begin with ideas for parents. I cannot stress enough that our efforts alone, within the confines of our individual families, will not suffice. Yes, we need to talk with our kids. Yes, we need to teach media literacy skills. Yes, we need to say "no" more often. Yes, we need to teach our children to look critically at media messages. But whatever we do alone won't be enough. Therefore, I'm also going to include suggestions for educators, health care professionals, advocacy groups, foundations, concerned citizens, and policy makers.

WHAT PARENTS CAN DO AT HOME

- Before we can help children deal with their vulnerability to advertising and marketing, we have to understand our own. In the process, we need to look honestly at what matters to us. If our values are primarily materialistic, it's likely that our children's values will be materialistic as well. The more we understand and try to change our own consumption patterns, including tendencies to overspend or to turn to products for gratification, the better our position for helping children cope.

- We need to find ways for children to spend time away from advertising. Depending on our inclinations and opportunities, we can spend more time with them in nature, doing art projects, in community service, working for social causes, and/or in churches, mosques, synagogues, or other religious venues. We can read to our kids, or play cards or board games with them. We can cook together. We can make music or do art projects as a family. We can get in the habit of doing things together that do not involve media.

- Talk to children about advertising, including product placement, as they encounter it. While young children can't fully grasp the purpose of advertising, they will begin to pick up your attitudes about it.

- Before trips to the grocery store, prepare kids ahead of time about what purchases you will and won't be making. It's easier to set limits when you can say, "Remember, we already talked about what cereals and snacks we were going to buy."

- Most holidays that involve gift giving are rooted in spiritual or cultural traditions that can often get lost for children in a deluge of presents. Find ways to help children find meaning in celebration that extends beyond the commercial.

- Participate in national events such as TV Turn Off week and Buy Nothing Day.

HOW PARENTS CAN LIMIT TELEVISION AND WHY IT'S IMPORTANT

In spite of the growing popularity of computers, television is still the primary and most effective means advertisers have for reaching children. Setting limits on television is the single most effective thing we can do to reduce children's exposure to advertising. In the short run, it's easier to plop young kids in front of the tube. But it is a choice that comes at a cost.

Television is primarily a tool for marketing. The more children watch it, the more they are being barraged by marketing messages, including those that are encouraging them to nag.

- The easiest way to limit television viewing is to remove them from children's bedrooms or refrain from putting them in. Having to share television time with other family members may lead to conflicts, but it can also help children learn important skills such as negotiation, cooperation, and compromise.
- We can limit television by limiting the number of hours children are allowed to watch. These rules are easier to enforce if they are in place from the time children are little, but they can be instituted when children are older as well.
- We can limit exposure to advertising by cutting down on the number of televisions we have in our homes. It's more likely that a family will have five televisions than it is that they will have just one. Do we need five television sets? Do we need more than one?[13]
- Keeping television off during meals not only cuts down on exposure to advertising, but gives us another opportunity for spending commercial-free time with our kids.
- Parents of babies and very young children can heed the American Academy of Pediatrics' suggestion that children under two be kept away from screens as much as possible. What children do learn from watching television—and from watching you watch television—is to turn to a screen for pleasure and stimulation. Don't be sucked in by video or computer toys for young children that claim to raise their IQ or make them smarter. They don't.
- When TV serves as background noise while children play, it actually interferes with their concentration in a way that may have negative effects on their developing intelligence. If you like watching TV, try videotaping programs and watching them when your kids are taking a nap or after they go to bed at night.
- If possible (and this is easier for two-parent families and those who can afford babysitters) avoid taking your young children with you when you shop at mega toy stores such as Toys "R" Us. These trips can be a nightmare for young children who have trouble with im-

pulse control and can't readily understand why you aren't buying them the things they want.

- Children are also targets for marketing in computer and video games as well as on the Internet. For that reason, we can keep computers out of their bedrooms as well. If a quiet place is available for homework, there is no reason for kids to have a computer in their rooms.

WHAT PARENTS CAN DO IN THE COMMUNITY

As children grow, they begin to make friends and get invited, independent of you, to other people's homes. They are suddenly exposed to different sets of values and rules, including rules about media, that might be quite different from your own. "But everyone else has one," becomes a common complaint. Once this happens, limiting children's exposure to marketing becomes much more difficult.

- Begin sharing your concerns about advertising to children with other parents. This has the benefit of finding allies among the parents of your children's friends and finding out ahead of time what your children might encounter at someone else's house. If you can find neighbors and other parents who share at least some of your feelings about commercialism, you might be able to get in the habit of setting rules together about the amount and kinds of media your kids will consume while they are together. It's easier for groups of parents, or even a few parents, to set certain kinds of limits than it is to do it alone.
- If your family belongs to a religious organization, find out what the clergy, the board, and the religious school head are doing about commercialism in the lives of children. Try to interest them in addressing commercialism on a regular basis and in a variety of ways. These could include workshops for kids as well as lectures or workshops for adults on a variety of topics—from marketing violence to marketing values.
- If you belong to a book group, select books for discussion that will educate you about the impact of marketing on the lives of children and families. *Rich Media, Poor Democracy; Deadly Persuasion; No Logo;* and *The High Cost of Materialism* address commercialism from a variety of points of view.

WHAT PARENTS CAN DO IN SCHOOLS

Many people believe that schools are the most effective arena for fighting commercialism in children's lives, not just because there is a prevailing philosophy that schools should be for the purpose of education, not marketing, but because they also provide a great platform for activism and advocacy. The Center for Commercial-Free Public Education, which closed for lack of funding, did a wonderful job of helping parents successfully challenge commercial intrusions in their children's schools. Other grassroots groups, such as the Citizens for Commercial-Free Schools in Seattle, have been doing a great job of fighting this problem on a local level.

- Take a long hard look at the kind of marketing going on in your local school. Are there pouring contracts with Coca-Cola or Pepsi? Does your school have Channel One? Are your teachers using other corporate-sponsored materials? Is the administration handing out ad-saturated daily planners? In recent years, grassroots efforts initiated by parents and parent groups have resulted in schools and school districts that refuse to enter into pouring contracts or refuse to renew them, schools banning soda entirely, and schools getting rid of Channel One. These battles are most readily won by building a base of support. Try to find parents, teachers, principals, and school board members who are sympathetic and will work with you.

- Parents, teachers, and administrators can use PTA meetings as a time to educate others about marketing. Several excellent videos are available, including *The Merchants of Cool,* the PBS *Frontline* program about marketing on MTV; *Wrestling with Manhood,* about the WWE; and *Captive Audience,* about marketing in schools, both of which were produced by the Media Education Foundation.

- Find out what laws are on the books or being considered that affect marketing in schools (including on school buses) and work with existing coalitions that are challenging those laws. Start your own coalition if none exists.

- Run for the school board and/or support local and state candidates who are working to stop marketing in schools. Work with the public health community in your town, county, or state to prevent passage of laws that would ease restrictions or laws that have already been passed that might need to be changed.

WHAT PARENTS CAN DO IN THE MARKETPLACE

In recent years, parents have been able to convince corporations to remove specific products from their shelves. Diane Samples, a mother and media activist in Connecticut, was shocked to find a Budweiser slogan emblazoned on clothes in the children's department of JC Penney. After she contacted the media, JC Penney removed the clothing.[14] Parents successfully got Abercrombie and Fitch to stop marketing thong underwear to ten-year-olds.[15] Last Easter, as a result of protests, Kmart and other national chain stores pulled Easter baskets containing machine-gun-toting soldiers and hand grenades off their shelves.[16] Whether or not you accomplish your immediate goal of getting a company to stop marketing a product, your actions can inspire other people to act as well.

- Last Christmas, a toy called *The Forward Command Post* depicting a bombed-out house caused a flurry of protest. They were removed from JC Penney and other stores.[17] If something concerns you, contact an advocacy group by phone or e-mail and see if they can help you mount a protest.

- Begin working with existing advocacy groups on an ongoing basis. Appendix 1 contains a list of groups who focus on a variety of issues relating to children and commercialism. Many offer opportunities for taking direct action to express your views either to corporations or to the government. Sometimes even the threat of on organized consumer protest is enough. Joe Kelly, the former director of Dads and Daughters, describes his shock when he wrote a letter to the head of Campbell's Soup to complain about a commercial showing preteen girls on a diet. A few days later he heard back from the CEO saying that the commercial had been pulled.

- Write letters to the editors of local and national newspapers and op-ed pieces that take a stand against commercialism as it harms children.

- Work for candidates at a city, state, and local level who support limiting the amount of marketing that reaches children.
- If you allocate some of your income for charitable donations, find an
  advocacy group whose mission matches your concerns and write
  them a check. Most of these organizations run on tight budgets and
  even a small donation can make a difference. Depending on the issues they address, many are not likely to be receiving corporate donations. Contributions from individuals and private foundations
  are their only source of funding.

WHAT FOUNDATIONS THAT CARE ABOUT CHILDREN AND FAMILIES CAN DO

Private foundations can make a significant difference in protecting children from commercial exploitation. If your organization focuses on children's health, education, or general well-being, it's likely that your work is
being undermined by marketing to kids. The same is true if you care about
the environment, or promoting civic involvement, or preventing family
stress.

- Fund research. My colleagues in academia say that the reason they
  have stopped conducting research on marketing to children is because they can't get funding for it. Corporations won't fund it, and
  at this point, neither does the government. The research that was
  done on tobacco marketing played a significant role in regulating tobacco marketing aimed at children. It would be helpful to replicate
  some of that research in other areas of concern. It would be particularly helpful to fund research that looks at children's responses to
  specific marketing techniques, rather than looking just at marketing
  violence, alcohol, tobacco, or food, for instance. The research that
  does exist focuses on those issues. As a result, it's easy to ignore the
  underlying relationship between marketing and various public
  health problems.
- Fund advocacy, including newsletters, books, and other publications about this issue. There are organizations around the country
  doing an extremely effective job of educating the public, raising
  public awareness, and organizing grassroots efforts that will eventu-

ally have an impact on policy. Most of them are struggling for support. They need your help. I've listed the organizations with whose work I am familiar in an appendix.

WHAT PROFESSIONALS WHO WORK WITH CHILDREN AND
FAMILIES CAN DO

- Think about children's exposure to marketing as a factor in health problems ranging from obesity to family stress. The American Academy of Pediatrics suggests doing a media screening to get a sense of how much time children spend with media, and what kind of media they are consuming. Encourage parents to limit children's exposure to commercial media and urge them to keep television out of their children's rooms.

- Professional organizations such as the American Psychological Association, or the American Academy of Child and Adolescent Psychiatry can be good advocates for children. Large organizations can be bureaucratic and slow to take action, but they have a good deal of clout. Work within your professional organization to develop a policy on marketing to children, including one that can be used as a means of affecting national policy. Putting issues about commercialism on the agenda at national professional conferences is good way to raise awareness among your colleagues and to find allies who share your concerns.

- Some professionals find it more effective to work outside of professional organizations. While psychologists and nutritionists, for instance, have been at the forefront of efforts to end or at least regulate advertising to children, some members of both these professions earn their living working for or consulting to companies who market to kids. You may decide to work with activists to try to hold your profession accountable for its contribution to escalating commercialism in children's lives. A letter to the American Psychological Association signed by sixty psychologists working with Commercial Alert served as an impetus for the organization to appoint a task force on advertising to children, most likely because it garnered a great deal of media attention.

- Work to prevent corporate sponsorship of, or corporate partnerships with, your professional organization if they create a conflict of interest for working on behalf of children. Coca-Cola's current sponsorship of the PTA[18] is an example. It's clearly beneficial for Coke in that it undermines the ability of local parent teacher associations to convince school boards not to sign soft drink contracts. It is also likely to insure that the PTA will not participate in any efforts to effect any government policies that might hinder the Coca-Cola company's ability to market in schools—Coca-Cola's million-dollar research grant to the American Academy of Pediatric Dentistry is equally questionable.[19]

- Collaborate across disciplines. Write papers not just for professional journals but for newspapers and magazines as well. Kelly Brownell, a psychologist from Yale, and David Ludwig, a pediatrician at Boston Children's Hospital, have written several op ed pieces together raising concerns about food marketing and childhood obesity.

- Collaborate with activists. Your work can inform theirs and vice versa. The steering committee of SCEC consists of activists as well as psychologists, educators, a lawyer, a nutritionist, and a former advertising executive. We each contribute a different kind of expertise.

WHAT MEMBERS OF THE CLERGY CAN DO

The messages embedded in marketing to children undermine most mainstream religious values. Yet at least in public dialogue, it is the religious right that speaks out most often about marketing to children as a threat to religious teaching, mostly focusing on precocious sexuality. The mainstream clergy has a significant role to play in ending children's exploitation by marketers. By speaking out publicly about the messages embedded in marketing to children, such as consumerism, "me-first"-ism, the notion that adults are idiots, and the premise that things can make us happy, you can help reclaim values from extremist groups.

- Begin to incorporate education about commercial media and marketing into discussions among adults and children in your congregation. You can educate your congregants about the impact of marketing to children, especially by helping them take a close look at the values promoted in child-targeted marketing that are counter to your religion's teachings.

• National religious organizations and coalitions are in a wonderful position to facilitate grassroots efforts that address marketing to children, to raise public awareness, and to influence policy.

WHAT POLICY MAKERS CAN DO

There's no way of getting around the fact that government policies, or the lack of them, have contributed to the fact that we are raising children in the middle of a marketing maelstrom aimed directly at them. Policies created and policies defeated by both Democrats and Republicans have enabled marketers to target children, as have policies endorsed and condemned by the extreme right and left. Politically, this issue cuts in funny ways.

Marketing to children assaults the sanctity of the family, undermines family and religious values, and targets children with ads for provocative clothing and sexually explicit media—issues traditionally associated with conservatives. If you really care about these, do something about marketing to children.

Marketing to children undermines democratic values by encouraging passivity, conformity, and selfishness, threatens the quality of public education, inhibits free expression, and contributes to public health problems such as childhood obesity, tobacco addiction, and underage drinking— issues traditionally associated with liberals. If you really care about these, do something about marketing to children.

Some issues associated with marketing to children—violence, for example—are often characterized as bipartisan concerns. If you care about violence, do something about marketing to children.

In order to stop marketing's assault on family and religious values, the Right is going to have to bite the bullet and support government regulation of corporations. In order to stop marketing's assault on democratic values and its contribution to major public health problems, the Left is going to have to rethink its definition of free speech as it applies to child-targeted advertising.

We should stop marketing to children. Short of that, there are lots of policies we could put in place that would significantly reduce the amount of advertising to which children are exposed each day. At first glance, some of these may look to be unrelated to advertising, but they are not.

Support . . .

- **Campaign finance reform:** When the FTC attempted to ban marketing to children under eight, Congress responded to pressure from corporate interests and took away the agency's power to regulate advertising to children. If you care about children's exposure to violence, precocious sexuality, fast food, or messages that undermine family values, you should support campaign finance reform.

- **Adequately funded public schools:** Schools should be commercial-free zones. Adequate funding would reduce the pressure school boards feel to enter into contracts with beverage companies and would limit the amount of soda children are encouraged to buy. In addition, schools would not feel pressured to bring Channel One or other corporate-sponsored programs and materials into the classroom. This would not only reduce the amount of advertising in children's lives, it would provide more assurance that the materials from which children learn lessons are subject to community review and reflect community standards.

- **Adequately funded after-school programs:** After-school programs provide kids with after-school prosocial activities away from commercial media, reducing the amount of advertising to which they are exposed.

Some policies address commercialism and children directly.

Support . . .

- **Adequately funded public media, including television, radio, and Internet sites for children.** A fully funded public media system would provide programming to promote prosocial behavior and enable public television to create programs for children that are not funded through product licensing, food advertising, and promotions. Even if the rest of television remains commercialized, public television would provide a truly commercial-free alternative for children and families. There are several interesting proposals for how to do this. Here are three of my favorites: (1) Tax corporations for advertising to children and use the money to fund public media for children. (2) Begin charging a fee to corporations for their use of the public's digital broadcasting span. Money from fees could go to support commercial-free broadcasting. (3) Require that at least one of the child channels leased by each media company be commercial-free.

- **Re-regulation of children's television:** Returning to the regulation of children's television as it existed before 1984 would prohibit companies from creating children's programs for the purpose of selling toys and other products. Since many of the de facto program-length commercials in existence today are centered around violence and violent toys, this could have a significant effect on the amount of violence to which young children are exposed.

- **Rating systems that are consistent across media and extend to the products licensed by media programs:** Toys, clothing, and accessories should carry the same rating as the programs they advertise.

Other Policy Recommendations

- **As recommended by the American Medical Association, limit televised alcohol ads to after ten o'clock at night.** Programs that feature actors smoking cigarettes or consuming alcohol should be rated R.

- **Regulate market research conducted with and about children in the same manner that academic research is regulated.** Any research conducted in an academic institution, even if it is privately funded, is subject to review by a committee to ensure that research subjects are adequately informed of the nature of the research and its potential harms. The government was able to regulate research in academia because most academic institutions receive government funding. However, many advertising agencies and corporations do have government contracts. It could be argued that their research could be regulated as well.

- **When used to enhance marketing to children, the following advertising strategies should be made illegal:**
  - Product placement in television programs, web sites, videos, and movies that target children.

- Viral marketing in the form of marketing that involves hiring or bribing minors to sell or promote products to other children.
- Viral marketing in the form of hiring people to enter on-line chat rooms unidentified for the purpose of promoting a product.
- Marketing to children that encourages them to disrespect adults.
- Program-length commercials.

LET'S BAN MARKETING TO CHILDREN.

If we agree that it needs to be eliminated, we can begin to quibble about the age at which that ban should take place. In her campaign for the U.S. Senate, Senator Hillary Clinton recommended that marketing should be banned to children under five. That is the age when children begin to understand the difference between a commercial and a television program. Before it was stripped of its power to regulate children's television, the FTC recommended a ban on advertising to children eight and under. That's the age at which children begin to get a firm grasp that the intent of commercials, and every decision made within that commercial, is to persuade them to buy something. Commercial Alert, in its Parents' Bill of Rights, includes a provision banning advertising to children twelve and under. As evident in COPPA, the Children's Online Privacy Protection Act, the law seems to recognize a distinction between teenagers and children.

As yet, no one is recommending that it be banned until the age of sixteen. But, *in the interests of children,* that's not unreasonable. The frontal cortex, which controls higher cognitive processes—including those that affect judgment—is not fully developed until the late teens.

Banning marketing to children may seem to be quite radical, but it really isn't. The United States regulates marketing to children less than most other industrial democracies. Sweden, Norway, and Finland ban marketing to children under age twelve. In Canada, the province of Quebec bans marketing to children under age thirteen. A proposal in the British House of Commons suggests banning marketing to preschool children.

Greece prohibits ads for toys between 7 A.M. and 10 P.M. Ads for toy guns and tanks are not allowed at any time. In the Flemish-speaking areas of Belgium, no advertising is allowed within five minutes of a children's television program shown on a local station.[20] New Zealand bans junk-food marketing to kids.[21] Advertising regulations proposed by the European Union would ban commercials suggesting that children's acceptance by peers is dependent on their use of a product.[22]

Advertising to children in this country is pervasive, expanding, unchecked, and unregulated. It harms children and undermines parents. It needs to be stopped. Children are so assaulted by marketing that it has reached a point where parents can no longer cope with it alone. In the process of being unprotected in the marketplace, children themselves are commodities sold as audiences to corporations.

Given the kinds of products marketed to children, as well as the intended and unintended messages embedded in advertising campaigns, people from all political and religious persuasions have a vested interest in helping families cope. Parents have a role to play. So do health care professionals, educators, businesses, legislators, and concerned citizens.

Let's stop marketing to children. It's not just that our kids are consuming. They are being consumed.

Appendix
Resources

Stop Commercial Exploitation of Children (SCEC)

www.commercialexploitation.org
Judge Baker Children's Center
3 Blackfan Circle
Boston, MA 02115
617-232-8390 x2303
Fax: 617-232-7343
scec@jbcc.harvard.edu
SCEC is a national coalition of health care professionals, educators, businesses, advocacy groups, parents, and concerned citizens working together to counter the commercial exploitation of children through action, advocacy, research, education, and collaboration.

Action Coalition for Media Education (ACME)

www.acmecoalition.org
505-828-3377
robw@acme.org
ACME is an independently funded international strategic network/membership coalition linking media educators, students, health advocates, researchers, media reformers, independent media makers, community organizers, and others working together to achieve three interrelated goals: critical media literacy education for classrooms and communities, independent media production, and media-related political reform.

Alliance for Childhood

www.allianceforchildhood.net
P.O. Box 44
College Park, MD 20741
301-779-1033
The Alliance for Childhood is a partnership of individuals and organizations committed to fostering and respecting each child's inherent right to a healthy, developmentally appropriate childhood.

American Academy of Child and Adolescent Psychiatry: The Television and Media Committee

www.aacap.org
3615 Wisconsin Avenue NW
Washington, DC 20016-3007
202-966-7300
Fax: 202-966-2891
AACAP is a professional organization of specialized physicians dedicated to promoting the mental health of children through education and advocacy.

American Academy of Pediatrics Committee on Public Education

www.aap.org/visit/cmte11.htm
141 Northwest Point Boulevard
Elk Grove Village, IL 60007
847-434-4000
Fax: 847-434-8000
The American Academy of Pediatrics is an organization of 57,000 primary care pediatricians, pediatric medical subspecialists, and pediatric surgical specialists dedicated to the health, safety, and well-being of infants, children, adolescents, and young adults. The AAP Committee on Public Education develops policy to educate pediatricians and the public about the impact of media on children and adolescents.

Association for Curriculum and Supervision Development (ACSD)

www.ascd.org
1703 N. Beauregard Street
Alexandria, VA 22311
800-933-2723
ASCD is a diverse, international community of educators, forging covenants in teaching and learning for the success of all learners.

Campaign for Tobacco Free Kids

www.tobaccofreekids.org
1400 Eye Street NW, Suite 1200
Washington, DC 20005
202-296-5469
Fax: 202-296-5427
The Campaign for Tobacco-Free Kids is fighting to free America's youth from tobacco and to create a healthier environment. The Campaign is one of the nation's largest non-governmental initiatives ever launched to protect children from tobacco addiction and exposure to secondhand smoke.

Canadians Concerned About Violence in Entertainment (C-CAVE)

www.c-cave.com
167 Glen Road
Toronto, Ontario
Canada, M4W 2W8
416-961-0853
Fax: 416-929-2720
C-CAVE provides public education on what the research on media violence shows. The organization believes the public has a right to know that the overwhelming weight of findings points toward harmful effects.

Center for Digital Democracy (CDD)

www.democraticmedia.org
1718 Connecticut Avenue NW, Suite 200
Washington, DC 20009
CDD is committed to preserving the openness and diversity of the Internet
in the broadband era, and to realizing the full potential of digital communications through the development and encouragement of noncommercial,
public-interest programming.

Center for the New American Dream

www.newdream.org
6930 Carroll Avenue, Suite 900
Takoma Park, MD, 20912
877-683-7326
Fax: 301-891-3684
The Center for the New American Dream helps Americans consume responsibly to protect the environment, enhance quality of life, and promote
economic justice. Working with individuals, institutions, communities,
and businesses to conserve natural resources, counter the commercialization of our culture, and promote positive changes in the way goods are produced and consumed.

Center for Science in the Public Interest (CSPI)

1875 Connecticut Avenue NW, Suite 300
Washington, DC 20009
202-332-9110
Fax: 202-265-4954
www.cspinet.org
CSPI is a consumer advocacy organization whose twin missions are to
conduct innovative research and advocacy programs in health and nutrition, and to provide consumers with current, useful information about
their health and well-being.

Children Now: Children and the Media Program

www.childrennow.org/media/
1212 Broadway, 5th Floor
Oakland, CA 94612
510-763-2444
Fax: 510-763-1974
The Children and the Media Program at Children Now works to improve the quality of news and entertainment media both for children and about children's issues, paying particular attention to media images of race, class, and gender. The program seeks to accomplish its goals through media industry outreach, independent research, and public policy development.

Citizens' Campaign for Commercial-Free Schools (CCCS)

www.scn.org/cccs
Seattle, Washington
CCCS opposes advertising and corporate marketing in Washington public schools. It is an all-volunteer, nonprofit organization focusing on research, education, lobbying, and direct action.

Commercial Alert

www.commercialalert.org
4110 SE Hawthorne Boulevard #123
Portland, OR 97214
503-235-8012
Fax: 503-235-5073
Commercial Alert's mission is to keep the commercial culture within its proper sphere, and to prevent it from exploiting children and subverting the higher values of family, community, environmental integrity and democracy.

Commercialism in Education Research Unit (CERU)

www.schoolcommercialism.org
P. O. Box 872411
Tempe, AZ 85287-2411
480-965-1886
Fax: 480-965-0303

CERU conducts research, disseminates information, and helps facilitate dialogue between the education community, policy makers, and the public at large about commercial activities in schools. Mixing commercial activities with public education, CERU raises fundamental issues of public policy, curriculum content, the proper relationship of educators to the students entrusted to them, and the values that the schools embody.

Common Sense Media

www.commonsensemedia.org
500 Treat Avenue #100
San Francisco, CA 94110
415-643-6300
Fax: 415-643-6310
info@commonsensemedia.org
Common Sense Media is a national membership organization of parents, educators, and kids who are concerned about the quality of today's media and its impact on children. It is a nonpartisan, nonprofit organization. Their mission is to give people a choice and a voice about the media they consume.

Concerned Educators Acting for a Safe Environment (CEASE)

www.peaceeducators.org
55 Frost Street
Cambridge, MA 02140
617-661-8347
CEASE is a network of parents, teachers, and other concerned individuals who are dedicated to creating a safe world for our children. It works to end the violence that permeates our society, to remove the root causes of this violence by advocating for peace, justice, and economic opportunity, and to redirect national priorities and funding from the military and corporate interests to human services and environmental opportunity.

Dads and Daughters

www.dadsanddaughters.org
34 E. Superior Street, Suite 200
Duluth, MN 55802
218-722-3942 or 888-824-DADS
Fax: 218-728-0314
Dads and Daughters is the national advocacy nonprofit for fathers and
daughters. DADs inspires fathers to actively and deeply engage in the lives
of their daughters and galvanizes fathers and others to transform the pervasive cultural messages that devalue girls and women.

Foundation for Taxpayer and Consumer Rights (FTCR)

www.consumerwatchdog.org
1750 Ocean Park Boulevard, Suite 200
Santa Monica, CA 90405
310-392-0522
Fax: 310-392-8874
FTCR combines legislative advocacy, litigation, and grassroots organizing
to protect the rights and pocketbooks of consumers and taxpayers.
FTCR's issue areas include health care reform, corporate accountability,
insurance reform, energy, privacy, and holding politicians accountable to
the public.

Free Press

www.mediareform.net
26 Center Street
Northampton, MA 01060
866-666-1533
Fax: 413-585-8904
info@mediareform.net
Free Press is a national organization working to increase informed public
participation in crucial media policy debates. The ultimate aim of Free
Press is to generate a range of policies that will produce a more competitive
and public interest–oriented media system with a strong nonprofit and
noncommercial sector.

Infact

www.infact.org
46 Plympton Street
Boston, MA 02118
617-695-2525
Fax: 617-695-2626
Since 1977, Infact has been exposing life-threatening abuses by transnational corporations and organizing successful grassroots campaigns to hold corporations accountable to consumers and society at large.

Judge Baker Children's Center

www.jbcc.harvard.edu
3 Blackfan Circle
Boston, MA 02115
617-232-8390 x2329
Fax: 617-232-7343
Judge Baker Children's Center is a nonprofit organization dedicated to improving the lives of children whose emotional and behavioral problems threaten to limit their potential. The center strives to provide services of the highest standard, to search for new knowledge, to teach, and to apply and disseminate knowledge to promote healthy development.

Kids Can Make a Difference

www.kidscanmakeadifference.org
1 Borodell Avenue
Mystic, CT 06355
860-245-3620
Fax: 860-245 3651
Kids Can Make a Difference is an innovative educational program for middle school and high school students. It helps them understand the root causes of hunger and poverty and how they—as individuals—can take action.

The Lion and Lamb Project

www.lionlamb.org
4300 Montgomery Avenue, Suite 104
Bethesda, MD 20814
301-654-3091
Fax: 301-654-2394
The mission of the Lion & Lamb Project is to stop the marketing of violence to children. They do this by helping parents, industry, and government officials recognize that violence is not child's play—and by galvanizing concerned adults to take action.

Media Education Foundation (MEF)

www.mediaed.org
60 Masonic Street
Northampton, MA 01060
800-897-0089
Fax: 800-659-6882
The Media Education Foundation is a nonprofit educational organization devoted to media research and production of resources to aid educators and others in fostering analytical media literacy.

Motherhood Project

www.watchoutforchildren.org
Institute for American Values
1841 Broadway, Suite 211
New York, NY 10023
212-246-3942
Fax: 212-541-6665
The mission of the Motherhood Project is to put the importance of mothering on the national agenda and to foster a renewed sense of purpose, passion, and power in the work of mothering in both the private and public spheres. A key goal of the Motherhood Project is to help mothers meet the challenges of raising children in an age increasingly driven by the values of commerce and technology.

National Institute for Media and the Family

www.mediafamily.org
606 24th Avenue South, Suite 606
Minneapolis, MN 55454
888-672-5437 or 612-672-5437
The National Institute on Media and the Family is a national resource for
research, education, and information about the impact of media on children and families.

New Mexico Media Literacy Project

www.nmmlp.org
6400 Wyoming Boulevard NE
Albuquerque, NM 87109
505-828-3129
Fax: 505-828-3142
An outreach project of the Albuquerque Academy, the New Mexico Media
Literacy Project has brought the media literacy message to hundreds of
thousands of children and adults across New Mexico and the nation.

New Moon Publishing

www.newmoon.org
34 E. Superior Street
Duluth, MN 55082
216-728-5507
Fax: 218-728-0316
New Moon: The Magazine for Girls and Their Dreams is the imaginative,
intelligent, and girl-created publication that brings girls' voices into the
public arena. New Moon is for every girl who wants her voice heard and
her dreams taken seriously. The Girls Editorial Board, comprised of 15
girls ages 8–14, makes all of the major decisions from content to layout for
the magazine.

Obligation, Inc.

www.obligation.org
3100 Lorna Road, Suite 311
Birmingham, AL 35216
205-822-0080
Fax: same as above
Obligation, Inc. is a media watchdog organization specializing in child advocacy with a focus on commercial-free schools.

Praxis Project

www.thepraxisproject.org
1750 Columbia Road NW, Second Floor
Washington, DC 20009
202-234-5921
Fax: 202-234-2689
The Praxis Project provides technical assistance, training, strategic consultation, and other kinds of support to advance community media and policy advocacy on health issues. The organization works with communities to identify solutions that shift individual blame to institutional and systemic approaches.

Stay Free!

www.stayfreemagazine.org
390 Butler Street, 3rd Floor
Brooklyn, NY 11217
718-398-9324
Stay Free! is a nonprofit print magazine focused on American media and consumer culture.

Slow Food USA

www.slowfoodusa.org
434 Broadway, 6th Floor
New York NY 10013
212-965-5640

Slow Food USA focuses on the food culture in schools. It works in support of school gardens and farm-to-cafeteria programs that bring to schools fresh, good-tasting organic foods produced with sustainable agriculture practices.

Teachers Resisting Unhealthy Children's Entertainment (TRUCE)

www.wheelock.edu/truce/truce.htm
TRUCE produces and provides an annual guide for teachers and parents to help them in selecting toys that are educationally and developmentally appropriate for young children.

TV-Turnoff Network

www.tvturnoff.org
1200 29th Street NW
Lower Level #1
Washington, DC 20007
202-333-9220
Fax: 202-333-9221
TV Turnoff Network is a national nonprofit group that encourages children and adults to watch much less television in order to promote healthier lives and communities. With an array of programs capped off by the annual national celebration of TV-Turnoff Week, TV-Turnoff Network has helped millions to turn off TV and turn on life.

Notes

INTRODUCTION

1. David Barboza, "If You Pitch It, They Will Eat," *New York Times*, 3 August 2003, sec. 3, p. 1.
2. Patricia Winters Lauro, "Coaxing the Smile that Sells: Baby Wranglers in Demand in Marketing for Children," *New York Times*, 1 November 1999, sec. C, p. 1.
3. Children ages five to fourteen directly influence $196 billion and indirectly influence over $400 billion in family spending annually. Reported in: Packaged Facts, *The Kids Market, March 2000* (New York: Kalorama Information, 1999), 7.
4. Karen Stabiner, "Get 'Em While They're Young; With Kid Flavors, Bright Colors and Commercials that Make Children Masters of Their Universe, Advertisers Build Brand Loyalty that Will Last a Lifetime," *Los Angeles Times Magazine*, 15 August 1993, 12.
5. Bob Garfield, "Top 100 Advertising Campaigns," *Advertising Age Special Issue: The Advertising Century*, 1999, 18 ff.
6. Charles K. Atkin, "Television Advertising and Socialization to Consumer Roles," in *Television and Behavior: Ten Years of Scientific Progress and Implications for the Eighties*, ed. David Pearl (Rockland, MD: National Institute of Mental Health, 1982), 191–200.
7. Diane Levin and Susan Linn, "The Commercialization of Childhood: Understanding the Problem and Finding Solutions," in *The Psychology of Consumerism*, eds. Tim Kasser and Allen Kanner (Washington, DC: American Psychological Association, 2004), 213–232.
8. Dale Kunkel, "Children and Television Advertising," in *The Handbook of Children and Media*, eds. Dorothy G. Singer and Jerome L. Singer (Thousand Oaks, CA: Sage, 2001), 375–393.
9. Rhonda Ross et al., "When Celebrities Talk, Children Listen: An Experimental Analysis of Children's Responses to TV Ads with Celebrity Endorsement," *Journal of Applied Developmental Psychology* 5 (3) (1984): 185–202.

10. Donald F. Roberts, Uhla G. Foehr, Victoria Rideout, and Molly Ann Brodie, *Kids and Media @ the New Millennium* (Menlo Park, CA: Henry J. Kaiser Family Foundation, 1999), 78.

11. Dale Kunkel, "Children and Television Advertising," 376.

12. Donald F. Roberts et al., *Kids and Media,* 61.

13. Ibid., 22.

14. Ibid., 21.

15. Ibid., 9.

16. Ibid., 13.

17. Victoria Rideout, Elizabeth Vandewater, and Ellen Wartella, *Zero to Six: Electronic Media in the Lives of Infants, Toddlers and Preschoolers* (Menlo Park, CA: The Henry F. Kaiser Family Foundation, 2003), 5.

18. D.C. Denison, "The Year of Playing Dangerously," *Boston Globe Magazine,* 8 December 1985, 14–16, 99–107, 110.

19. Robert W. McChesney, *Rich Media, Poor Democracy: Communication Politics in Dubious Times* (Urbana: University of Illinois Press, 1999).

20. Edward S. Herman and Noam Chomsky, *Manufacturing Consent: The Political Economy of the Mass Media* (New York: Pantheon Books, 2002).

21. For a broader presentation of this trend, see Robert Kuttner, *Everything for Sale: The Virtues and Limits of Markets* (Chicago: University of Chicago Press, 1996).

22. Dennis Kelly, "A Corporate Hand for Troubled Students," *USA Today,* 26 September 1989, 4D.

23. Julie Edelson Halpert, "Dr. Pepper Hospital? Perhaps, for a Price; Company Names Are Busting Out All Over," *New York Times,* 18 February 2001, sec. 3, p. 1.

24. American Library Association, "WWF Entertainment Joins Teen Read Week Effort," ALA news release, July 2001. Available at http://www.ala.org/news/v7n9/trw_wwf.html. Accessed 31 October 2002.

25. An excellent presentation of this point is made in Alex Molnar, *Giving Kids the Business: The Commercialization of America's Schools* (Boulder, CO: Westview Press, 1996).

26. Richard Rothstein, "When States Spend More," *American Prospect* 9 (36) (1998): 72–79.

27. Kathy McCabe, "City Schools Squeezed by Budget Cuts: Schools Merged, Programs Axed," *Boston Globe,* 31 July 2003, sec. Globe North, p. 1.

28. Richard Rothstein, "The Myth of Public School Failure," *American Prospect* 4(13), 21 March 1993. Available at http://www.prospect.org/print/V4/13/rothstein-r.html.

29. Susan E. Linn and Alvin F. Poussaint, "The Trouble with Teletubbies," *American Prospect* 10 (44), May/June 1999, 18–25.

30. Susan Linn and Alvin F. Poussaint, "The Truth About Teletubbies," *Zero to*

Three Bulletin: Special Issue on Babies, Toddlers, and the Media, Fall 2001, 24–29.

31. Bob Sperber, "Wendy's Collars Clifford, Pals for '02 Effort," *Brandweek* 42 (24), 11 June 2001, 6.

32. From a brochure published by Common Sense Media, available at www. commonsensemedia.org: "View From the Family Room: Parents Speak on the Media That Affects Our Kids' Lives," the 2003 Common Sense Media Poll of American Parents, conducted by Penn, Schoen & Berland, and American Viewpoint.

33. Center for a New American Dream, "Kids and Commercialism Survey," poll commissioned by the Center for a New American Dream and conducted on 20–21 July 1999 by EDK Associates, New York. Press release available at http://www.newdream.org/campaign/kids/press-release.html. Accessed 9 July 2003.

34. A good discussion and review of the literature about the psychological costs of materialism can be found in Tim Kasser, *The High Price of Materialism* (Cambridge: MIT Press, 2002).

35. Melissa Preddy, "Toy Aisle Reflects Our Money Woes," *The Detroit News,* 1 December 2003, B1.

36. Marian Burros, "Dental Group Is Under Fire for Coke Deal," *New York Times,* 4 March 2003, sec. A, p. 16.

37. Caroline E. Mayer, "Sold on Summer: Why Retailers Sponsor Kids' Activities," *Seattle Times,* 5 August 2003, A3.

CHAPTER 1: NOTES FROM THE UNDERGROUND

1. *KidScreen* web site: www.kidscreen.com. Accessed 16 September 2002.

2. Kid Power Food & Beverage Marketing 2004—PREMAILER. Available at http://www.kidpowerx.com/cgiin/teplates/10648563952383422851500004/document.html?topic=445&event=3708&document=34513. Accessed 2 September 2003.

3. Our efforts led to the founding of a national coalition called Stop Commercialization of Childhood (SCEC). I discuss our efforts and the efforts of others to stop the onslaught of advertising on children in chapter 12.

4. A live-action program using real actors instead of animated characters.

5. The Joester Loria Group web site: http://redtrail.com/jl_net/case.htm. Accessed 3 October 2002.

6. TV Parental Guidelines, TV Parental Guidelines Monitoring Board, Washington, D.C. Available at http://www.tvguidelines.org/ratings.asp. Accessed 16 September 2002.

7. Caroline Marshall, "Keith Reinhard: DDB Worldwide's Chief Has Forged a Top Creative Network. What's Next? Caroline Marshall Asks." *Campaign,* 26 April 2001.

8. Michael McCarthy, " 'Whassup?!' Four Buddies Find Fame As Their Personal Greeting Enters the Pop Culture Lexicon in an Ad Campaign," *USA Today,* 14 March 2000, 6B. The quote is attributed to *Entertainment Tonight.*

9. Laurel Wentz et al., "Cannes of Beer: 'Whassup?!' Wins Grand Prix," *Advertising Age* 71 (27), 26 June 2000, 1.

10. Scott Donaton, " 'Whassup' With That, Disney? Station Plays a Bud-Like Song," *Advertising Age* 72 (26), 25 June 2001, 17.

11. Roshan D. Ahuja, Mary Walker, and Raghu Tadepalli, "Paternalism, Limited Paternalism and the Pontius Pilate Plight When Researching Children," *Journal of Business Ethics* 32 (2001), 81–92.

12. Pontius Pilate, the Roman military governor of Judea, personally believed that Jesus of Nazareth did not deserve to be condemned, but rather than follow his own ethics (and his wife's urgings), he sentenced Jesus to death because it was in his job description to do so.

13. David Klein and Scott Donaton, "The Advertising Century: Top Ten Advertising Icons," *Advertising Age,* 1999. Available at http://www.adage.com/century/ad_icons.html. Accessed 1 September 2003.

14. The 1992 version of the American Psychological Association's Ethical Principles of Psychologists and Code of Conduct, Principle F (Social Responsibility) reads: "Social Responsibility: Psychologists are aware of their professional and scientific responsibilities to the community and the society in which they work and live. They apply and make public their knowledge of psychology in order to contribute to human welfare. Psychologists are concerned about and work to mitigate the causes of human suffering. When undertaking research, they strive to advance human welfare and the science of psychology. Psychologists try to avoid misuse of their work. Psychologists comply with the law and encourage the development of law and social policy that serve the interests of their patients and clients and the public. They are encouraged to contribute a portion of their professional time for little or no personal advantage."

15. A comparison of the 1992 and the 2003 versions of the American Psychological Association's Ethical Principles of Psychologists and Code of Conduct can be found on the APA web site: http://www.apa.org/ethics/codecompare.html.

16. Dan S. Acuff, with Robert H. Reiher, *What Kids Buy and Why: The Psychology of Marketing to Kids* (New York: Free Press, 1997), 16.

17. Judann Pollack, "Foods Targeting Children Aren't Just Child's Play: Shape-Shifting Foods, 'Interactive' Products Chase Young Consumers," *Advertising Age,* 1 March 1999, 16.

18. Shelly Reese, "The Quality of Cool," *Marketing Tools,* July 1997, 34.

19. Rachel Geller, chief strategic officer of the Geppetto Group, quoted in Amy Frazier, "Prom Night Means Teen Independence, Buying Spree for Parents and Kids: Geppetto Group Finds Teens Ready to Break Away, Buy, Buy, Buy," *Selling to Kids* 3 (8), 15 April 1998.

20. Amy Frazier, "Market Research Ages 6 and Up: Savvy Gen Y-ers—Challenge, Involve Them," *Selling to Kids* 4 (4), 3 March 1999.

21. Paul Kurnit, of Griffin Bacal, quoted in Duncan Hood, "Is Advertising to Kids Wrong? Marketers Respond," *KidScreen,* November 2000, 16.

22. David Leonhardt and Karen Kerwin, "Hey Kid, Buy This! Is Madison Avenue Taking 'Get 'Em While They're Young' Too Far?" *Business Week,* 30 June 1997, 62.

23. Paul Kurnit quoted in Duncan Hood, "Is Advertising to Kids Wrong?" 16.

24. Janice Rosenberg, "Brand Loyalty Begins Early: Savvy Marketers 'Surround' Kids to Build Connection," *Advertising Age,* 12 February 2001, S2.

25. U.S. Department of Health and Human Services, *The Surgeon General's Call to Action to Prevent and Decrease Overweight and Obesity* (Rockville, MD: U.S. Department of Health and Human Services, Public Health Service, Office of the Surgeon General, 2001).

26. Dina L.G. Borzekowski and Thomas N. Robinson, "The 30-Second Effect: An Experiment Revealing the Impact of Television Commercials on Food Preferences of Preschoolers," *Journal of the American Dietetic Association* 101 (1) (2001), 42–46.

27. Paul Kaplowitz et al., "Earlier Onset of Puberty in Girls: Relation to Increased Body Mass Index and Race," *Pediatrics* 108 (2001), 347–353.

28. Richard P. Nelson, Jeffrey Brown, Wallace Brown, et al., "Improving Substance Abuse Prevention, Assessment and Treatment Financing for Children and Adolescents," *Pediatrics* 108 (2001), 1025–1029.

29. Sue Dibb, Witness Statement, *Helen Steel and David Morris v. McDonalds,* statement of advertising researcher, witness for the defense, November 1994. Available at http://www.mcspotlight.org/cgi-bin/zv/people/witnesses/advertising; shdibb_sue.html. Accessed 10 September 2003.

30. Food Commission, "Sweet Persuasion: We Investigate Children's Television Advertising," *The Food Magazine,* June 1990, 12–18.

CHAPTER 2: A CONSUMER IN THE FAMILY

1. Charles Atkin, "Observation of Parent-Child Interaction in Supermarketing Decision Making," *Journal of Marketing* 42 (1978): 41–45.

2. James McNeal, *Kids as Customers: A Handbook of Marketing to Children* (New York: Lexington Books, 1992), 12.

3. Judann Pollack, "Foods Targeting Children Aren't Just Child's Play: Shape-Shifting Foods, 'Interactive' Products Chase Young Consumers," *Advertising Age,* 1 March 1999, 16.

4. Elena Morales, "The Nag Factor: Measuring Children's Influence," *Admap,* March 2000, 35–37.

5. Western Media International, "The Fine Art of Whining: Why Nagging Is a Kid's Best Friend," *Business Wire,* 11 August 1998.

6. This is put out by Packaged Facts, through MarketResearch.com. Available at http://www.marketresearch.com/vendors/viewvendor.asp?SID=12952634-267242518-254306348&vendorid=768. Accessed 1 September 2003.

7. Elena Morales, "The Nag Factor," 35.

8. Amy Frazier, "Market Research: The Old Nagging Game Can Pay Off for Marketers," *Selling to Kids 3* (8), 15 April 1998.

9. Lucy Hughes, creator of the Nag Factor Study and vice president of Initiative Media Worldwide, in an interview by producer Mark Achbar for the documentary film *The Corporation,* produced by Big Picture Media, 2003.

10. Center for a New American Dream, "Thanks to Ads, Kids Won't Take No, No, No, No, No, No, No for an Answer," poll conducted in May 2002 by Widmeyer Communications. Press release available at http://www.newdream.org/campaign/kids/press-release2002.html. Accessed 6 November 2002.

11. Amy Frazier, "Market Research."

12. Jonathan Eig, "Edible Entertainment—Food Companies Grab Kids by Fancifully Packaging Products as Toys, Games," *Wall Street Journal,* 24 October 2001, B1.

13. Linda Neville, "Kids' Brands Must Exercise Pest Control," *Brand Strategy* 2 November 2001, 17.

14. Ibid.

15. Ibid.

16. MASSPIRG, "Excessive Packaging," Available at: http://www.grrn.org/resources/excess_packaging.html. Accessed 6 November 2002.

17. Linda Neville, "Kids Brands Must Exercise Pest Control."

18. Duncan Hood, "Is Advertising to Kids Wrong? Marketers Respond," *KidScreen,* November 2000, 16.

19. Ibid.

20. Lucy Hughes.

21. Ibid.

CHAPTER 3: BRANDED BABIES

Portions of this chapter first appeared in articles I wrote with Alvin Poussaint that appeared in the *American Prospect* (1999) and *Zero to Three* (2001).

1. Warner Home Video press release: "Eh Oh! Guess Who's Coming to Video! Teletubbies Celebrate Their Exclusive Video Releases with Big Hugs for Babies," *Business Wire,* 1 September 1998. Available at http://www.businesswire.com.

2. Amanda Burgess, "Branding Ages Down," *KidScreen,* 1 October 2000, 64.

3. Julia Fein Azoulay, "Brand Aware," *Childrens Business* 15 (6) (June 2001): 46–48.

4. Ibid.

5. Ibid.

6. Duncan Hood, "Is Advertising to Kids Wrong? Marketers Respond," *Kid-Screen,* November 2000, 15.

7. According to statistics from the CPB and PBS, two-thirds of all preschoolers and half of all kindergartners watch PBS. Viewing PBS children's programs is only slightly less common among children whose parents have less than a high school education and poverty-level or near-poverty-level incomes than among children whose parents have more education and higher incomes. See PBS Research, "Table 15: Four-Week Daypart Trends in the Public TV Audience: October 2000," *PBS National Audience Report,* Fall 2000. (Original data source for the table: Nielsen Television Index, survey covering September 30–October 27, 2002.)

8. Bradley S. Greenberg, "Minorities and the Mass Media," in *Perspectives on Mass Media Effects,* eds. Jennings Bryant and Dolf Zillmann (Hillsdale, NJ: Erlbaum, 1986), 165–188.

9. Walt Belcher, "Masterpieces and Oil Will Mix on PBS," *The Tampa Tribune,* 25 January 1996, Baylife, 4. Mobil eventually dropped sponsorship of the program altogether in 2002 (see Elizabeth Jensen, "When Image Isn't Enough: Weak Economy Is Driving Exxon Mobil, Other Companies Away from PBS Sponsorship in Favor of Direct Ads, Leaving Stations Scrambling for Funds," *Los Angeles Times,* 31 January 2003, Calendar, 1).

10. Microsoft press release, "Microsoft, PBS Introduce Groundbreaking Enhancement to Television Technology; Microsoft ActiMates Interactive Barney to Interact With 'Barney & Friends' on PBS," *PR Newswire,* 18 September 1997. Accessed on Lexis/Nexis, 30 August 2003.

11. Brooks Boliek, "Duggan Puts His Brand on PBS with New Bucks: Pubcaster Chief Rises to Fiscal Challenge," *Hollywood Reporter,* 19 August 1998. accessed Lexis/Nexis.

12. Marcia Diamond, director, Program Underwriting Policy, PBS, "Underwriting Guidelines Change," memo to general managers, program directors, development directors, and program information directors, 1 May 1998.

13. Abigail Klingbeil, "Galleria Sale in Works: New Owner Would Add Theater and Restaurants," *Journal News,* 11 December 2002, 1A.

14. Leslie Kaufman, "PBS Is Expanding Its Brand From the Television Screen to the Shopping Mall," *New York Times,* 27 June 2002, sec. C, p. 10.

15. Ibid., quoting PBS executive Judy L. Harris.

16. Ibid., quoting Mark Rivers, director of strategic development for Mills.

17. Mills Corporation, "St. Louis Mills Enters America's Heartland," *Business Wire,* 27 June 2002.

18. Judy L. Harris, quoted in Mills Corporation/PBS press release, "PBS and the Mills Corporation Forge Groundbreaking Cause-Marketing Alliance for PBS Kids," *Business Wire*, 27 June 2002. accessed Factiva, 29 July 2003.

19. Ibid.

20. Judy L. Harris, quoted in Leslie Kaufman, "PBS Is Expanding," 10.

21. David W. Kleeman, *One Mission, Many Screens: A PBS/Markle Foundation Study on Distinctive Roles for Children's Public Service Media in the Digital Age,* 17 April 2002, 18.

22. PBS Kids, *Clifford the Big Red Dog,* available at http://pbskids.org/Clifford. Accessed 31 August 2003.

23. David Lieberman, "How to Sell to Kids Without Selling Out," *USA Today*, 27 November 2000, 6B.

24. Michael Starr and Kate Perrotta, "Uh-Oh, Eh-Oh! Teletubby Show Goes Belly-Up," *New York Post*, 13 February 2001, 3.

25. PBS Kids, "Teletubbies: Background." Available at http://pbskids.org/teletubbies/background.html. Accessed 13 September 2003.

26. From personal correspondence with Dorothy Singer, 11 August 2003, citing Deborah S. Weber of Fisher-Price and Dorothy G. Singer of Yale University, "Media Use by Infants and Toddlers: Results of a Survey," report submitted to Fisher-Price, Inc., 2002.

27. Victoria Rideout, Elizabeth Vandewater, and Ellen Wartella, *Zero to Six: Electronic Media in the Lives of Infants, Toddlers and Preschoolers* (Menlo Park, CA: The Henry F. Kaiser Family Foundation, 2003), 5.

28. Personal communication with Dan Anderson, June 2003.

29. Daniel R. Anderson et al., "Estimates of Young Children's Time with Television: A Methodological Comparison of Parent Reports with Time-Lapse Video Home Observation," *Child Development* 56 (1985), 1345–1357.

30. Andrew Meltzoff, "Immediate and Deferred Imitation in Fourteen- and Twenty-Four-Month-Old Infants," *Child Development* 56 (1988): 62–72.

31. Rachel Barr and Harlene Hayne, "Developmental Changes in Imitation from Television During Infancy," *Child Development* 70 (5) (1999): 1067–1081.

32. Rachel Barr, "Deferred Imitation from Television During Infancy: The effect of repeated exposure," symposium paper presented at the European Conference on Developmental Psychology, Milan, Italy, August 2003. A description of the study and its findings is available at the Early Learning Project at Georgetown University website, http://cfdev.georgetown.edu/research/elp/findings_study.cfm?findings_id=17. Accessed 3 September 2003.

33. Daniel Anderson and Stephen Levin, "Young Children's Attention to 'Sesame Street,' " *Child Development* 47 (1976): 806–811.

34. Georgetown Early Learning Project, "Findings."

35. Erica Goode, "Babies Pick Up Emotional Clues From TV, Experts Find," *New York Times*, 21 January 2003, sec. F, p. 5.

36. A good discussion about marketing's manipulation of emotions and its relationship to what we are learning about the brain can be found in David Walsh, "Slipping Under the Radar: Advertising and the Mind," paper presented at the World Health Organization Conference, "Health: Marketing and Youth," Fabrica, Treviso, Italy, 18 April 2002. Available at http://www.who.int/health-mktg/walshpaper.pdf.

37. David Walsh, "Slipping Under the Radar."

38. Microsoft, "Welcome to the ActiMates Teletubbies Web Page!" Available at http://www.Microsoft/Teletubbies/default.htm. Accessed 24 May 1999.

39. Frances Rauscher, Gordon Shaw, and Katherine Ky, "Listening to Mozart Enhances Spatial-Temporal Reasoning: Towards a Neurophysiological Basis," *Neuroscience Letters* 185 (1995): 44–47.

40. Frances Rauscher et al., "Music Training Causes Long-Term Enhancement of Preschool Children's Spatial-Temporal Reasoning," *Neurological Research* 19 (1997): 2–8.

41. For more information, see Stephanie M. Jones and Edward Zigler, "The Mozart Effect: Not Learning from History," *Journal of Applied Developmental Psychology* 23 (3) (2002): 355–372.

42. Elliott Minor, "Child Advocates Kick Off 'Better Brains for Babies,' " *Associated Press Newswire,* 14 October 1998. accessed Factiva, 22 May 2003.

43. Stephanie M. Jones and Edward Zigler, "The Mozart Effect."

44. Joseph R. Zanga, "Message From the American Academy of Pediatrics: TV & Toddlers," *Healthy Kids* (August/September 1998): 3.

45. Baby Gourmet press release: "There Is Something New in the Produce Aisle . . . Baby Gourmet Video Series Launched in Albertson's Stores Nationwide!" *Business Wire,* 13 December 2002. accessed Factiva, 22 May 2003.

46. Mark Waller, "Experts Still Favor Parents Over Products," *Star Tribune* (Minneapolis), 7 May 2001, Variety, 3E.

47. See Alliance for Childhood, *Fools's Gold: A Critical Look at Computers in Childhood* (College Park, MD: Alliance for Childhood, 2000).

48. Jeffrey Stranger and Natalia Gridina, *Media in the Home: The Fourth Annual Survey of Parents and Children* (Philadelphia: Annenberg Public Policy Center, 1999).

49. Susan Linn and Alvin Poussaint, "Spare the Babies from 'Teletubbies' and Toy Tie-In Marketing," *Los Angeles Times,* 18 January 1999, B5; Susan Linn and Alvin Poussaint, "The Trouble with Teletubbies: The Commercialization of PBS," *American Prospect* 44 (May/June 1999): 18–25; Susan Linn and Alvin Poussaint, "The Truth about Teletubbies," *Zero to Three* (October/November 2001): 24–29.

50. Joseph R. Zanga, "Message from the AAP."

51. PBS Kids, "Teletubbies: Introduction," publicity materials for *Teletubbies,* the Ready to Learn Service, PBS, 26 September 1997.

52. The Write News, "Teletubbies Say 'Eh-Oh' to the Internet on Their First Official Website," 7 April 2003. Available at http://www.writenews.com/1998/040798.htm. Accessed 31 July 2003.

53. Interview with Anne Wood, PBS, "Teletubbies on PBS: Meet the Show's Creator." Available at http://www.pbs.org/teletubbies/about/interview.html. Accessed 4 January 1999.

54. PBS, "PBS Partners with Ragdoll Productions and the Itsy Bitsy Entertainment Company to Air Innovative Preschool Series *Teletubbies.*" Available at http://www.pbs.org/insidepbs/news/teletubbies.html. accessed 4 January 1999.

55. Lynne Heffley, "Telly Trouble? The British Toddler-TV Hit 'Teletubbies' Has Critics Babbling. It Premieres Monday on PBS," *Los Angeles Times,* 4 April 1998, 1.

56. James Collins, "Tube for Tots: Move Over, Barney. You've Now Got Some Company," *Time,* 24 November 1997, 96ff.

57. Gloria Goodale, "Entertainment's Message: 'Buy Me!' " *Christian Science Monitor,* 12 June 1998, B1.

58. PBS Ready to Learn Service, "Watching Teletubbies," promotional materials, undated.

59. "BBC Results Buoyed by Kids' Brands," *Kids TV* 3 (14), 3 July 2000. accessed Factiva, 1 September 2003.

60. "A Big Buildup for Bob: Hasbro Plans New Toys Based on a Hit British TV Show," *Providence Journal-Bulletin,* 21 April 2000, 1F.

61. Joan Verdon, "Taking Home Tinky Winky," *Bergen County Record,* 17 May 1998, L02.

62. Stuart Elliott, "Teletubbies Switch Fast-Food Alliance," *New York Times,* 4 April 2000, sec. C, p. 16.

63. Tish Rabe and Theodor Seuss Geisel, *Oh Baby, the Places You'll Go! A Book to Be Read in Utero* (New York: Random House, 1997).

CHAPTER 4: ENDANGERED SPECIES

1. D.W. Winnicott, *Playing and Reality* (New York: Basic Books, 1971), 51.

2. Versions of the section on *Harry Potter* first appeared in *Commonwealth Magazine* and the *Boston Globe:* Susan Linn, "Harry, We Hardly Knew Ye," *Common Wealth,* Spring 2000, 92–94; Susan Linn, "J.K. Rowling and the Golden Calf," *Boston Globe,* 8 July 2000, F3.

3. For an excellent discussion on how big business is transforming children's relationship to books, see Daniel Hade, "Storyselling: Are Publishers Changing the Way Children Read?" *Horn Book* 78 (5), September/October 2002, 509–19.

4. "Harry Potter and the Merchandising Gold," *Economist* 367 (8329), 21 June 2003, 64.

5. Karen Raugust, "Licensing Hotline," *Publishers Weekly* 250 (14), 7 April 2003, 25.
6. Ibid.
7. Kelly D. Brownell, Ph.D., and Katherine Battle Horgen, *Food Fight: The Inside Story of the Food Industry, America's Obesity Crisis, and What We Can Do About It* (New York: Contemporary Books, 2004), 121.
8. Warren Kornblum, quoted in David Finnigan, "Hollywood Gets Humble," *Brandweek* 42 (24), 11 June 2001, 28.
9. There's a whole literature on the relationship of play to health. See D.W. Winnicott, *Playing and Reality*; Erik Erikson, *Childhood and Society* (New York: Norton, 1962).
10. Lisa Fickenscher, "Stock Watch: 4Kids Entertainment Sheds One-Hit Wonder Tag; Yu-Gi-Oh Follow-Up to Pokémon Inks Fox Television Development Deal," *Crain's New York Business,* 7 October 2002, 55.
11. Ibid.
12. Mars Marx Toys "Fort Apache Deluxe Western Playset" description available at http://www.marxtoys.com/marxtoys/playsets1.htm, accessed 3 September 2003.
13. See Gerard Jones, *Killing Monsters: Why Children Need Fantasy, Superheroes, and Make-Believe Violence* (New York: Basic Books, 2002).
14. Patricia Marks Greenfield et al., "The Program-Length Commercial," in *Children and Television: Images in a Changing Sociocultural World,* eds. Gordon Berry and Joy Keiko Asamen (Newbury Park, CA: Sage, 1993), 53–72.
15. Ibid.
16. A good discussion of deregulation and its impact on play can be found in Diane Levin, *Remote Control Childhood? Combating the Hazards of Media Culture* (Washington, DC: National Association for the Education of Young Children, 1998).
17. Play Date Inc., "Play Date 2002: Best Selling Toys Overall." Available at http://www.playdateinc.com/playdate2002/overall.asp. Accessed 5 November 2002.
18. Joester Loria Group, "Care Bears Case Study." Available at http://www.joester loriagroup.com/clients/cs_carebears.asp. Accessed 28 August 2003.
19. Constance Hays, "Aided by Clifford and the Care Bears, Companies Go After the Toddler Market," *New York Times,* sec. C, p. 5.
20. Scholastic.com, Teacher Store, "Clifford's Kit for Personal and Social Development." Available at http://click.scholastic.com/teacherstore/catalog/product/product.jhtml?skuid=sku3932910&catid=&catType. Accessed 6 September 2003.
21. Ibid.

CHAPTER 5: STUDENTS FOR SALE

1. Ed Winter, quoted in Pat Wechsler, "This Lesson Is Brought to You By . . ." *Business Week,* 30 June 1997, 68.
2. Kate Zernike, "Coke to Dilute Push in Schools for Its Products," *New York Times,* 14 March 2001, sec. A, p. 14.
3. American Coal Foundation, "Unlocking Coal's Potential Through Education: Our Mission." Available at http://www.afc-coal.org/. Accessed 11 September 2003.
4. Pizza Hut, "Book It! Time for Kids." Available at http://www.bookit program.com. Accessed 11 September 2003.
5. Susan Campbell, "The Hazards of Learning to Speak for Yourself," *Hartford Courant,* 19 June 2001, Life, D2.
6. Project 2000, Inc., "Mariott Hospitality Public Charter High School." Available at http://project2000inc.org/mariott.htm. Accessed 11 September 2003.
7. Francis Beckett, "Schools, United States—Schools with High Hopes for Low Achievers: Francis Beckett Finds Determined US Efforts to Lure the Truants Back," *Guardian,* 26 October 1992, E4.
8. Alex Molnar, "What's in a Name? The Corporate Branding of America's Schools: Year 2001-2002." *Fifth Annual Report on Trends in Schoolhouse Commercialism* (Tempe, AZ: Commercialism in Education Research Unit [CERU], Education Policy Studies Laboratory, University of Arizona, 2002), 29.
9. Ryan Kim, "Schools May Sell Naming Rights; District Considers Proposal to Raise Funds," *San Francisco Chronicle,* 18 January 2003, A1.
10. Enola Aird, "Reading, Writing, 'Rithmetic—and Marketing," *Newsday,* 12 June 2001, A39.
11. It's important to note that until 2002 schools did not even need parental permission to allow market research firms to mine students for their ideas. That changed with a provision in the federal No Child Left Behind Act, which reauthorizes the Elementary and Secondary Education Act ("Student Privacy Protections Added in ESEA Reauthorization Bill," *Education Technology News,* 19 (2), 16 January 2002).
12. Pat Wechsler, "This Lesson Is Brought to You."
13. Alex Molnar, *Giving Kids the Business: The Commercialization of America's Schools* (Boulder, CO: Westview Press, 1996), 39.
14. Inger L. Stole, "Advertisers in the Classroom: A Historical Perspective," paper presented at the Association for Consumer Research annual conference, Columbus, Ohio, 1999.
15. Elizabeth A. Fones-Wolf, *Selling Free Enterprise: The Business Assault on Labor and Liberalism, 1945-60* (Urbana: University of Illinois Press, 1994), 204. She cites *New York Times,* January 4, 1959, and others.

16. Alex Molnar, "What's in a Name?" 5.

17. Rod Taylor, senior vice president at CoActive Marketing, Great Neck, NY, quoted in Carrie MacMillan, "Readin', Writin', and Sellin'," *Promo* 15 (10), 1 September 2002, 24.

18. General Accounting Office, *Public Education: Commercial Activities in Schools—Report to Congressional Requesters* (Washington, DC: United States General Accounting Office, 2000), 26.

19. For a full discussion of this, see Robert Kuttner, *Everything for Sale: The Virtues and Limits of Markets* (Chicago: University of Chicago Press, 1996).

20. Jen Lin-Liu, "Hornbeck Steps Down as Superintendent, Two Take Over," Associated Press State and Local Wire, 14 August 2000.

21. Dan Russakoff, "Finding the Wrongs in Naming Rights: School Gym Sponsorship Sparks Furor," *Washington Post,* 16 December 2001, A3.

22. Alison Gendar and David Saltonstall, "Lawyer Picked as Chancellor: Joel Klein has Federal, Business Background," New York *Daily News,* 30 July 2002, 3.

23. Gail Russell Chaddock, "Corporate Ways Invade Schools," *Christian Science Monitor,* 4 August 2000, 1.

24. Linda Shaw and Keith Ervin, "Olchefske Facing a Crisis That's Not Just About Money; Cool Businesslike Superintendent Must Balance the Books—and Regain Trust," *Seattle Times,* 17 November 2002, A1; Linda Shaw and Keith Ervin, "Under Fire, Olchefske Steps Down: Seattle Superintendent Quits Amid Financial Upheaval," *Seattle Times,* 15 April 2003, A1.

25. "Chicago's Budget Director Taking Schools Post in Philadelphia," Associated Press State and Local Wire, 13 July 2002.

26. Joel Babbit quoted in Ralph Nader, *Children First: A Parent's Guide to Fighting Corporate Predators* (Washington, DC: Children First, 1996), 64.

27. Joan Vennochi, "Budget Punishes Schools' Success," *Boston Globe,* 17 July 2003, A19.

28. Rick Collins, "Coming to Your Town Soon: A Debate Over Advertising on School Buses," *State House News Service,* 5 August 2002. Available at www.statehousenews.com.

29. Representative Bradley Jones quoted in ibid.

30. Dan Russakoff, "Finding the Wrongs."

31. Alex Molnar, *Giving Kids the Business,* 1.

32. Richard Rothstein, "When States Spend More," *American Prospect* 9 (36), 1 January 1998–1 February 1998, 72–79.

33. Ibid.

34. National Association of State Boards of Education, "Cost of President's Testing Mandate Estimated As High As $7 Billion," Washington, DC: National Association of State Boards of Education, 25 April 2001. Available at http://www.nasbe.org/Archives/cost.html. Accessed 20 July 2003.

35. National Governors Association and National Associations of State Budget Officers, "Executive Summary," *Fiscal Survey of States,* May 2002, ix.

36. Jean Brennan, ed., *The Funding Gap* (Washington D.C.: The Education Trust, August 2002).

37. Derek White, executive vice president of Alloy, quoted in Carrie MacMillan, "Readin', Writin', and Sellin'," 24.

38. Personal e-mail communication from Dorothy Wolden, 20 November 2000.

39. Alex Molnar, "Corporate Involvement in Schools: Time for a More Critical Look," Education Policy Studies Laboratory (EPSL) (Washington, DC: National Association of States Board of Education, Winter 2001). Available at http://www.asu.edu/educ/epsl/CERU/Documents/cace-01-01.html.

40. Deron Boyles, *American Education and Corporations: The Free Market Goes to School* (New York: Garland Publishing, 1998).

41. Consumers Union, "Evaluations," *Captive Kids: A Report on Commercial Pressures on Kids in School* (Washington, DC: Consumers Union, 1998), 3. Available at www.consumersunion.org/other/captivekids/evaluations.

42. American Petroleum Institute, "Classroom Energy! Lesson Plans." Available at http://www.classroom-energy.org/teachers/plans/index.html. Accessed 12 November 2002.

43. Consumers Union, "Evaluations."

44. Channel One, "About Channel One." Available at http://www.channelone.com/common/about/. accessed 14 September 2003.

45. Consumer Union, "Evaluations."

46. Steven Manning, "The Television News Show Kids Watch Most," *Columbia Journalism Review* 38 (6) (2000): 55–57.

47. Ibid.

48. Janice M. Barrett, "Participants Provide Mixed Reports About Learning from Channel One," *Journalism and Mass Communication Educator* 53 (2) (1998): 54–67.

49. Center for Commercial-Free Public Education, "Education Industry: What's on Channel One?" 8 July 1998. Available at http://www.corpwatch.org/issues/PID.jsp?articleid=888. Accessed 21 May 2003.

50. Max B. Sawicky and Alex Molnar, "The Hidden Costs of Channel One: Estimates for the Fifty States," Arizona State University, Education Policy Studies Laboratory (EPSL), April 1998. Available at http:// www.asu.edu/educ/epsl/CERU/ Documents/cace-98-02/CACE-98-02.htm.

51. Michael Morgan, "Channel One in the Public Schools: Widening the Gap," research report prepared for UNPLUG, University of Massachusetts at Amherst, Department of Communication, 13 October 1993.

52. Drew Tienne, "Exploring the Effectiveness of Channel One School Telecasts," *Educational Technology* 33 (5) (1993): 26–42.

53. Nancy Nelson Knupfer and Peter Hayes, "The Effects of the Channel One

Broadcast on Students' Knowledge of Current Events," in *Watching Channel One,* ed. Ann DeVaney (Albany, NY: SUNY Press, 1994): 42–60.

54. Ibid.

55. Mark Miller, "How to Be Stupid: The Teachings of Channel One," paper prepared for Fairness and Accuracy in Reporting (FAIR), January 1997, 1. Available at http://www.fair.org/extra/9705/ch1-miller.html.

56. William Hoynes, "News for a Captive Audience: An Analysis of Channel One," *Extra!* (published by FAIR, May/June 1997: 11–17.

57. Steven Manning, "The Television News Show Kids Watch Most."

58. Ibid.

59. Channel One, "About Channel One."

60. Mark Miller, "How to Be Stupid."

61. Roy F. Fox, "How Do Kids Respond to Commercials?" in *Harvesting Minds: How TV Commercials Control Kids* (Westport, CT: Praeger, 1996): 39–59.

62. Bradley S. Greenberg and Jeffrey E. Brand, "Television News Advertising in Schools: The 'Channel One' Controversy," *Journal of Communication* 43 (1) (1993): 143–151.

63. Roy F. Fox, "How Do Kids Respond," 92.

64. Jeffrey E. Brand and Bradley S. Greenberg, "Commercials in the Classroom: The Impact of Channel One Advertising," *Journal of Advertising Research* 34 (1) (1994): 18–21.

65. Kelly D. Brownell and Katherine Battle Horgen, *Food Fight: The Inside Story of the Food Industry, America's Obesity Crisis, and What We Can Do About It* (New York: Contemporary Books, 2004).

66. Judith Jones Putnam and Jane E. Allshouse, "In 1945, Americans Drank More Than Four Times as Much Milk as Carbonated Soft Drinks; in 1997, They Downed Nearly Two and a Half Times More Soda Than Milk," Figure 8 in *Food Consumption Prices and Expenditures, 1970–1997* (Washington, DC, Food and Rural Economics Division, Economics Research Services, U.S. Department of Agriculture, 1999): 49.

67. David S. Ludwig, Karen E. Peterson, and Steven L. Gortmaker, "Relation Between Consumption of Sugar-Sweetened Drinks and Childhood Obesity: A Prospective, Observational Analysis," *Lancet* 357 (17 February 2001): 505–508.

68. Amanda Purcell, "Prevalence and Specifics of District-Wide Beverage Contracts in California's Largest School Districts," report commissioned by the California Endowment, April 2002, 3.

69. Ibid.

70. General Accounting Office, "Public Education," 4.

71. NPR, Morning Edition, "Analysis: Soda Machines Used to Raise Money for Schools." National Public Radio transcript for 18 October 2002.

72. Mindy Spar, "Local School Focus of 'Now,' " *Post and Courier* (Charleston, SC), 18 October 2002, TV3.

73. NPR, "Analysis: Soda Machines."

74. Steven Manning, "Counting Cokes and Candy Bars," Cleveland *Plain Dealer*, 25 March 1999, 9B; Kate Zernike, "Coke to Dilute Push in Schools."

75. Amanda Purcell, "Prevalence and Specifics," 9.

76. Ibid.

77. Marc Kaufman, "Fighting the Cola Wars in Schools," *Washington Post*, 23 March 1999, Z12.

78. U.S. Department of Agriculture, "Food Sold in Competition with USDA Meal Programs: A Report to Congress," 12 January 2001. Available at http://www. fris.usda.gov/end/lunch/CompetitiveFoods/report_congress.htm. Accessed November 15, 2002.

79. Kate Zernike, "Coke to Dilute Push in Schools."

80. "Sports Authority: Soft Drink Deal Reached," *Pittsburgh Post Gazette* 28 June 2003, D5.

81. Sherri Day, "Coke Moves with Caution to Remain in Schools," *New York Times,* 3 September 2003, sec. C, p. 1.

82. Richard Rothstein, "Lessons: For Schools' Ills, the Sugar Pill," *New York Times,* 21 August 2002, sec. B, p. 8.

83. Correspondence with Gary Boyes via e-mail, November/December 2002.

84. "West Salem Cheerleader in Hot Water with Pepsi," Associated Press State and Local Wire, 3 November 2002.

85. Marion Nestle addresses in depth the commercialization of school food services and the other ways food marketers target children in school in her book *Food Politics: How the Food Industry Influences Nutrition and Health* (Berkeley: University of California Press, 2002), 188-195.

86. Diane Brockett, "School Cafeterias Selling Brand-Name Junk Food: Who Deserves a Break Today?" *Education Digest* 64 (2) (1998): 56-59.

87. Jane Levine, "Food Industry Marketing in Elementary Schools: Implications for School Health Professionals," *Journal of School Health* 69 (7) (1999): 290-291.

88. "Battle of the Bulge; Fast Food Is King at Arroyo High," editorial, *San Francisco Chronicle,* 29 July 2003, D4.

89. Jane Levine and Joan Gussow, "Nutrition Professionals' Knowledge of and Attitudes Toward the Food Industry's Education and Marketing Programs in Elementary Schools," *Journal of the American Dietetic Association* 8 (1999): 973-976.

90. Jane Levine, "Nutrition Professionals' Knowledge."

91. Personal communication.

92. ABC News, World News Saturday, "Profile: Controversy Over Company-

Sponsored School Field Trips," 11 May 2002. Transcript from Factiva, 22 July 2003.

93. Field Trip Factory, "Be a Sports Authority: Fitness, Safety & Teamwork." Available at http://www.fieldtripfactory.com/tsa/. Accessed 22 July 2003.

94. Alisa Hauser Kraft, "Buy, Baby Bunting," *Chicago Reader,* 32 (37) 13 June 2003, 1, 20–22.

95. Julia Silverman, "When Strapped Schools Can't Pay for Field Trips, Corporations Step In," Associated Press Newswire, 15 October 2002.

96. Ibid.

97. Pete Johnson, Sports Authority sales manager, quoted in Minnesota Public Radio: Marketplace Morning Report, "Profile: School Field Trips to Stores and Shopping Centers," 4 September 2002. Transcript from Factiva, 22 May 2003.

98. Caroline E. Mayer, "A Growing Market Strategy: Get 'Em While They're Young; Firms Sponsor School Activities and Books," *Washington Post,* 3 June 2002, A1.

99. "In-School Marketing Programs Focus on Educating Rather Than Selling," *Youth Markets Alert 1,* 14 (4), 1 April 2002, 1.

100. ABC News, "Profile: Controversy Over Company-Sponsored School Field Trips."

CHAPTER 6: THROUGH THICK AND THIN

1. "100 Leading National Advertisers," *Advertising Age,* special issue, 74 (25), 23 June 2003, 2.

2. Joan Voight, "Don't Look Back: Major Advertisers Are Driving a Recovery in Media. TV's the First to Benefit," *Adweek* (Eastern Edition) 43 (39), 30 September 2002.

3. Gregg Cebryznski and Amy Zuber, "Burger Behemoths Shake Up Menu Mix, Marketing Tactics," *Nation's Restaurant News,* 5 February 2001, 1.

4. Stephanie Thompson, "Cap'n Goes AWOL as Sales Flatten; Quaker Redirects Cereal Brand's Marketing Budget to Focus on Kids," *Advertising Age,* 22 November 1999, 8.

5. Richard Troiano and Katherine Flegal, "Overweight Children and Adolescents: Description, Epidemiology, and Demographics," *Pediatrics,* March 1998, 497–504.

6. Centers for Disease Control, "CDC's KidsMedia: Physical Activity and Youth." Available at: http://www.cdc.gov/kidsmedia/background.htm. Accessed 28 May 2003.

7. American Diabetes Association, "Type 2 Diabetes in Children and Adolescents," *Pediatrics* 105 (3) (2000): 671–680.

8. Carlos J. Crespo et al., "Television Watching, Energy Intake, and Obesity in U.S. Children: Results from the Third National Health and Nutrition Examination Survey, 1988–1994," *Archives of Pediatric and Adolescent Medicine* 155 (3) (2001): 360–365.

9. Barbara A. Dennison, Tara A. Erb, and Paul L. Jenkins, "Television Viewing and Television in Bedroom Associated with Overweight Risk Among Low-Income Preschool Children," *Pediatrics* 109 (2002): 1028–1035.

10. Steven L. Gortmacher et al., "Television Viewing as a Cause of Increasing Obesity Among Children in the United States, 1986–1990," *Archives of Pediatric Adolescent Medicine* 150 (1996): 356–362.

11. William H. Dietz, "You Are What You Eat—What You Eat Is What You Are," *Journal of Adolescent Health Care* 11 (1990): 76–81.

12. Thomas N. Robinson, "Reducing Children's Television Viewing to Prevent Obesity: A Randomized Controlled Trial," *Journal of the American Medical Association* 282 (16) (1999): 1561–1567.

13. Jerome D. Williams, Cheryl Achterberg, and Gina Pazzaglia Sylvester, "Targeting Marketing of Food Products to Ethnic Minority Youths," in *Prevention and Treatment of Childhood Obesity: Annals of the New York Academy of Sciences,* Vol. 699, eds. C.L. Williams and S.Y.S. Kimms (New York: New York Academy of Sciences, 1993), 107–114.

14. "100 Leading National Advertisers."

15. Ibid.

16. Krista Kotz and Mary Story, "Food Advertisements During Children's Saturday Morning Television Programming: Are They Consistent with Dietary Recommendations?" *Journal of the American Dietetic Association* 94 (1994): 1296–1300.

17. "Favorite Brands Team with Nickelodeon," *Professional Candy Buyer* 7 (2) (1999): 51.

18. Bob Brown of MarketResearch.com, quoted in: Tiffany Kjos, "Marketers Compete Fiercely for Spending on Kids," *Knight Ridder Tribune Business News,* 15 April 2002, 1.

19. Lisa Rant, "Baby Bottles," *Beverage Aisle* 10 (9) (2001): 68.

20. Ibid.

21. Everyone seems to agree that drinking fruit juice in moderation is healthy for babies and children over six months. According to the American Academy of Pediatrics, children are the prime consumers of juice. The AAP has voiced concern that babies and toddlers may be drinking too much juice, citing as a factor its easy portability, in the form of covered cups and juice boxes (exactly the form of juice packaging the article cited in note 19 extols). Among other potential health problems, sipping juice throughout the day may be harmful to young children's teeth. American Academy of Pediatrics, "The Use and Misuse of Fruit Juice in Pediatrics (RE0047)," 107 (5) (2001): 1210–1213.

22. Julie Halpin from the Geppetto Group quoted in Lisa Rant, "Baby Bottles," 68.
23. In September 2003, the Food Standards Agency in Great Britain published a report on food advertising and promotion to children that included a review of the literature of its effects on children. The report concluded advertising has an impact on children's purchase behavior, consumption, and preferences. The report also found that the effects were independent of other factors and influenced both brand selection and category of food. Gerald Hastings, Martine Stead, Laura McDermott, et al., *Review of Research on Effects of Food Promotion to Children: Final Report. 22 September 2003* (London: Food Standards Agency), 3. The report can be found at http://www.foodstandards.gov.uk/ healthiereating/promotion/readreview/.
24. For a good review of research on the impact of food advertising on children's food preferences, see: Katherine Battle Horgen, Molly Choate, and Kelly D. Brownell, "Television Food Advertising: Targeting Children in a Toxic Environment," in *Handbook of Children and the Media,* eds. Dorothy Singer and Jerome Singer (Thousand Oaks, CA: Sage, 2001), 447–461.
25. Dina L.G. Borzekowski and Thomas N. Robinson, "The 30-Second Effect: An Experiment Revealing the Impact of Television Commercials on Food Preferences of Preschoolers," *Journal of the American Dietetic Association* 101 (1) (2001): 42–46.
26. Kraft Foods, "Kraft Cares: Helping to Get Kids Moving." Available at www.kraft.com. Accessed 2 October 2002.
27. General Mills, "Community Action." Available at: http://www.generalmills. com/corporate/about/community/#Nutrition. Accessed 28 May 2003.
28. From a chart provided by Margo Wootan, director of nutrition policy at the Center for Science in the Public Interest (CSPI).
29. Ira Dreyfuss, "Federal Government Starts Ad Campaign to Try to Teach Kids to Play," Associated Press Newswire, 1 July 2002.
30. Lisa Mills, quoted in Nanci Hellmich, "Sedentary Kids Called to Action," *USA Today,* 17 July 2002, 6D.
31. David Shea, creative director for Frankel, quoted in Ira Dreyfuss, "Federal Government Starts Ad Campaign to Try to Teach Kids to Play."
32. Ira Dreyfuss, "Federal Government Starts Ad Campaign."
33. Ira Teinowitz and Wayne Friedman, "U.S. Launches $125 Million Push to Combat Obesity," *Advertising Age,* 17 June 2002, 4, 42.
34. "100 Leading National Advertisers."
35. Ira Teinowitz and Wayne Friedman, "U.S. Launches $125 Mil Push to Combat Obesity."
36. "100 Leading National Advertisers."
37. Nancy Hellmich, "Sedentary Kids Called to Action," 6D.
38. Jeffrey E. Brand and Bradley S. Greenberg, "Commercials in the Classroom: The Impact of Channel One Advertising," 18–21.

39. Margaret Spillane, "Unplug It! (Group Called 'Unplug' Opposes the Use of Channel One in Schools)," editorial, *The Nation,* 259 (17) 21 November 1994, 600.

40. "Lose the TV, Gain a Brain," editorial, *Seattle Times,* 26 September 2001, B6.

41. Russ Baker, "Stealth TV; Channel One—and Lots of Advertising—Seeps into America's Schools," *American Prospect,* 12 February 2001, 28.

42. Chris Gowar and Richard Rees, "Eatertainment Puts Brands on the Plate," *Brand Strategy,* 9 January 2002, 26.

43. Lisa Piasecki, quoted in Stephanie Dunnewind, "Eatertainment for Kids: 'Toy' Foods in Many Shapes are Targeted for Children," *Seattle Times,* 20 September 2000, G1.

44. Dianna Marder, "Marketers Tempt Kids with Colourful Food," *Toronto Star,* 9 January 2002, Entertainment, 2.

45. Gene Del Vecchio quoted in Mary Ellen Kuhn, "Connecting with Kids: Understanding a Child's Psyche Is a Good Place to Start When Courting this Appealing Demographic Segment," Special Report, *Confectioner* 86 (10) (2002): 18(5).

46. Timothy Coffey, in a segment produced by Kitty Pilgrim on CNN for "Lou Dobbs Tonight: Moneyline News Hour," 29 July 2003. Downloaded from Factiva, 6 August 2003.

47. M.K. Lewis and A.J. Hill, "Food Advertising on British Children's Television: A Content Analysis and Experimental Study with Nine-Year-Olds," *International Journal of Obesity* 22 (1998): 206–214.

48. For a good discussion of this phenomenon, see Jean Kilbourne, "The More You Subtract the More You Add," in *Deadly Persuasion* (New York: Free Press, 1999), 128–154; and Mary Pipher, "Worshipping the Gods of Thinness," in *Reviving Ophelia* (New York: Ballantine Books, 1994), 167–185.

49. William H. Dietz, "You Are What You Eat—What You Eat Is What You Are," *Journal of Adolescent Health Care* 11 (1990): 76–81.

50. G.B. Schreiber et al., "Weight Modification Efforts Reported by Black and White Preadolescent Girls: National Heart, Lung, and Blood Institute Growth and Health Study," *Pediatrics* 98 (1996): 63–70.

51. Sharon Rubinstein and Benjamin Caballero, "Is Miss America an Undernourished Role Model?" Letter, *Journal of the American Medical Association* 283 (2000): 1569.

52. Patricia Owens, "Weight and Shape Ideals: Thin is Dangerously In," *Journal of Applied Social Psychology* 30 (2000): 979–990.

53. A.P. Verri et al., "Television and Eating Disorders: Study of Adolescent Eating Behavior," *Minerva Pediatrica* 49 (6) (1997): 235–243.

54. Josep Toro, Manuel Salamero, and E. Martinez, "Assessment of Sociocultural Influences on the Aesthetic Body Shape Model in Anorexia Nervosa," *Acta Psychiatrica Scandinavica* 89 (3) (1994): 147–151.

55. Mary C. Martin and Patricia F. Kennedy, "Advertising and Social Comparison: Consequences for Female Preadolescents and Adolescents," *Psychology and Marketing* 10(6), November–December 1993, 513–530.

56. Anne E. Becker et al., "Eating Behaviours and Attitudes Following Prolonged Exposure to Television Among Ethnic Fijian Adolescent Girls," *British Journal of Psychiatry* 180 (2002): 509–514.

57. Harrison G. Pope Jr. et al., "Evolving Ideals of Male Body Image as Seen Through Action Toys," *International Journal of Eating Disorders* 26 (1999): 65–72.

58. Kevin L. Norton et al., "Ken and Barbie at Life Size," *Sex Roles* 34 (3/4) (1996): 287–294.

CHAPTER 7: PEACE-KEEPING BATTLE STATIONS AND SMACKDOWN!

1. Mike Snider, "Video Games: Grand Theft Auto: Vice City," *USA Today*, 27 December 2002, 8D.

2. From ToysRUs.com at Amazon.com. Available at http://www.amazon.com/exec/obidos/ASIN/B00005RF53/ref%3Dnosim/namebrandtoy-20/103-1333579-1894214. Accessed 1 October 2003.

3. For a good discussion of the impact of violent media and violent toys on children and their play, see Nancy Carlsson-Paige and Diane Levin, *Who's Calling the Shots: How to Respond Effectively to Children's Fascination with War Play and War Toys* (Philadelphia: New Society Publishers, 1990).

4. Nancy Carlsson-Paige and Diane Levin, *Who's Calling the Shots*.

5. Newton N. Minow and Craig L. Lamay, *Abandoned in the Wasteland: Children, Television, and the First Amendment* (New York: Hill and Wang, 1996), 27.

6. Ibid.

7. Bruno Bettleheim, *The Uses of Enchantment: The Meaning and Importance of Fairy Tales* (New York: Vintage Books, 1977).

8. Joanne Cantor has researched and written extensively about media-induced fear. See: Joanne Cantor, *"Mommy I'm Scared": How TV and Movies Frighten Children and What We Can Do to Protect Them* (San Diego: Harvest, 1998).

9. Joanne Cantor, *"Mommy I'm Scared,"* see 5–48.

10. Alvin Poussaint, conversation with author.

11. Glenn G. Sparks, "Developmental Differences in Children's Reports of Fear Induced by the Mass Media," *Child Study Journal* 16 (1986): 55–66.

12. Brad J. Bushman and L. Rowell Huesmann, "Effects of Televised Violence on Aggression" in *The Handbook of Children and Media*, eds. Dorothy G. Singer and Jerome L. Singer (Thousand Oaks, CA: Sage, 2001), 238.

13. Jenny Deam, "Targeting Kid Consumers Children and Parents Find Ads' Influence Tough to Shut Out," *Denver Post*, 23 July 2002, F1.

14. "Special Report: Youth Marketing: Farrell: Cool is About the Spirit of the Individual," *Strategy,* 11 May 1998, B3.

15. Kid Power Exchange, "Heard on the Playground: Think Like a Kid." Available at http://www.kidpowerx.com/newsletter/issues/0402/0303.htm#articles. Accessed 18 March 2003.

16. *The Merchants of Cool,* a PBS *Frontline* production describes this phenomenon and its consequences quite well. Airdate 27 February 2001. See http://www.pbs.org/wgbh/frontline/shows/cool.

17. David L. Siegel, Timothy J. Coffey, and Gregory Livingston, "Finding Tweens at the Grass Roots Level," in *The Great Tween Buying Machine: Marketing to Today's Tweens* (New York: Paramount Market Publishing, 2001), 169–185.

18. Brandon Tarkitoff quoted by Newton N. Minow and Craig L. Lamay, *Abandoned in the Wasteland,* 30.

19. Diane Levin, *Teaching Young Children in Violent Times: Building a Peaceable Classroom,* second edition (Washington, DC: National Association for the Education of Young Children, 2003).

20. Kathryn Shattuck, "For Young Viewers; Power Rangers With Personality Plus," *New York Times,* 2 March 2003, sec. 13, p. 59. According to this article, "Power Ranger Ninja Storm" was scheduled to be shown at 8:30 A.M. on Saturdays and Sundays. When I checked the ABCKIDs website, the times ranged from 6:00 A.M. to 11:30 A.M. depending on the time zone.

21. Wrestling Information Archive, "Wrestling Television Listings." Available at http://www.100megsfree4.com/wiawrestling/pages/other/wrestv.htm. Accessed 7 February 2003.

22. Walter Gantz, "Indiana University: WWF 'Raw' Study," Brutality Isn't Child's Play (BICP) web site. Available at: http://www.bicp.org/unistudy.html. Accessed 11 February 2002.

23. *Wrestling with Manhood: Boys, Bullying and Battering,* featuring Sut Jhally and Jackson Katz, Media Education Foundation, 2002, videocassette.

24. In 2001, 8 percent of students reported that they had been bullied at school in the last 6 months, up from 5 percent in 1999 according to National Center for Education Statistics, "Indicators of School Crime and Safety, 2002: Nonfatal Student Victimization—Student Reports." Available at http://nces.ed.gov/pubs2003/schoolcrime/6.asp?nav=1. Accessed 20 February 2003.

25. Tonja Nansel et al., "Bullying Behaviors Among US Youth: Prevalence and Association with Psychosocial Adjustment," *Journal of the American Medical Association,* 285 (16) (2001): 2094–2100.

26. Federal Trade Commission, *Marketing Violent Entertainment to Children: A Review of Self-Regulation and Industry Practices in the Motion Picture, Music Recording and Electronic Game Industries,* September 2000, 50.

27. In February 2003, Congressman Joe Baca (D-CA) introduced a bill that would

ban violent video game sales to minors. As of this writing, it is sitting with the House Judiciary Committee. Similar laws passed at the state level in Missouri and in Washington State were overturned in federal appeals court.

28. WWE Parents, "Get R.E.A.L." Available at http://www.wweparents.com/real/index.html. Accessed 20 February 2003.

29. WW Entertainment, "Word Wrestling WWE Entertainment and Simon & Schuster Announce New Publishing Partnership." Available at http://www.wwecorpbiz.com/media/0108.html. Accessed 12 February 2002.

30. Bethany McLean, "Inside the World's Weirdest Family Business," *Fortune*, 16 October 2000, 292ff.

31. Robert DuRant, Karen Sigmon Smith, and Erika Borgerding, "Watching Wrestling Positively Associate with Date Fighting," presented by Dr. Robert DuRant at the American Academy of Pediatrics meeting, 28 April 2001.

32. Daphne Lemish, "The School as a Wrestling Arena: The Modelling of a Television Series," *Communication*, 22 (4) (1997): 395–418.

33. American Academy of Pediatrics, *Joint Statement on the Impact of Entertainment Violence on Children*, Presented at the Congressional Public Health Summit, Washington, DC, 26 July 2000.

34. Ibid.

35. L. Rowell Huesmann, "Longitudinal Relations Between Children's Exposure to TV Violence and Their Aggressive and Violent Behavior in Young Adulthood: 1977–1992," *Developmental Psychology*, 39 (2) (2003): 201–221.

36. John Murray, "TV Violence and Children's Brains—More Reasons for Advocacy and Policy Reform," *The Advocate*, 24 (1) (2001): 1–4.

37. Federal Trade Commission, *2001 Marketing Violent Entertainment to Children: A One-Year Follow-Up Review of Industry Practices in the Motion Picture, Music Recording and Electronic Game Industries: A Report to Congress* (Washington, DC: Federal Trade Commission, December 2001).

38. "Florida Teen Gets Life Sentence in Wrestling Death of 6-Year-Old," *Jet* 99 (26 March 2001): 16–18.

39. "Wrestling Company, Tate Lawyer Settle Defamation Suit," Associated Press Newswires, 3 July 2002. Downloaded from Factiva, 3 January 2003.

40. Recording Industry of America Association, "RIAA/Gold & Platinum." Available at http://www.riaa.org/Gold-Search_Results.cfm?start=1#. Accessed 8 May 2003.

41. Jill Pesselnick, "Aerosmith, Clapton Are Certified Platinum," *Billboard*, 19 May 2001, 66.

42. Andrew Bary, "World Wrestling May Get Up Off the Mat," *Wall Street Journal Sunday*, 17 November 2002, 3.

43. A good discussion can be found in Marie-Louise Mares, and Emily H. Woodard, "Prosocial Effects on Children's Social Interactions," in *The Hand-*

book of *Children and Media,* eds. Dorothy G. Singer and Jerome L. Singer (Thousand Oaks, CA: Sage, 2001), 183–203.

44. Ibid.

45. According to data supplied by A.C. Neilsen, an average of 1,457,000 children watch *The Simpsons* each week.

46. Paul E. McGhee, *Humor: Its Origin and Development* (San Francisco: W.H. Freeman, 1979), 83. According to McGhee, children do not grasp irony until they reach adolescence and are able to understand abstractions.

47. Shelly Dews, et al., "Children's Understanding of the Meaning and Functions of Verbal Irony," *Child Development* 67 (1996): 3071–3085.

48. Dolf Zillmann and Jennings Bryant, "Guidelines for the Effective Use of Humor in Children's Educational Television," in *Humor and Children's Development: A Guide to Practical Applications* (New York: Haworth Press, 1989), 201–221.

49. Andy Meisler, "Ehhh, What's Up, Toons? More Adult, Just as Loony," *New York Times,* 22 February 1998, sec. 13, p. 3.

CHAPTER 8: FROM BARBIE AND KEN TO BRITNEY, THE BRATZ, AND BEYOND

1. Paul Kaplowitz, "Earlier Onset of Puberty in Girls: Relation to Increased Body Mass Index and Race," *Pediatrics* 108 (2) (2001): 347–353.

2. Elizabeth Terry and Jennifer Manlove, *Trends in Sexual Activity and Contraceptive Use Among Teens* (Washington, DC: National Campaign to Prevent Teen Pregnancy, 2000). Available at http://www.teenpregnancy.org/resources/reading/fact_sheets/bestthfs.asp. Accessed 11 October 2003.

3. Centers for Disease Control, Youth Risk Behavior Surveillance System (YRBSS), "Percentage of Students Who Have Had Sexual Intercourse: 2001, United States, Grouped by Grade." Available at http://apps.nccd.cdc.gov/YRBSS/GraphV.asp. Accessed 22 July 2003.

4. "New National Survey of Parents and Kids: Bullying, Discrimination and Sexual Pressures 'Big Problems' for Today's Tweens and Younger Kids," *PR Newswire,* 8 March 2001. Downloaded from Factiva, 12 June 2003.

5. J.D. Brown, B.S. Greenberg, and N.L. Beurkel Rothfuss, "Mass Media, Sex, and Sexuality," *Journal of Adolescent Health Care* 11 (1993): 62–70.

6. Kaiser Family Foundation, *Sex Education in America: A View from Inside the Nation's Classrooms* (Menlo Park, CA: Henry J. Kaiser Family Foundation, 2000), 3.

7. Anna Mulrine, "Risky Business," *U.S. News and World Report* 132 (18), 27 May 2002, 42.

8. Ibid.

9. Ibid.

10. Michael J. Sutton et al., "Shaking the Tree of Knowledge for Forbidden Fruit:

Where Adolescents Learn About Sexuality and Contraception," in *Sexual Teens, Sexual Media: Investigating Media's Influence on Adolescent Sexuality,* eds. Jane D. Brown et al. (Mahwah, NJ: Erlbaum, 2002), 25–55.

11. National Campaign to Prevent Teen Pregnancy, *Not Just Another Thing to Do: Teens Talk About Sex, Regret, and the Influence of Their Parents* (Washington, DC: National Campaign to Prevent Teen Pregnancy, 2000).

12. Jane D. Brown, Carolyn Tucker Halpern, and Kelly Ladin L'Engle, *Mass Media as Sexual Surrogate Peer?* unpublished manuscript, School of Journalism and Mass Communication, University of North Carolina at Chapel Hill, 2003.

13. Kristen Anderson Moore, Anne Driscoll, and Laura Duberstein Lindberg, *A Statistical Portrait of Adolescent Sex, Contraception, and Childbearing* (Washington, DC: National Campaign to Prevent Teen Pregnancy, 1998), 11.

14. Ibid.

15. National Campaign to Prevent Teen Pregnancy.

16. Jean Kilbourne, *Deadly Persuasion: Why Women and Girls Must Fight the Addictive Power of Advertising* (New York: Free Press, 1999), 260.

17. Ibid.

18. Chelsey Goddard, "Media Effects on Adolescent Sexuality," Advocates for Youth, January 1995. Accessed on Lexis-Nexis, 24 May 2002. Goddard cites J. Bryant, "Effects of Massive Exposure to Sexually Oriented Prime-Time Television Programming on Adolescents' Moral Judgment," in *Media, Children and the Family: Social Scientific, Psychodynamic, and Clinical Perspectives* (Hillsdale, NJ: Erlbaum, 1994): 183–195.

19. Aletha C. Huston et al., *Big World, Small Screen: The Role of Television in American Society* (Lincoln, NE: University of Nebraska Press, 1992), 135–136.

20. American Psychological Association, *Violence and Youth: Psychology's Response, Volume I: Summary Report of the American Psychological Association Commission on Violence and Youth* (Washington, DC: American Psychological Association, 1993), 32.

21. This incident occurred during an episode of *Raw Is War,* aired on TNN on 5 March 2001.

22. This episode aired on TNN on 10 February 2003.

23. Julia Fein Azoulay, "The Changing Scene of the American Tween," *Children's Business* 38 (18), 1 March 2003, 38.

24. Rachel Geller, chief strategic officer of the Geppetto Group, quoted in "Reading Tween the Lines," *Cablevision.* 11 June 2001, 26.

25. "Reading Tween the Lines," *Cablevision.*

26. Midge Pierce, vice president for programming at WAM!, quoted in "Reading Tween the Lines," *Cablevision.*

27. "Latchkey Kid Is King in Marketing Realm, Clout Carries Over to Buying by Parents," *Chicago Tribune,* 31 July 1988, C3.

28. Philip H. Dougherty, "Rodale Press Prepares a Magazine for Lipton," *New York Times,* 9 May 1988, sec. D., p. 11.

29. Ibid.

30. Marshall Cohen, senior vice president for research at Nickelodeon, quoted in "Latchkey Kid Is King in Marketing Realm, Clout Carries over to Buying by Parents," *Chicago Tribune,* 31 July 1988, C3.

31. Samantha Critchell, "4–9: Tweens Hear Fashion's Beat," Associated Press, 9 April 2001.

32. Julee Greenberg, Katherine Bowers, and Kristin Young, "What the Girls Like and Want (Results from Teens and Tweens Conference)," *WWD,* 28 March 2002, 8.

33. Betsey Johnson quoted in Samantha Critchell, "4–9; Tweens Hear Fashion's Beat," Associated Press, 9 April 2001.

34. Andrea Braverman, "Tween Scene: Trends in Apparel Sales to 7-14-Year-Olds," *Body Fashions Intimate Apparel* 31 (11) (2001): 11.

35. "Thongs for Tots," editorial, *Seattle Times,* 30 May 2002, B6.

36. Ibid.

37. Samantha Critchell, "4–9: Tweens Hear Fashion's Beat."

38. Julee Greenberg, et al., "What the Girls Like and Want."

39. Joan Anderman, "Lolitas with a Beat: Behind the Gloss that Preteen Girls Love Are the Sexy Lyrics that Older Men Write," *Boston Globe,* 23 January 2000, D1.

40. Ibid.

41. Chuck Taylor, "Preteens: A Lucrative, If Vulnerable, Market—Accessing the 'Tween' Audience Reaches Fever Pitch With More Music," *Billboard,* 12 May 2001. Accessed on Lexis-Nexis, 13 June 2003.

42. Ibid.

43. Ibid.

44. Joan Anderman, "Lolitas with a Beat."

45. Douglas A. Gentile, *Teen-Oriented Radio and CD Sexual Content Analysis* (Minneapolis, MN: National Institute on Media and the Family, 1999).

46. Mary Pipher, *Reviving Ophelia* (New York: Ballantine Books, 1994): 33–34.

47. Joan Anderman, "Lolitas with a Beat."

48. I imagine that by this book's publication date, the videos will have changed. I viewed them on April 20, 2003.

49. S. Robert Lichter, Linda S. Lichter, and Daniel R. Amundson, *Sexual Imagery in Popular Culture* (Washington, DC: Center for Media and Public Policy, 2000). Available at http://www.cmpa.com/archive/sexpopcult.htm. Accessed 11 April 2003.

50. Gina M. Wingood et al., "A Prospective Study of Exposure to Rap Music Videos and African American Female Adolescents' Health," *American Journal of Public Health* 93 (3), 437–439.

51. *True Love* video downloaded from lilromeo.com on 15 April 2003.

52. Louis Chunovic, "Marketers Turning 'Tween' into Green: Preteens a Growing Target for Advertisers," *Electronic Media* 21 (31), 6.

53. *True Love* video.

54. Josh Rottenberg, "Puppy Love," *New York Times*, 30 June 2002, sec. 6, p. 22.

55. Bella English, "Parents Guide Their Children Through Eminem's '8 Mile,' " *Boston Globe*, 12 November 2002, E1.

56. *The Merchants of Cool*, a PBS *Frontline* production, provides a good example of how this happens.

57. Miriam Bar-on, "Sexuality, Contraception, and the Media," *Pediatrics* 95 (2) (2001): 298–300.

58. Dale Kunkel et al., *Sex on TV 3: A Biannual Report of the Kaiser Foundation* (Santa Barbara: University of California and the Henry J. Kaiser Family Foundation, 2003). Available at http://www.kff.org.

59. Ibid.

60. Penguin Group (USA) Inc., "News: Alloy Online and Penguin Putnam Form Alloybooks, a New Teen Imprint." Available at http://www.penguinputnam. com/static/packages/us/about/press/press06.htm. Accessed 16 September 2003.

61. Alloy.com, "Real Life." Available at http://appjava.alloy.com/advicenew/ disclaimer.html. Accessed 13 June 2003.

62. Alloy.com, "Health: Sex?'s." Available at http://www.alloy.com/reallife/health/ sexquestions/moreinfo/index.html. Accessed 6 April 2003.

63. Alloy.com. Available at http://appjava.alloy.com/advicenew/SexQuestion.jsp? articleID=1589&from=140. Accessed 14 April 2003.

64. Alloy.com. Available at http://appjava.alloy.com/advicenew/SexQuestion.jsp? articleID=1593&from=80. Accessed 14 April 2003.

65. Alloy.com. Available at http://appjava.alloy.com/advicenew/SexQuestion.jsp? articleID=1593&from=70. Accessed 14 April 2003.

66. Alloy.com. Available at http://appjava.alloy.com/advicenew/SexQuestion.jsp? articleID=1593&from=40. Accessed 14 April 2003.

67. Alloy.com. Available at http://appjava.alloy.com/advicenew/SexQuestion.jsp? articleID+1593&from=30. Accessed 14 April 2003.

68. Alloy.com. Available at http://appjava.alloy.com/advicenew/SexQuestion.jsp? articleID=1593&from=0jenn. Accessed 14 April 2003.

69. Andrea Braverman, "Tween Scene."

70. Bettijane Levine, "The Next Wave in Literature? Roxy Girl Makes Surf Clothes and Now Books. Not Everyone Appreciates the Tie-In," *Los Angeles Times*, 5 April 2003, Calendar, part 5, p. 1.

71. "Student Advantage and Alloy Forge Youth Marketing Relationship; Alloy Acquires S.A. Events and Promotions Group," *PR Newswire*, 8 May 2002.

72. "Financial Reports: Alloy, Brookstone, Restoration Hardware," *Catalog Age*, 19 March 2003. Accessed on Lexis-Nexis 21 April 2003.

73. Bettijane Levine, "The Next Wave in Literature."

74. Jane Brown, personal communication.

75. "Welcome to Bratzpack.com." Available at http://www.bratzpack.com/. Accessed 16 September 2003.

76. Deborah Roffman, "Way Too Much Fantasy With That Dream House," *Washington Post*, 22 December 2002, B1.

77. ToysRUs.com, "What Toy Does Your Four-Year-Old Want this Year? Toys "R" Us and Toysrus.com Pick the Hottest Toys," 17 October 2002. Available at http://www.shareholder.com/toy/releaseDetail.cfm?ReleaseID=92763. Accessed 7 October 2003.

CHAPTER 9: MARKETING, MEDIA, AND THE FIRST AMENDMENT

1. An excellent history of the debates about media violence is included in Newton Minnow and Craig Lemay, *Abandoned in the Wasteland: Children, Television and the First Amendment* (New York: HarperCollins, 1995).

2. Ibid.

3. Larry Rohter, "A 'No Children' Category to Replace the 'X' Rating," *New York Times*, 27 September 1990, A1.

4. Amy Jordan and Emily Woodward, *Parents' Use of the V-Chip to Supervise Children's Television Use* (Philadelphia: Annenberg Public Policy Center, University of Pennsylvania, 2003), p. 2.

5. The books that I found the most useful include: *Rich Media, Poor Democracy* by Robert W. McChesney (see note 13); *Before Push Comes to Shove*, by Nancy Carlsson-Paige and Diane Levin (see note 16); *Mayhem* by Sissela Bok; and *Abandoned in the Wasteland* by Newton Minnow and Curtis Lemay (see note 1).

6. The First Amendment says: "Congress shall make no law respecting an establishment of religion, or prohibiting the free exercise thereof; or abridging the freedom of speech, or of the press; or the right of the people peaceably to assemble, and to petition the government for a redress of grievances."

7. Robert McChesney makes a very good case for this argument in his *Rich Media, Poor Democracy* (see note 13).

8. The information that follows in the text is adapted from an article of mine that was published in the *Boston Globe*: Susan Linn, "How About 'The Sopranos' Sell . . . Soda?" *Boston Sunday Globe*, 21 May 2000, E5.

9. Sonia Reyes, "Into the Mouths of Babes," *Brandweek*, 26 May 2002.

10. Gloria Goodale, "Advertisers Fund Family-Friendly TV, Win Kudos," *Christian Science Monitor*, 15 October 1999, 19.

11. For a thorough discussion of the ramifications of U.S. media policy, read Robert McChesney's *Rich Media, Poor Democracy* (see note 13). Minow and Lemay's *Abandoned in the Wasteland* contains a good discussion on the context of children's media issues.

12. I am indebted to Angela Campbell, director of the Georgetown Law Center, for clarifying this point.

13. Robert McChesney, *Rich Media, Poor Democracy* (Urbana: University of Illinois Press, 1999), 146-158.

14. Robert McChesney, quoted in Jeffrey Scheuer, *The Sound Bite Society: Television and the American Mind* (New York: Four Walls Eight Windows, 1999), 188.

15. Ibid.

16. Nancy Carlsson-Paige, Diane E. Levin, and Celeste Henriquez (illustrator), *Before Push Comes to Shove: Building Conflict Resolution Skills With Children* (New York: Redleaf Press, 1998).

17. Henry Cohen, *Freedom of Speech and Press: Exceptions to the First Amendment,* Congressional Information Service, Inc., 5 June 2001.

18. American Academy of Pediatrics, *Joint Statement on the Impact of Entertainment Violence on Children,* presented at the Congressional Public Health Summit, Washington, DC, 26 July 2000.

19. Kansas State, Media Relations & Marketing, "K-State Professor 'Maps' Brains for Effect of TV Violence on Youth," press release Manhattan, KS: Kansas State University, 22 February 2001. Available at http://www.mediarelations. ksu.edu/WEB/News/NewsReleases/brainmapping22201.html. Accessed 31 March 2003.

20. Diane Penner, "Video's Effects on Teens Studied," *Indianapolis News/Indianapolis Star,* 3 December 2002, B01.

21. Amy Jordan and Emily Woodward, "Parents' Use of V-Chip."

22. Tobi Elkin, "Replay TV Seeks Shop; Riney Won't Defend Business," *Advertising Age* 71 (42) (2000): 1.

CHAPTER 10: JOE CAMEL IS DEAD, BUT WHASSUP WITH THOSE
BUDWEISER FROGS?

1. Bridget F. Grant and Deborah A. Dawson, "Age at Onset of Alcohol Use and Its Association with DSM-IV Alcohol Abuse and Dependence: Results from the National Longitudinal Alcohol Epidemiological Survey," *Journal of Substance Abuse* 9 (1997): 103-110.

2. David J. DeWit et al., "Age at First Alcohol Use: A Risk Factor for the Development of Alcohol Disorders," *American Journal of Psychiatry* 157 (5) (2000): 745-750.

3. A good discussion of the profitability of alcoholism can be found in Jean Kilbourne's book *Deadly Persuasion: Why Women and Girls Must Fight the Addictive Power of Advertising* (New York: Free Press, 1999), 156-157.

4. Susan E. Foster et al., "Alcohol Consumption and Expenditures for Underage Drinking and Adult Excessive Drinking," *Journal of the American Medical Association* 289 (8) (2003): 989-995.

5. Centers for Disease Control, "Chronic Disease Prevention: Targeting Tobacco Use: The Nation's Leading Cause of Death: At a Glance, 2003." Available at http://www.cdc.gov/ncedphp/aag/aag_osh.htm. Accessed 12 May 2003.
6. Sakid A. Khuder, Hari H. Dayal, and Anand B. Mutgi, "Age at Smoking Onset and Its Effect on Smoking Cessation," *Addictive Behavior* 24 (5) (1999): 673-677.
7. Sherry A. Everett et al., "Initiation of Cigarette Smoking and Subsequent Smoking Behavior Among U.S. High School Students," *Preventive Medicine* 29 (5) (1999): 327-333.
8. Naomi Breslau and Edward Peterson, "Smoking Cessation in Young Adults: Age at Initiation of Cigarette Smoking and Other Suspected Influences," *American Journal of Public Health* 86 (2) (1996): 214-220.
9. Harriet A. Washington, "Burning Love: Big Tobacco Takes Aim at LGBT Youths," *American Journal of Public Health* 92 (7) (2002): 1086-1095.
10. U.S. Department of Health and Human Services, *Preventing Tobacco Use Among Young People: A Report of the Surgeon General* (Atlanta, GA: U.S. Department of Health and Human Services, Public Health Service, Centers for Disease Control and Prevention, National Center for Chronic Disease Prevention and Health Promotion, Office on Smoking and Health, 1994).
11. SAMHSA, U.S. Department of Health and Human Services, "Alcohol Use," *Office of Applied Studies: Summary of Findings from the 2000 National Household Survey on Drug Abuse* (Washington, DC: U.S. Department of Health and Human Services, September 2001).
12. Ross Atkin, "Keeping Kids 'Clean,'" *Christian Science Monitor,* 4 December 2002, 11.
13. Laura Kann, Steven A. Kinchen, Barbara I. Williams, et al., "Youth Risk Behavior Surveillance—United States, 1999," *Morbidity and Mortality Weekly Report* 49 (SS05) (2000): 1-96.
14. Center for Science in the Public Interest, "Fact Sheet: Young People and Alcohol," *Alcohol Policies Project.* Available at http://www.cspinet.org/booze/liquor_branded_advertising_FS2.htm. Accessed 15 May 2003.
15. Center for Alcohol Marketing and Youth (CAMY), *Television: Alcohol's Vast Adland* (Washington, DC: Georgetown University, 18 December 2002).
16. Jean Kilbourne, *Deadly Persuasion: Why Women and Girls Must Fight the Addictive Power of Advertising* (New York: Free Press, 1999), 155-179.
17. Beer Industry, "The Beer Industry's Advertising and Marketing Code." Available at http://www.beerinstitute.org/admarkcode.htm. Accessed 30 April 2003. Models in commercials must be at least twenty-five and look to be reasonably over twenty-one.
18. Jeff Becker, "Statement from the Beer Institute Regarding Today's Report on Alcohol Industry Advertising Practices," *PR Newswire,* 17 December 2002. Accessed on Lexis-Nexis on 12 May 2003.

19. Susan E. Foster, "Alcohol Consumption and Expenditures."

20. National Center on Addiction and Substance Abuse at Columbia University, *Teen Tipplers: America's Underage Drinking Epidemic* (New York: Columbia University, revised February 2003).

21. The proportion of people who began drinking in the eighth grade or younger jumped 33 percent from 1975 to 1999. See National Center on Addiction and Substance Abuse at Columbia University, *The Economic Value of Underage Drinking and Adult Excessive Drinking to the Alcohol Industry: A CASA White Paper* (New York: Columbia University, February 2003).

22. Bridget F. Grant and Deborah A Dawson, "Age at Onset of Alcohol Use."

23. Lloyd D. Johnston, Patrick M. O'Malley, and Jerald G. Bachman, *Monitoring the Future: National Results on Adolescent Drug Use: Overview of Key Findings, 2000* (NIH Publication No. 03-5374) (Bethesda, MD: National Institute on Drug Abuse, 2003), 30, 42.

24. National Center on Addiction and Substance Abuse at Columbia University, *The Economic Value of Underage Drinking.*

25. Ibid.

26. Janet M. Evans and Richard F. Kelly, *Self-Regulation in the Alcohol Industry: A Review of Industry Efforts to Avoid Promoting Alcohol to Underage Consumers* (Washington, DC: Federal Trade Commission, September 1999). Available at http://www.ftc.gov/reports/alcohol/alcoholreport.htm.

27. Center for Alcohol Marketing and Youth (CAMY), *Television: Alcohol's Vast Adland.*

28. CAMY, "Top 15 Teen Television Programs and Alcohol Ads," 7, table 2.

29. Data of courtesy A.C. Neilsen, showing the number of children between two and eleven watching *Survivor Africa* and *Friends* for the 2001-2002 season.

30. Thomas N. Robinson et al., "Television and Music Video Exposure and Risk of Adolescent Alcohol Use," *Pediatrics* 102 (5) (1998). Available at http://www.pediatrics.org/cgi/content/full/102/5/e54.

31. Center for Alcohol Marketing and Youth (CAMY), *Radio Daze: Alcohol Ads Tune in Underage Youth* (Washington, DC: Georgetown University, 2 April 2003).

32. Center for Alcohol Marketing and Youth (CAMY), *Overexposed: Youth a Target of Alcohol Advertising in Magazines* (Washington, DC: Georgetown University, 24 September 2002). Nearly one-third of the $350 million spent on print advertising by the alcohol industry went to ten magazines with a youth readership of 25 percent or more. Half went to advertising in magazines whose teen readers comprise more than 15 percent. As CAMY explains in their research, since the youth population of this country is about 15 percent, any media that attract an audience comprising more than 15 percent of their total market can be thought of as having a significant teen component.

33. CAMY, 24 September 2002. Obviously, magazines get passed on, so it's likely that even more kids read *Sports Illustrated* than the number quoted.

34. Jean Kilbourne, *Deadly Persuasion: Why Women and Girls Must Fight the Addictive Power of Advertising*, 155–157.

35. Michael D. Slater et al., "Male Adolescents' Reactions to TV Beer Advertisements: The Effects of Sports Content and Programming Context," *Journal of Studies on Alcohol* 57 (4) (1996): 425–433.

36. U.S. Department of Health and Human Services, "Tobacco, Alcohol, and Illicit Drug Use: Racial and Ethnic Differences Among U.S. High School Seniors, 1976–2000," *Public Health Reports [Suppl 1]*, 117 (2002): S67–S75.

37. Thomas Lee, "Coors Kicks Off Go-Younger Blitz With NFL Sponsorship," *St. Louis Post-Dispatch*, 18 August 2002: E.1.

38. Douglas A. Gentile et al., "Frogs Sell Beer: The Effects of Beer Advertisements on Adolescent Drinking Knowledge, Attitudes, and Behavior," paper presented at the Biennial Conference of the Society for Research in Child Development, Minneapolis, MN, April 2001.

39. Bruce Horovitz and Melanie Wells, "Ads for Adult Vices Big Hit with Teens," *USA Today*, 31 January 1997, 1A.

40. David Jernigan and James O'Hara, "Alcohol Advertising and Promotion," in *Reducing Underage Drinking: Issues and Interventions*, Committee on Developing a Strategy to Reduce and Prevent Underage Drinking (Washington, DC: National Academies Press, in press).

41. Ibid.

42. Janet M. Evans and Richard F. Kelly, "Self-Regulation in the Alcohol Industry."

43. Nat Ives, "A Trade Group Tries to Wean the Alcohol Industry from Full-Figured Twins and Other Racy Images," *New York Times*, 6 March 2003, sec. C, p. 7.

44. Erica W. Austin and Beth Nach-Ferguson, "Sources and Influences of Young School-Age Children's General and Brand-Specific Knowledge about Alcohol," *Health Communication* 7 (1995): 1–20.

45. Attributed to James McNeal in Stephanie Dunnewind, "Eatertainment for Kids: 'Toy' Foods in Many Shapes are Targeted for Children," *Seattle Times*, 20 September 2000, G1.

46. Dan S. Acuff, with Robert H. Reiher, *What Kids Buy and Why: The Psychology of Marketing to Kids* (New York: Free Press, 1997), 73.

47. Laurie Leiber, *Commercial and Character Slogan Recall by Children Aged 9 to 11 Years: Budweiser Frogs versus Bugs Bunny* (Berkeley: Center on Alcohol Advertising, 1996).

48. Constance L. Hays, "Spots for Adults Appeal to Children," *New York Times*, 26 March 1998: sec. D, p. 5.

49. Joel W. Grube and Lawrence Wallack, "Television Beer Advertising and

Drinking Knowledge, Beliefs, and Intentions Among Schoolchildren," *American Journal of Public Health* 84 (1994): 254–259.

50. Edward Jacobs et al., "Alcohol Use and Abuse: A Pediatric Concern," *Pediatrics* 108 (1) (2001): 185–189.

51. Bruce A. Christiansen and Mark S. Goldman, "Alcohol-Related Expectancies Versus Demographic/Background Variables in the Prediction of Adolescent Drinking," *Journal of Consulting and Clinical Psychology* 83 (51) (1983): 249–257.

52. Paris M. Miller, Gregory T. Smith and Mark S. Goldman, "Emergence of Alcohol Expectancies in Childhood: A Possible Critical Period," *Journal of Studies on Alcohol* 51 (4) (1990): 343–349.

53. Doug Halonen, "Alcohol Ads Under Pressure," *Electronic Media* 21 (51) (2002): 22.

54. Jernigan and O'Hara, "Alcohol Advertising and Promotion."

55. Michael McCarthy, "Sponsors Line Up for 'Survivor' Sequel: Sydney May Be Over, but Popular CBS Series Lures Advertisers to the Outback," *USA Today*. 9 October 2000, 1B.

56. Ed Bark, "Branded: Networks Maximize the Plugs," *Newark Star-Ledger*, 9 August 2002, 59.

57. Thomas Lee, "Coors Kicks Off Go-Younger Blitz."

58. Bernard Stamler, "A New Campaign for Courvoisier, Brand of Napoleon, Looks for Younger, Hipper Customers," *New York Times*, 29 August 2000, C8.

59. Lynette Holloway, "Media: Hip-Hop Sales Pop: Pass the Courvoisier and Count the Cash," *New York Times*, 2 September 2002, C1.

60. Center for Media Education, "Alcohol Advertising Targeted at Youth on the Internet: An Update," Washington, DC, December 1998. Available at http://www.cme.org/publications/alcohol_tobacco/alcrep.html. Accessed 27 May 2003.

61. Jack Daniels Co., "School of Hard Cola." Available at http://www.jdhardcola.com. Accessed 30 August 2003.

62. Doc Otis's Hard Lemon brand literature, "Lower Calories Lower Carbs." Available at http://docotis.com/. Accessed 30 August 2003.

63. Coors Light product information. Available at http://www.coorslight.com/noentry.html. Accessed 30 August 2003.

64. Center for Alcohol Marketing and Youth (CAMY), *State Alcohol Advertising Laws: Current Status and Model Policies* (Washington, DC: Georgetown University, 10 April 2003), Appendix, 11.

65. Dina L. G. Borzekowski et al., "The Perceived Influence of Cigarette Advertisements and Smoking Susceptibility Among Seventh Graders," *Journal of Health Communication* 4 (1999): 105–118.

66. Siobhan McDonough, "Study: Alcohol Ads Reaching Teens," *Associated Press Online*, 24 September 2002.

67. James Twitchell, quoted in Joyce Wolkomir, "You Are What You Buy," *Smithsonian Magazine* 31 (7) (2000): 102.

68. "A Treaty Against Tobacco," editorial, *Boston Globe*, 22 May 2003, sec. A, p. 22.

69. Jean Kilbourne, *Deadly Persuasion*, 184.

70. See, for example: Gordon Fairclough, "Corporate Focus: R.J. Reynolds Lowers Forecasts," *Wall Street Journal*, 9 September 2002; and the company's periodic reports to the U.S. Securities and Exchange Commission at www.sec.gov/edgar/searchedgar/webusers.htm.

71. Campaign for Tobacco-Free Kids, "Tobacco Company Marketing to Kids," Washington, DC, 8 October 2002. Available at www.tobaccofreekids.org/research/factsheets/pdf/0008.pdf. Philip Morris quote is cited as: Philip Morris, Special Report, "Young Smokers: Prevalence, Trends, Implications, and Related Demographic Trends," 31 March 1981, Bates No. 1000390803, http://www.pmdocs.com.

72. Campaign for Tobacco-Free Kids, "Tobacco Company Marketing to Kids." R.J. Reynolds quote is cited as: R.J. Reynolds, "Planned Assumptions and Forecast for the Period 1977-1986," 15 March 1976, Bates No. 502819513-9532, http://www.rjrtdocs.com.

73. Lorillard Corp., memo from executive T.L. Achey to former Lorillard president Curtis Judge, about the Newport brand, dated August 30, 1978, Bates No. TINY0003062. Available at http://www.tobaccoinstitute.com.

74. Paul M. Fischer et al., "Brand Logo Recognition by Children Aged 3 to 6 Years: Mickey Mouse and Old Joe the Camel," *Journal of the American Medical Association* 266 (22) (1991): 3145-3148.

75. Joseph R. DiFranza et al., "Cartoon Camel Promotes Cigarettes to Children," Journal of the American Medical Association 266 (1991): 3149-3153.

76. Jean Kilbourne does an excellent job of showing how tobacco companies exploit girls. Jean Kilbourne, *Deadly Persuasion: Why Women and Girls Must Fight the Addictive Power of Advertising*, 180-216.

77. Joseph A. Califano Jr., "The Wrong Way to Stay Slim," *New England Journal of Medicine* 333 (18) (1995): 1214-1216.

78. Campaign for Tobacco-Free Kids, "Tobacco Company Marketing to Kids."

79. John E. Calfee, "The Ghost of Cigarette Advertising Past," *Cato Review of Business and Government* 20 (3) (1997). Available at http://www.cato.org/pubs/regulation/reg20n3d.html. Accessed 15 September 2002.

80. Kimberly Thompson and Fumie Yokota, "Depiction of Alcohol, Tobacco and Other Substances in G-Rated Animated Feature Films," *Pediatrics* 107 (6) (2001): 1369-1374.

81. James D. Sargent et al., "Effect of Seeing Film on Tobacco Use Among Adolescents: A Cross Sectional Study," *British Medical Journal* 323 (2001): 1394-1397.

82. Diane Turner-Bowker, Massachusetts Department of Public Health, and William L. Hamilton, ABT Associates, Inc., "Cigarette Advertising Expendi-

tures Before and After Master Settlement Agreement: Preliminary Findings," unpublished paper, 15 May 2000.

83. Lisa Girion and Myron Levin, "R.J. Reynolds Fined for Ads Aimed at Teens Tobacco: Judgment of $20 Million for Magazine Pitches Is First Financial Penalty for Violation of 1998 National Settlement," *Los Angeles Times*, 7 June 2002, C1.

84. Conversation with Dr. Elizabeth Wheelan, director, American Council of Science and Health, 15 May 2003.

85. Charles King III, Michael Siegel, and Linda G. Pucci, "Exposure of Black Youths to Cigarette Advertising in Magazines," *Tobacco Control* 9 (1) (2000): 64–70.

86. Campaign for Tobacco-Free Kids, "Tobacco Company Marketing to Kids."

87. Lois Biener and Michael B. Siegel, "The Role of Advertising and Promotion in Smoking Initiation," in *Changing Adolescent Smoking Prevalence, Smoking and Tobacco Control* (Washington, DC: National Cancer Institute, November 2001) Monograph No. 14, NH Pub. No. 02-5086: 202–212.

88. Campaign for Tobacco-Free Kids, "Tobacco Company Marketing to Kids."

89. N. Evans et al., "Influence of Tobacco Marketing and Exposure to Smokers on Adolescent Susceptibility to Smoking," *Journal of the National Cancer Institute* 87 (20) (1995): 1538–1545.

90. Campaign for Tobacco-Free Kids, "Tobacco Company Marketing to Kids."

91. John P. Pierce et al., "Does Tobacco Marketing Undermine the Influence of Recommended Parenting in Discouraging Adolescents from Smoking?" *American Journal of Preventive Medicine* 23 (2) (2002): 73–81. The researchers interviewed twelve- to fourteen-year-olds who were not smokers. There were already studies showing that some kids were more susceptible to tobacco marketing than others and showing that those more susceptible were more likely to smoke. The kids were then divided into two groups. Those with parents whose style of parenting was characterized by traits commonly identified in child development literature as effective were placed in one group. Those with parents who were perceived as not parenting effectively were placed in another. Susceptibility to tobacco advertising was based on questions such as: In the past year have you exchanged coupons for an item with a tobacco brand name or logo on it? Received as a gift or for free any item with a tobacco brand or logo on it? Purchased any item with a tobacco brand or logo on it? Do you have a favorite cigarette advertisement? The researchers also tested recall of cigarette commercials. For the kids whose parents were determined to be lax in their parenting, other factors were more significant than ads in their decision to smoke.

92. Joel B. Cohen, "Playing to Win: Marketing and Public Policy at Odds Over Joe Camel," *Journal of Public Policy Marketing* 19 (2) (2000): 155–167.

93. "Media Week Allstars 2000—Advertiser of the Year—Budweiser," *Media Week*, 5 January 2001, 15.

CHAPTER 11: IF VALUES ARE RIGHT, WHAT'S LEFT?

1. Daniel J. Wakin, "Video Game Created by Militant Group Mounts Simulated Attacks Against Israeli Targets," *New York Times,* 18 May 2003, 24.
2. Mary Wiltenburg, "More Than Playing Games," *Christian Science Monitor,* 3 April 2003, 14.
3. America's Army, "Defense Briefing." Available at http://www.americas army.com/operations/missions.php. Accessed 17 September 2003.
4. Reed Stevenson, "U.S. Army Creates Video Game to Train Soldiers," Reuters News, 15 May 2003, 1.
5. Ibid.
6. Ibid.
7. Wiltenburg, "More Than Playing Games."
8. Liz Paley, from Grey Advertising, quoted in Karen Stabiner, "Get 'Em While They're Young: With Kid flavors, Bright Colors and Commercials That Make Children Masters of Their Universe, Advertisers Build Brand Loyalty That Will Last a Lifetime," *Los Angeles Times Magazine,* 15 August 1993, 12.
9. Kate MacArthur, "BK Push Banks on Big Kids," *Advertising Age* 72 (7) 12 February 2001, 10.
10. Jon Hanson and David Yosifon, unpublished paper. Available at http:// 141.211.44.51/centersandprograms/olin/papers/Winter%202003/Hanson %20040303.pdf. Accessed 21 June 2003.
11. Burger King, "Nutritional Wizard." Available at: http://Burgerking.com/Food/ Nutrition/NutritionalTable/index.html. Accessed 17 September 2003.
12. Deirdre Donahue, "Struggling to Raise Good Kids in Toxic Times: Is Innocence Evaporating in an Open-Door Society?" *USA Today,* 1 October 1998, 1D.
13. Gail S. Goodman and Christine Aman, "Children's Use of Anatomically Detailed Dolls to Recount an Event," *Child Development* 61 (1991): 1859–1871.
14. James McNeal, *Kids as Customers: A Handbook of Marketing to Children* (New York: Lexington Books, 1992), 12.
15. Tim Kasser, *The High Price of Materialism* (Cambridge: MIT, 2002).
16. Ibid.
17. Ibid.
18. James B. Twitchell, *Lead Us into Temptation* (New York: Columbia University Press, 1999), 30.
19. Ron Harris, "Children Who Dress for Excess: Today's Youngsters Have Become Fixated with Fashion, the Right Look Isn't Enough—It Also Has to Be Expensive," *Los Angeles Times,* 12 November 1989, sec. A, p. 1.
20. Judann Pollack, "Foods Targeting Children Aren't Just Child's Play: Shape-Shifting Foods, 'Interactive' Products Chase Young Consumers," *Advertising Age,* 1 March 1999, 16.

21. Daniel Dumoulin, "Brands: The New Religion," *Brand Strategy*, 2 January 2003, 35.

22. Mindy F. Ji, "Children's Relationships to Brands: 'True Love' or 'One-Night Stand'?" *Psychology & Marketing* 19 (4) (2002): 369–387.

23. Marc Gobe, *Emotional Branding: The New Paradigm for Connecting Brands to People* (New York: Allworth Press, 2001).

24. Laurie Lieber, *Commercial and Character Slogan Recall by Children Aged 9 to 11 Years: Budweiser Frogs versus Bugs Bunny* (Berkeley: Center on Alcohol Advertising, 1996).

25. Andy Bohjalian quoted in Karen Stabiner, "Get 'Em While They're Young."

26. Karen Stabiner, "Get 'Em While They're Young."

27. Archbishop Rowan Williams, *Lost Icons: Reflections on Cultural Bereavement* (Harrisburg, PA: Morehouse Publishing, 2000).

28. Frank Rich, "Never Forget What?" *New York Times*, 14 September 2002, sec. A, p. 15.

29. Bloomberg Business News, "Brand Loyalty is the New Holy Grail for Advertisers; Marketing: Making Sure the Customer Keeps Coming Back Is Viewed as Path to Maximum Profit," *Los Angeles Times*, 18 July 1996, D8.

30. Karen Stabiner, "Get 'Em While They're Young."

31. Carl F. Mela, Sunil Gupta, and Donald R. Lehmann, "The Long-Term Impact of Promotion and Advertising on Consumer Brand Choice," *Journal of Marketing Research* 34 (1997): 248.

32. D.W. Rajecki et al., "Violence, Conflict, Trickery, and Other Story Themes in TV Ads for Food for Children," *Journal of Applied Social Psychology*, 24 (19) (1994), 1685–1700.

33. Neil Postman, *Amusing Ourselves to Death: Public Discourse in the Age of Show Business* (New York: Viking, 1985), vii–viii.

CHAPTER 12: ENDING THE MARKETING MAELSTROM

1. Allen Kanner and René G. Soule, "Globalization, Corporate Culture and Freedom," in *Psychology and Consumer Culture: The Struggle for a Good Life in a Materialistic Society*, eds. Tim Kasser and Allen Kanner (Washington, DC: American Psychological Association, 2004), 49–69.

2. Comments attributed to Dave Siegel, president of WonderGroup in "Heard on the Playground," a feature of the e-newsletter "Youth University," published by WonderGroup. Available at http://www.youthuniversity.com/archive/ v22_ 2003.html#Playground. Accessed 18 March 2003.

3. Rachel Geller, chief strategic officer of the Geppetto Group, quoted in: Amy Frazier, "Prom Night Means Teen Independence: Buying Spree for Parents and Kids—Geppetto Group Finds Teens Ready to Break Away, Buy, Buy, Buy," *Selling to Kids* 3 (8), 15 April 1998.

3. Shelly Reese, "The Quality of Cool," *Marketing Tools*, July 1997, 34.

4. Applied Research and Consulting, "Shrink Rap: Forbes.com." Available at http://www.arc.com/press.htm. Accessed 30 June 2003.

5. Constance Hays, "P.T.A. Under Fire for Letting Advertiser Use Its Name," *New York Times*, 1 September 1998, 18A.

6. French fries are called "chips" in England.

7. Editorial, "Selling To—and Selling Out—Children," *The Lancet* 360 (28 September 2002): 959.

8. Golden Marble Awards. Available at http://www.goldenmarble.com. Accessed 15 September 2003. The last time I checked the web site it read, "Here at Kid-Screen, we pride ourselves on producing top-notch events and conferences that super-serve the industries we cater to. So after tinkering with the process and format of the Golden Marble Awards over the past couple of years, we've decided to take this year off to sit back and re-evaluate the project so that we can be sure we're still giving you exactly what you need."

9. Kesa Dillon, "Decked Out," *Sports Illustrated for Women*, 3 (6) (2001): 44.

10. Lee Bailey, "Action and Reaction: Sponsoring Action-Sports Starts Isn't Just a Way to Grade Some Publicity," *DNR*, 14 April 2003, 16.

11. "Marketing Mix: Global Pulse," *Marketing*, 21 March 2002, 48.

12. An interesting discussion of teenage activism can be found in: Alissa Quart, *Branded* (New York: Perseus, 2002): 189–224.

13. Donald F. Roberts, et al., *Kids & Media @ the New Millennium* (Menlo Park, CA: Henry J. Kaiser Family Foundation, 1999).

14. Denise Lavoie, "Retailers Removes Boy's Clothes Bearing Brewer's Slogan," Associated Press State and Local Wire, 31 October 2000.

15. Editorial, "Sex Sells; A&F's T&A," *San Francisco Chronicle*, 2 June 2002, D4.

16. Molly Freedenberg, "Military Easter Baskets Have Some Up in Arms," *Ventura County Star (California)*, 5 April 2003, A8.

17. Stop Commercial Exploitation of Children, "One for the Grassroots." Available at http://www.commercialexploitation.com/newsletter/winter2002.htm. Accessed 15 September 2003.

18. Derrick Z. Jackson, "Slim Chances of NFL Fighting Obesity," *Boston Globe*, 5 September 2003, A19.

19. Marian Burros, "Dental Group is Under Fire for Coke Deal," *New York Times*. 4 March 2003, 16A.

20. David Rowan, "Hard Sell, Soft Targets," *London Times*, 18 October 2002, sec. 2, p. 6.

21. Mark Metherell, "Doctors Urged to Look at TV's Role in Obesity," *Sydney Morning Herald*, 9 December 2002, 3.

22. Mark Metherell, "EU Commission Targets Unfair Businesses Practices," *Sydney Morning Herald*, 19 June 2003, 3.

Suggested Reading

Bok, Sissela. *Mayhem: Violence as Public Entertainment.* Reading, PA: Addison-Wesley, 1998.

Boyles, Deron. *American Education and Corporations: The Free Market Goes to School.* New York: Garland Publishing, 2000.

Brown, Jane D., Jean R. Steele, and Kim Walsh-Childers eds. *Sexual Teens, Sexual Media: Investigating Media's Influence on Adolescent Sexuality.* Mahwah, NJ: Lawrence Erlbaum Associates, 2002.

Brownell, Kelly D. and Katherine Battle Horgan. *Food Fight: The Inside Story of the Food Industry, America's Obesity Crisis, and What We Can Do About It.* New York: Contemporary Books, 2003.

Cantor, Joanne. *"Mommy I'm Scared:" How TV and Movies Frighten Children and What We Can Do to Protect Them.* San Diego: Harvest, 1998.

Carlsson-Paige, Nancy and Diane Levin. *Before Push Comes to Shove: Building Conflict Resolution Skills With Children.* St. Paul: Redleaf Press, 1998.

————. *Who's Calling the Shots: How to Respond Effectively to Children's Fascination with War Play and War Toys* (Philadelphia: New Society Publishers, 1990).

Giroux, Henry A. *Stealing Innocence: Corporate Culture's War on Children.* New York: Palgrave, 2000).

————. *The Mouse that Roared: Disney and the End of Innocence.* New York: Rowman and Littlefield, 1999.

Fones-Wolf, Elizabeth A. *Selling Free Enterprise: The Business Assault on Labor and Liberalism.* Urbana: University of Illinois Press, 1994.

Fox, Roy. *Harvesting Minds: How TV Commercials Control Kids.* Westport: Praeger, 1996.

Herman, Edward, and Noam Chomsky. *Manufacturing Consent: The Political Economy of Mass Media.* New York: Pantheon, 2002.

Jones, Gerard. *Killing Monsters: Why Children NEED Fantasy, Super-Heroes, and Make-Believe Violence.* New York: Basic Books, 2002.

Kalle, Lasn. *Culture Jam: How to Reverse America's Suidal Consumer Binge—and Why We Must.* New York: William Morrow, 1999.

Kasser, Tim. *The High Price of Materialism.* Cambridge: MIT Press, 2002.

Kasser, Tim, and Allen D. Kanner, eds. *Psychology and Consumer Culture: The Struggle for a Good Life in a Materialistic Society.* Washington, DC: APA Books, 2004.

Kelly, Joe. *Dads and Daughters: How to Inspire, Understand, and Support Your Daughter When She's Growing Up So Fast.* New York: Broadway Books, 2002.

Kilbourne, Jean. *Deadly Persuasion: Why Women and Girls Must Fight the Addictive Power of Advertising.* New York: Free Press, 1999.

Klein, Naomi. *No Logo: Taking Aim at the Brand Bullies.* New York: Picador, 1999.

Kuttner, Robert. *Everything for Sale: The Virtues and Limits of Markets.* Chicago: University of Chicago Press, 1996.

Ledbetter, James. *Made Possible by . . . the Death of Public Broadcasting in the United States.* New York: Verso, 1997.

Levin, Diane, E. *Teaching Young Children in Violent Times: Building a Peaceable Classroom.* Cambridge: Educators for Social Responsibility, 2003.

———. *Remote Control Childhood? Combating the Hazards of Media Culture.* Washington, DC: National Association for the Education of Young Children, 1998.

McChesney, Robert W. *Rich Media, Poor Democracy: Communication Politics in Dubious Times.* Urbana: University of Illinois Press, 1999.

Minow, Newton N., and Craig L. Lamay. *Abandoned in the Wasteland: Children, Television, and the First Amendment.* New York: Hill and Wang, 1996.

Molnar, Alex, *Giving Kids the Business: The Commercialization of America's Schools.* Boulder, CO: Westview Press, a division of HarperCollins, 1996.

Nader, Ralph. *Children First: A Parent's Guide to Fighting Corporate Predators.* Washington, DC: Children First, 1996.

Nestle, Marion. *Food Politics: How the Food Industry Influences Nutrition and Health.* Berkeley: University of California Press, 2002.

Pipher, Mary. *Reviving Ophelia: Saving the Selves of Adolescent Girls.* New York: Ballentine Books, 1994.

Postman, Neil. *Amusing Ourselves to Death: Public Discourse in the Age of Show Business.* New York: Viking, 1985.

Quart, Alissa. *Branded: The Buying and Selling of American Teenagers.* New York: Perseus, 2002.

Ravitch, Diane, and Joseph Viteritti, eds. *Kids Stuff . . . Marketing Sex and Violence to America's Children.* Baltimore: Johns Hopkins University Press, 2003.

Scheur, Jeffrey. *The Sound Bite Society: Television and the American Mind*. New
    York: Four Walls Eight Windows, 1999.
Schlosser, Eric. *Fast Food Nation: The Dark Side of the All-American Meal*. Boston:
    Houghton Mifflin, 2001.
Singer, Dorothy G., and Jerome L. Singer, eds. *The Handbook of Children and Media*.
    Thousand Oaks, CA: Sage, 2001.
William, Rowan. *Lost Icons: Reflections on Cultural Bereavement*. Harrisburg, PA:
    Morehouse Publishing, 2000.
Winnicott, Donald, W. *Playing and Reality*. New York: Basic Books, 1971.

Index

Burger King, 7, 76, 98
  advertising budget, 95, 96–97
  "Big Kids Meals," 179–81
  children's programming and promotions at,
    7, 39, 58
  school sales by, 89
Bush, George W., administration of, 127, 190
Business Week, 26, 75
Busta Rhymes, 166

Cahn, Alice, 56, 57
Califano, Joseph, 171
California Endowment, 85
Callaway, Nicholas, 65–66
Calvin and Hobbes, 65
Camels, 170–71, 173
campaign finance reform, 216
Campaign for Tobacco Free Kids
Campbell, Angela, 150
Campbell's Soup, 211
Canadians Concerned About Violence in
    Entertainment, 223
candy:
  marketing of, 95, 101–2
  vending machines in schools, *see* vending
    machines in school
Candy (song), 134
Captive Audience, 210
Captive Kids! (Consumer Union), 7
Car and Driver, 162
Care Bears, 73
Carlsson-Paige, Nancy, 106–7
Carnegie Commission on Educational
    Television, 44
Carter, Aaron, 134
Carter administration, 151
Cartoon Network, 176
Catholicism, 186, 187
CBS, 165–66
celebrities:
  marketing using, 111
  music industry, 133–38
censorship, *see* First Amendment, free speech
    guarantees of
Center for Alcohol Marketing and Youth,
    Georgetown University, 162

Center for a New American Dream, 8
Center for Commercial-Free Public
    Education, 200, 203, 210
Center for Digital Democracy, 176, 224
Center for Eating and Weight Disorders, Yale
    University, 85
Center for Media and Public Affairs, 136
Center for Media and the Family, 134
Center for Media Education, 166, 200
Center for Science in the Public Interest, 224
Center for the New American Dream, 200, 224
Centers for Disease Control (CDC), 99, 127,
    159, 160
Chanel, 187
Channel One, 7, 76, 77–78, 81–84, 200, 202,
    205, 210, 216
charitable donations, 212
Chicago school system, 77
Chicago Tribune, 130
child development, *see* developmental stages of
    children
Children Now, 225
Children's Advertising Review Unit (CARU),
    197
Children's Online Privacy Protection Act, 200,
    217
"Children's Relationship to Brands: 'True
    Loves' or 'One Night Stand,' 187
Children's Television Act of 1990, 200
Chomsky, Noam, 150
Christian Science Monitor, 57, 177
Chuck E. Cheese, 7
Chucky, 108
cigarette advertising, *see* tobacco, marketing of
Cinnamon Toast Crunch, 189
Citizens' Campaign for Commercial-Free
    Schools, 225
Citizens for Commercial-Free Schools in
    Seattle, 210
Clairol, 2
Clifford the Big Red Dog, 7, 47, 74
Clinton, Hillary, 199, 217
Coca-Cola, 9, 13, 76, 86, 151, 152, 155, 200,
    214
  advertising budget, 95
  pouring-rights contracts, 85, 86, 210